THE BOOK OF JOHN

the **Smart Guide** to the **Bible** series

BE SMART · BE INSPIRED ™

Lin Johnson

Larry Richards, **General Editor**

NELSON BOOKS
A Division of Thomas Nelson Publishers
Since 1798

www.thomasnelson.com

The Book of John
The Smart Guide to the Bible™ Series
© 2006 by GRQ, Inc.

Published by Nelson Reference, a Division of Thomas Nelson, Inc., P.O. Box 141000, Nashville, Tennessee 37214.

Originally published by Starburst Publishers under the title *John: God's Word for the Biblically-Inept*. Now revised and updated.

General Editor: Larry Richards
Managing Editor: Lila Empson
Associate Editor: W. Mark Whitlock
Scripture Editor: Deborah Wiseman
Assistant Editor: Amy Clark
Design: Diane Whisner

Library of Congress Cataloging-in-Publication Data
ISBN 1-4185-0991-4

Printed in the United States of America
06 07 08 09   9 8 7 6 5 4 3 2 1

Introduction

Welcome to *The Book of John—The Bible Smart Guides*™. It's part of a series that makes the Bible easy to understand even for people who know little or nothing about it. This commentary is different from other commentaries and Bible study books. It won't bore you or put you to sleep or discourage you with a lot of big words and religious terms. My goal is to help you discover that knowing and studying the Bible is enjoyable. And in the process of using this book, you will learn God's Word.

To Gain Your Confidence

The Book of John—The Bible Smart Guides™ is for people who want an easy-to-read, verse-by-verse study of the most popular book in the Bible. You'll find Bible verses, icons, and brief chunks of information to help you understand the text and how it relates to you today. You'll meet Jesus Christ when he lived here on earth. As you get to know him from John's perspective, I hope you will want to read the other books about his life and teachings *(The Book of Matthew, The Book of Mark, The Book of Luke)*.

What Is the Bible?

Although we treat it as one book, the Bible is a collection of sixty-six books. They were written by many different authors over a period of about 1,500 years. These books are grouped in two sections: the Old Testament with thirty-nine books and the New Testament with twenty-seven books. The Old Testament was written mostly in Hebrew between 1400 BC and 400 BC. It begins with God's creation of the world and tells the history of the Jewish people until they returned to the land of Israel after captivity to other nations. Then four hundred years went by, during which God did not give us any Bible books. This period of silence was followed by the New Testament, written in Greek between AD 40 and AD 100.

It tells about Jesus' birth, life, teachings, death and resurrection, and about the church, which was started by people who believed Jesus was the Son of God.

Many years after the Bible was written, Bible experts divided the books into chapters and verses. Now it's quick and easy to find a reference. So if someone refers to John 3:16, you can locate the book of John, find the third chapter, and then find verse 16 without having to scan through pages of text.

Why Study the Bible?

One reason to study the Bible is because God gave it to us so we can know him. It's his primary way of communicating to humans—his letters to us. Even though we can learn some things about him from nature, we can't really know him unless we read the Bible. It tells us what he is like and how he acts.

Another reason to study the Bible is because it gives answers to questions people have asked since the beginning of time. Questions like: How did the world begin? What is my purpose in life? Why do people act the way they do? What will happen to me when I die? Where is the world headed?

A third reason to study the Bible is because it's the best-selling and most influential book in history. Our literature is filled with references to Bible stories and people. Most of our laws are based on the Bible's moral code. An education is not complete without some knowledge of this book.

Still another reason to study the Bible is because it has power to change lives. No one can read it with an open mind and not be changed by the truth it contains. Ultimately, it will lead you to a personal relationship with the God of the universe.

Why Study John?

When a person's life generates a lot of interest, multiple biographies appear in bookstores. The person who has caused the most interest through the years is Jesus Christ. In fact, the first four biographies about him, called the Gospels, begin the New Testament.

These books are not normal biographies though. Instead, they present the message of eternal life through faith in the historic person of Jesus of Nazareth. As John put it, "Jesus did many other signs in the presence of His disciples, which are not written in this book; but these are written that you may believe that Jesus is the Christ, the Son of God, and that believing you may have life in His name" (John 20:30–31 NKJV).

The first three books—Matthew, Mark, and Luke—are called the synoptic Gospels since they are similar in content and approach. John, the fourth book, doesn't cover as many events but includes more of Jesus' teaching.

While the book of John focuses on Jesus' life, it is not an exhaustive biography. In other words, it doesn't tell everything there is to know about Jesus. It begins "in the beginning" with Jesus' relationship with God the Father. Then—unlike the other Gospels—John skips the details of Jesus' birth and goes right to his public ministry. To prove Jesus is the Son of God, John selected a few miracles from the many Jesus performed that are related to his main teaching.

A Comparison of the Four Gospels
Merrill C. Tenney

Although [John] deals with the same broad sequence of events to be found in the pages of the others, it is quite different in structure and in style. It contains no parables and only seven miracles, five of which are not recorded elsewhere. The discourses of Jesus in it are concerned chiefly with His person rather than with the ethical teaching of the kingdom. Personal interviews are multiplied, and Jesus' relationship to individuals is stressed more than His general contact with the public. The Gospel is strongly theological, and it deals particularly with the nature of His person and with the meaning of faith in Him.[1]

Gospel	Matthew	Mark	Luke	John
Author	Matthew	John Mark	Luke	John
Author's Job	Tax collector	Companion	Doctor	Fisherman
Author's Nationality	Jew	Jew	Gentile	Jew
Author's Focus	Disciple	Missionary	Missionary	Disciple
Readers	Jewish people	Romans	Greeks	The world
Author's View of Jesus	King	Servant	Son of Man	Son of God

Warren W. Wiersbe

Whereas the first three Gospels major on describing events in the life of Christ, John emphasizes the meaning of these events. For example, all four Gospels record the feeding of the 5,000 but only John records Jesus' sermon on "The Bread of Life" which followed that miracle when He interpreted it for the people.[2]

Who Wrote John?

John, the son of Zebedee and Salome and brother of James, was a fisherman on the Sea of Galilee when Jesus called him as one of his first disciples. He was one of the inner circle of three disciples who were privileged to be with Jesus for certain events. Thus he was an eyewitness to the events and teachings he wrote about.

John was called the "disciple whom Jesus loved." He was an intimate friend of Jesus, the one who leaned on Jesus' breast at the last Passover dinner just before Jesus' death. He was also the one Jesus asked to take care of his mother after his death.

John apparently had a temper since Jesus called him and his brother "Sons of Thunder." And he was selfish and ambitious. But later he was known as the apostle of love because one of his other books (1 John) focuses on this quality.

John was a thinker who focused on the big picture. He preferred to deal with abstract terms and concepts, rather than with actions like Mark. Throughout this Gospel, John emphasized contrasts like belief and unbelief, light and darkness, and love and hatred. He also highlighted symbols like the time Jesus turned water into wine.

Next to Paul, John wrote more New Testament books than anyone else—Gospel of John, 1 John, 2 John, 3 John, and Revelation. He penned John around AD 85–90. The oldest New Testament manuscript we have is a fragment of the Gospel of John copied a few years after it was originally written.

What Is John All About?

John is one of four selective biographies of Jesus Christ, God's Son. In it John tells about

- Jesus' existence before he was born here on earth
- Jesus' miracles
- Jesus' teachings
- Jesus' private teaching with his disciples
- Jesus' death and resurrection

A Word About Words

You will notice several interchangeable terms: Scripture, Scriptures, Word, Word of God, God's Word. All these mean the same thing and come under the broad heading called the Bible. I use each of these terms at various times. "Gospel" refers to one of four books that tell about Jesus and his life here on earth.

The word "Lord" in the Old Testament refers to Yahweh, God. In the New Testament, it refers to Jesus Christ, God's Son.

One Final Word

As you read the Bible text and the study helps in this book, you're going to learn a lot. You'll get acquainted with Jesus as he really is—not as people have described him or pictured him. But remember this: God didn't give us the Bible so we can collect a lot of facts to fill our heads. He gave it to us so we can have a personal relationship with him.

As you read and study John, do so prayerfully. When you ask God to speak to you through this book, he will. And when you finish it, you'll be surprised at how much you've learned and changed.

Understanding the Bible Is Easy with These Tools

To understand God's Word you need easy-to-use study tools right where you need them—at your fingertips. The Smart Guide to the Bible™ series puts valuable resources adjacent to the text to save you both time and effort.

Every page features handy sidebars filled with icons and helpful information: cross references for additional insights, definitions of key words and concepts, brief commentaries from experts on the topic, points to ponder, evidence of God at work, the big picture of how passages fit into the context of the entire Bible, practical tips for applying biblical truths to every area of your life, and plenty of maps, charts, and illustrations. A wrap-up of each passage, combined with study questions, concludes each chapter.

These helpful tools show you what to watch for. Look them over to become familiar with them, and then turn to Chapter 1 with complete confidence: You are about to increase your knowledge of God's Word!

Study Helps

The thought-bubble icon alerts you to commentary you might find particularly thought-provoking, challenging, or encouraging. You'll want to take a moment to reflect on it and consider the implications for your life.

Don't miss this point! The exclamation-point icon draws your attention to a key point in the text and emphasizes important biblical truths and facts.

death on the cross
Colossians 1:21–22

Many see Boaz as a type of Jesus Christ. To win back what we human beings lost through sin and spiritual death, Jesus had to become human (i.e., he had to become a true kinsman), and he had to be willing to pay the penalty for our sins. With his <u>death on the cross</u>, Jesus paid the penalty and won freedom and eternal life for us.

The additional Bible verses add scriptural support for the passage you just read and help you better understand the <u>underlined text</u>. (Think of it as an instant reference resource!)

How does what you just read apply to your life? The heart icon indicates that you're about to find out! These practical tips speak to your mind, heart, body, and soul, and offer clear guidelines for living a righteous and joy-filled life, establishing priorities, maintaining healthy relationships, persevering through challenges, and more.

This icon reveals how God is truly all-knowing and all-powerful. The hourglass icon points to a specific example of the prediction of an event or the fulfillment of a prediction. See how some of what God has said would come to pass already has!

What are some of the great things God has done? The traffic-sign icon shows you how God has used miracles, special acts, promises, and covenants throughout history to draw people to him.

Does the story or event you just read about appear elsewhere in the Gospels? The cross icon points you to those instances where the same story appears in other Gospel locations—further proof of the accuracy and truth of Jesus' life, death, and resurrection.

Since God created marriage, there's no better person to turn to for advice. The double-ring icon points out biblical insights and tips for strengthening your marriage.

The Bible is filled with wisdom about raising a godly family and enjoying your spiritual family in Christ. The family icon gives you ideas for building up your home and helping your family grow close and strong.

Isle of Patmos
a small island in the
Mediterranean Sea

something significant had occurred, he wrote down the substance of what he saw. This is the practice John followed when he recorded Revelation on the **Isle of Patmos.**

What does that word really mean, especially as it relates to this passage? Important, misunderstood, or infrequently used words are set in **bold type** in your text so you can immediately glance at the margin for definition. This valuable feature lets you better understand the meaning of the entire passage without having to stop to check other references.

the big picture

Joshua

Led by Joshua, the Israelites crossed the Jordan River and invaded Canaan (see Illustration #8). In a series of military campaigns the Israelites defeated several coalition armies raised by the inhabitants of Canaan. With organized resistance put down, Joshua divided the land among the twelve Israelite

How does what you read fit in with the greater biblical story? The highlighted big picture summarizes the passage under discussion.

what others say

David Breese

Nothing is clearer in the Word of God than the fact that God wants us to understand himself and his working in the lives of men.[5]

It can be helpful to know what others say on the topic, and the highlighted quotation introduces another voice in the discussion. This resource enables you to read other opinions and perspectives.

Maps, charts, and illustrations pictorially represent ancient artifacts and show where and how stories and events took place. They enable you to better understand important empires, learn your way around villages and temples, see where major battles occurred, and follow the journeys of God's people. You'll find these graphics let you do more than study God's Word—they let you *experience* it.

Chapters at a Glance

Part One
Jesus' Public Ministry

John 1: Jesus the Word

Chapter Highlights:
• Jesus the Creator
• John the Witness
• God Undercover
• John the Voice
• Jesus the Recruiter

Let's Get Started

Imagine you are in a room with no light or sound. You put your hand in front of your eyes and wriggle your fingers, but you see nothing and you hear nothing. Suddenly, someone turns on a light, and you see you are standing in the middle of a room as big as a football stadium. Everywhere you look, there are diamonds, gold coins, jewels, and priceless treasures—covering the floor around you, packed into corners, stacked to the ceiling.

Wouldn't that be wondrous? When God created the world, he did something infinitely more wondrous than filling a stadium with gold and jewels. He filled a void with life. Where once there was chaos, now spinning galaxies swirled into being. Where once there was darkness, now there was light. Where once there was deadness, now there was life—more creatures than you can imagine. And human beings.

But before all that creation, there was only God—God the Father, God the Son (Jesus), and God the Holy Spirit.

That's where the apostle John began this book about Jesus—long before Jesus was born. And John wasted no time in introducing his readers to Jesus. He got right to the point and stayed there until the end of the book.

Jesus Before His Birth

JOHN 1:1–2 *In the beginning was the Word, and the Word was with God, and the Word was God. He was in the beginning with God.* (NKJV)

John was a gutsy writer. He began this book with an amazing statement. His early readers, who were familiar with Scripture, would have recognized the opening words. The first book in the Bible, Genesis, begins with the same phrase. That book introduces the creation of the world and man; John introduces the Creator.

in the beginning
Genesis 1:1

always existed
John 8:58

creating
Genesis 1;
Colossians 1:16;
Hebrews 1:2

Godhead
three names and
natures of God in
one word

"The Word" refers to Jesus, as we'll discover later in this chapter. The Greek word *logos*, translated "Word," means the spoken word that communicates meaning, or a message. So Jesus communicates to us what God is like—his actions, thoughts, feelings, and attitudes. Jesus was "in the beginning with God." Unlike us, he always existed; his life didn't begin when he was born as a baby on earth. The word "with" indicates a personal relationship between two or more people. In other words, they are both God but not two different Gods.

> **what others say**
>
> **Lawrence O. Richards**
>
> In Greek philosophical thought *logos* was used of the rational principle or Mind that ruled the universe. In Hebrew thought "the word of God" was His active self-expression, that revelation of Himself to humanity through which a person not only receives truth about God, but meets God face-to-face.[1]

Jesus gave up his home in heaven and face-to-face company with God the Father to come to this earth to show us what God is like. He traded a place where everything is perfect for one where sin and suffering are prevalent. That was a huge move for him.

The Ultimate Creator

JOHN 1:3 *All things were made through Him, and without Him nothing was made that was made. (NKJV)*

Jesus was God's agent in creating everything—light, darkness, sky, water, land, vegetation, sun, moon, stars, animals, fish, birds, people—that is in the world. Even before he was born as a human, he showed us what God is like through creation. From creation, we can see that God is creative, orderly, and powerful.

The book of Genesis begins by describing God's creation of the world. But John says here that Jesus made everything. We don't know all the details of how the **Godhead** operates. (If we understood it all, we'd be God!) But we do know that John's statement makes Jesus equal with God—a fact that caused a lot of trouble when Jesus was here on earth.

life
John 5:26

Life from the Source

JOHN 1:4–5 *In Him was life, and the life was the light of men. And the light shines in the darkness, and the darkness did not comprehend it.* (NKJV)

Jesus not only showed us God in the creation of the world; he also showed us God in the creation of living creatures and people. Life, both physical and spiritual, originates in Jesus, a living, eternal Being. Through him, God makes his power and purpose known to people.

Light also originates in Jesus. The purpose of light is to banish darkness. When John used the terms "light" and "darkness," he was referring to good and evil, holiness and sin. Thus Jesus, who is morally pure, meaning sinless, became God's light in a spiritually dark world full of sin and evil behavior, thoughts, and attitudes. People in the world resisted the spiritual light Jesus brought partly because they didn't understand it. When they did catch glimpses of understanding, they saw that they had done bad things, and they didn't like that feeling. Although sin and darkness are powerful, they can't overcome or conquer Jesus' light. The light and holiness of Jesus are always more powerful than any forces of darkness and evil.

> ignorance as man moved from light to darkness. Willful rejection of the light of revelation through creation brought progressive darkness until men were ignorant of God. Jesus Christ came to dispel that ignorance. He who is God came in flesh so that men might see that revelation and come out of ignorance into knowledge.[3]

key point

John traces the themes of life and light throughout his book. To John, "life" means more than physical well-being. It has a spiritual dimension, enabling a believer to live abundantly in this life and to be sure of resurrection with God after death. When John uses "light," he focuses on spiritual understanding and guidance.

Themes of Life

Theme	Reference
John 1:4–5	Jesus is the source of all life
John 3:15	Jesus gives eternal life to those who believe in him
John 5:19–23	God the Father and God the Son have control over life and death
John 5:24	We move from eternal death to eternal life through faith in God
John 6:68	Only Jesus' words, which we have in the Bible, can produce eternal life
John 10:10	Jesus came to give us a full, satisfying life now and in eternity
John 12:23–26	Hanging on to our selfish desires will cost us eternal life
John 14:5–6	Jesus is the source of life, not death
John 15:12–13	The greatest demonstration of love for others is sacrificing our lives for them
John 17:3	Eternal life is personally knowing the one true God and Jesus Christ, his Son

Themes of Light

Theme	Reference
John 1:4–5	Jesus was God's light in a dark, sinful world
John 3:19	Jesus brought God's light to earth, but people prefer the darkness of evil because they are sinners
John 5:35	John the Baptist brought God's light to people, pointing them to Jesus
John 9:5	As the Light of the World, Jesus offers a way out of the darkness of sin
John 12:35–36	We will not have the opportunity to choose to follow Jesus' light forever

John the Witness

JOHN 1:6–9 There was a man sent from God, whose name was John. This man came for a witness, to bear witness of the Light, that all through him might believe. He was not that Light, but was sent to bear witness of that Light. That was the true Light which gives light to every man coming into the world. (NKJV)

John the Baptist
Malachi 3:1;
Mark 1:1–8

The John in these verses is <u>John the Baptist</u>, Jesus' cousin, not the author of this Bible book. God chose him for a specific ministry—to prepare the Jewish people for Jesus' coming and to point to Jesus. His job was to identify Jesus to the people as the "Light," to introduce him to the Jewish people, and to get them ready for his ministry. John preached that the time for the long-awaited, promised **Messiah**—who was written about in the **Hebrew Scriptures**—had come. He also called the people to **repentance** from their sin. His goal was to encourage them to trust Jesus for salvation from their sin.

Messiah
God's anointed King

Hebrew Scriptures
Old Testament

repentance
turning from sin

The Light John testified about was Jesus, who "gives light to every man." As the "true Light," he reveals people's sin.

what others say

Leon Morris

Testimony is a serious matter and it is required to substantiate the truth of a matter. It is clear that our author wants us to take what he writes as reliable. He is insistent that there is good evidence for the things he sets down. Witness establishes the truth.

It does more. It commits a man. If I take my stand in the witness box and testify that such-and-such is the truth of the matter I am no longer neutral. I have committed myself. John lets us see that there are those like John the Baptist who have committed themselves by their witness to Christ.[4]

John drew attention to Jesus, not himself. Isn't that just the opposite of us? We want to be sure people notice us. We want to take the credit, to be the star, to be the center of attention. But not John. Instead, he wanted people to notice Jesus, who is far more important.

God with Skin On

didn't believe
John 12:37

His own
Psalm 2:6–9

born again
John 3:5–7

Gentiles
non-Jewish people

sacrifice
Jesus' death

God's children
members of God's
kingdom

JOHN 1:10–13 *He was in the world, and the world was made through Him, and the world did not know Him. He came to His own, and His own did not receive Him. But as many as received Him, to them He gave the right to become children of God, to those who believe in His name: who were born, not of blood, nor of the will of the flesh, nor of the will of man, but of God. (NKJV)*

Jesus became a man and lived in our world. Although he created humans, the people of his day didn't know who he was—didn't know him as a friend or have a relationship with him—because they were blinded by sin. So they <u>didn't believe</u> he was the promised Messiah from God.

Jesus went to "<u>His own</u>" things or home. He had created this world. It was his. Within the world, Jesus chose to become a Jew. But sadly, leaders of the Jewish nation and many of his own Jewish people—as well as **Gentiles**—rejected him instead of welcoming him. They did not believe he was the Messiah whom God had promised to them.

Although most of the Jewish people rejected Jesus, some received him. They trusted him as the **sacrifice** for sin and, as a result, became **God's children**. To use a phrase Jesus used later in this book, they were <u>born again</u>. In this passage, John equates believing with receiving. Belief is more than mental assent.

No one automatically or naturally belongs to God. That relationship doesn't result from being born Jewish or Christian or Muslim or Russian or American. We don't become a child of God because of who our parents are. Instead, relationship with God is a supernatural gift from him through faith in Jesus. And we need to reach out and accept that gift, demonstrating that we believe it is real.

The word "belief" and its variants, "believed" and "believing," were important to John. He used them over eighty-eight times in this book. John wanted his readers to believe that Jesus was God's Son. When we believe this, we become God's adopted children.

human being
Philippians 2:5–9

glory
Hebrews 2:9

Moses
first leader of Jewish people

<blockquote>
what others say

Leon Morris

We might translate the opening words, "he came home." . . . When the Word came to this world He did not come as an alien. He came home. Moreover, He came to Israel. Had He come to some other nation it would have been bad enough, but Israel was peculiarly God's own people. The Word did not go where He could not have expected to be known. He came home, where the people ought to have known Him.[5]
</blockquote>

When God Became One of Us

JOHN 1:14 *And the Word became flesh and dwelt among us, and we beheld His glory, the glory as of the only begotten of the Father, full of grace and truth.* (NKJV)

Jesus, the eternal God, became—at a specific point in time—a <u>human being</u> and lived among humans without losing his deity to communicate to us what God is like. He became one of us while remaining God. This action is called the incarnation. In this verse, John equated the Word with Jesus, clearly defining who the Word is.

The author, John, was an eyewitness to Jesus' life and <u>glory</u>. He saw Jesus' awesomeness as the unique Son of God, a Son in a way that humans can't be. He is eternal, of the same essence as God the Father. "Full of grace and truth" means the same as "abounding in goodness and truth" (Exodus 34:6 NKJV), the description of God's glory as shown to **Moses**.

<blockquote>
what others say

Merrill C. Tenney

He expressed Himself in a human personality that was visible, audible, and tangible. He partook of flesh and blood with its limitations of space and time, and with its physical handicaps of fatigue, hunger, and susceptibility to suffering, so that He belongs to humanity as well as to God.[6]
</blockquote>

For John to say that God became a human being was a radical concept in his day. Jewish people believed humans could not become gods and vice versa. Greek philosophers taught that what is invisible is far more important than what we can see and touch. So to announce that "the Word became flesh and dwelt among us" was thinking outside the box.

Jesus, who is God, became a baby who cried, burped, and messed his diapers. He grew into a child who probably played in the mud, made enemies, and later broke girls' hearts. He worked with his hands, lost his earthly father, and got tired and hungry. He was like us.

Jesus is fully God and fully human. He didn't give up being God with all his perfection. And because he became a man, he understands our limitations and temptations. So he can help us get through the tough times if we ask him to.

Out with the Old, In with the New

JOHN 1:15–18 *John bore witness of Him and cried out, saying, "This was He of whom I said, 'He who comes after me is preferred before me, for He was before me.'" And of His fullness we have all received, and grace for grace. For the law was given through Moses, but grace and truth came through Jesus Christ. No one has seen God at any time. The only begotten Son, who is in the bosom of the Father, He has declared Him. (NKJV)*

These verses verse logically follow verses 7 and 8, since they continue the narrative about John the Baptist. Even though this <u>John was born</u> six months before Jesus and began his ministry first, Jesus was more important. He existed long before John was conceived and was greater than John because he was God. This statement was radical in Jesus' day since people believed that what or who came first chronologically was superior.

From Jesus we've received lots of blessings. God's grace or favor toward us—which we don't deserve and <u>can't earn</u>—can never be exhausted; there is an <u>unlimited supply</u> of it.

<u>God gave the Law</u>, the first five books of the Old Testament, to Moses and his people to show them his standards of right behavior and attitudes. If anyone could keep the Law (although that was impossible), doing so wouldn't make that person a child of God. In contrast to the Law, Jesus showed us God's attitude—love and faithfulness.

Although God is invisible and no human can see him, he has made himself known to us through Jesus. When Jesus made God known, he told God's story, disclosing who he is and giving a trustworthy account about him. Again John asserted that Jesus is God and that

John was born
Luke 1:57–80

can't earn
Ephesians 2:8–9

unlimited supply
James 4:6

God gave the Law
Exodus 20

he existed before he was born on earth. So John ended this section by coming full circle to how he began it: writing about "the Word" who "was in the beginning with God."

Levites
priests' assistants

what others say

Edwin A. Blum

Because of the fullness of His grace . . . one blessing after another (. . . lit., "grace in place of grace") comes to Christians as waves continue to come to the shore. The Christian life is the constant reception of one evidence of God's grace replacing another.[7]

Warren W. Wiersbe

John did not suggest that there was no grace under the Law of Moses, because there was. Each sacrifice [for sins] was an expression of the grace of God. The Law also revealed God's truth. But in Jesus Christ, grace and truth reach their fullness; and this fullness is available to us. . . . John hinted that a whole new order had come in, replacing the Mosaic system.[8]

John could have had a big ego since he was older than Jesus and because God chose him to introduce Jesus to the Jewish people. But he didn't. Instead, he humbly did his job of telling people to repent and of introducing people to Jesus.

Radical Preacher

JOHN 1:19–23 *Now this is the testimony of John, when the Jews sent priests and* **Levites** *from Jerusalem to ask him, "Who are you?" He confessed, and did not deny, but confessed, "I am not the Christ." And they asked him, "What then? Are you Elijah?" He said, "I am not." "Are you the Prophet?" And he answered, "No." Then they said to him, "Who are you, that we may give an answer to those who sent us? What do you say about yourself?" He said: "I am*
   'The voice of one crying in the wilderness:
   "Make straight the way of the LORD,"'
as the prophet Isaiah said." (NKJV)

John the Baptist was not your normal preacher. He lived in the desert, ate locusts and wild honey, wore a camel-hair robe, and told people to get their acts together. His lifestyle and message attracted

go to

Elijah
Malachi 4:5

the Prophet
Deuteronomy
18:15–18;
Acts 3:22–23

voice
Isaiah 40:3

priests
supervised worship
and offered sacrifices

baptize
perform water ritual
of initiation in the
faith

Pharisees
exclusive teachers of
religious law and
tradition

a lot of attention. That's why a committee of religious leaders—**priests** and Levites—from Jerusalem went out to the desert of Judea (see Appendix A) to investigate him. They plied John with questions, which he clearly answered.

Of course, since John wasn't acting normally, they wanted to know who he was. Keep in mind that Messiah fever raged back then. Everyone was looking for the Messiah who would free the Jewish people from Roman rule. First, John denied he was that expected Messiah. Second, he denied he was <u>Elijah</u>, an Old Testament prophet who the people thought would come back to announce the Messiah. Then, he denied he was <u>the Prophet</u>, another name for the expected Messiah. When the leaders ran out of true-false questions, they finally asked, "Who are you?" John answered by calling himself the <u>voice</u> of one crying in the wilderness.

"I'm a Nobody"

JOHN 1:24–28 *Now those who were sent were from the Pharisees. And they asked him, saying, "Why then do you baptize if you are not the Christ, nor Elijah, nor the Prophet?" John answered them, saying, "I baptize with water, but there stands One among you whom you do not know. It is He who, coming after me, is preferred before me, whose sandal strap I am not worthy to loose." These things were done in Bethabara beyond the Jordan, where John was baptizing.* (NKJV)

These big shots didn't go find John the Baptist so they could be preached at. Once they found out who he was, they wanted to know what he was doing—why he was baptizing. It was customary for religious leaders to **baptize** Gentiles who converted to Judaism. But they didn't baptize Jewish people, like John did. In doing so, John treated Jewish people like pagans, which was unheard of and offensive.

So in answer to the **Pharisees**' question, John pointed his inquisitors to Jesus, whose ministry would follow his and who was a much greater person. In fact, John said he was a nobody in comparison to Jesus. Untying sandals was a job that belonged to the least important household servant.

John ended this section by identifying the location as Bethabara, which was on the east bank of the Jordan River (see Appendix A). It is also called Bethany. This is not the same Bethany that is mentioned later in the book, a suburb of Jerusalem.

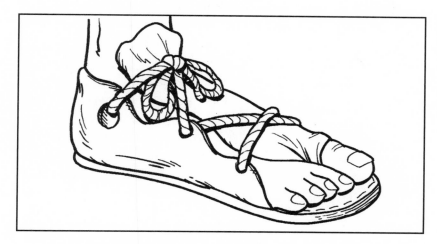

what others say

James Montgomery Boice

The delegation from Jerusalem could think of three things that John might claim to be, and the first of these quite obviously was "the Messiah." Was he the Messiah? We must remember as we read these words that the Jews were a people living under the dominion of Rome and that they were looking with great expectation for their deliverer, as any captive people do. . . . Moreover, there had been many messianic pretenders. . . . It would have been easy for John, who by this time had received quite an impressive following, to have announced that he was the Messiah. But not only did he reject the temptation, he even rejected it with the hint that the One who actually was the Messiah was present.[9]

Lamb Confession

JOHN 1:29–31 *The next day John saw Jesus coming toward him, and said, "Behold! The Lamb of God who takes away the sin of the world! This is He of whom I said, 'After me comes a Man who is preferred before me, for He was before me.' I did not know Him; but that He should be revealed to Israel, therefore I came baptizing with water." (NKJV)*

The day after the religious leaders questioned John, Jesus showed up while John was preaching and baptizing. So John introduced him

sacrificing lambs
Exodus 12–13;
Numbers 28:4

cousin
Luke 1

alighted
Matthew 3:13–17;
Mark 1:9–10;
Luke 3:21–22

as the Lamb of God—not the Great God of the Universe who created everyone and everything in it. The Jewish people, to whom he was preaching, would have recognized the title "Lamb of God," although many didn't get the true meaning of it. They were used to <u>sacrificing lambs</u> as a means to gain forgiveness for their sins. But they weren't expecting this human Lamb.

John clearly identified Jesus as the person to whom he referred earlier—the one who was greater even though he came later than John.

The people of Jesus' day, especially the religious leaders, had certain expectations about the Messiah that God had promised to send. Because of their political situation, they were looking for a political leader and didn't recognize him as a lamb who would die for their sins. Have your religious expectations kept you from seeing the real Jesus?

Look for the Dove

> JOHN 1:32–34 *And John bore witness, saying, "I saw the Spirit descending from heaven like a dove, and He remained upon Him. I did not know Him, but He who sent me to baptize with water said to me, 'Upon whom you see the Spirit descending, and remaining on Him, this is He who baptizes with the Holy Spirit.' And I have seen and testified that this is the Son of God."* (NKJV)

Jesus was John's <u>cousin</u>, and they probably spent a lot of time together as children and teens. When they were children, John didn't know Jesus was God's Son. He didn't discover that truth until Jesus came to him for baptism. God's sign that Jesus was the Son of God, the Lamb, was the Holy Spirit in the form of a dove who <u>alighted</u> on Jesus when John baptized him. And just in case John missed the sign, the dove was accompanied by God's voice saying, "This is My beloved Son, in whom I am well pleased" (Matthew 3:17 NKJV).

Can you imagine witnessing that scene? And hearing God's voice out loud? Many of us might have been tempted to keep it to ourselves so people wouldn't think we were crazy. But not John. Once he knew who Jesus really was, John told everyone who would listen—and did so with confidence.

Jesus the Recruiter

JOHN 1:35–39 *Again, the next day, John stood with two of his disciples. And looking at Jesus as He walked, he said, "Behold the Lamb of God!" The two disciples heard him speak, and they followed Jesus. Then Jesus turned, and seeing them following, said to them, "What do you seek?" They said to Him, "Rabbi" (which is to say, when translated, Teacher), "where are You staying?" He said to them, "Come and see." They came and saw where He was staying, and remained with Him that day (now it was about the tenth hour). (NKJV)*

disciples
followers

On the third day that John recorded of this week, John the Baptist again pointed people to Jesus as the Lamb of God. John said, "Hey, look! Here's Jesus. Don't miss him!"

John, who wrote this book, and Andrew were two of John the Baptist's **disciples** who were with him at this time. They immediately left John and followed Jesus, an action that pleased John instead of making him mad.

To be sure Andrew and John followed him for the right reasons, Jesus asked them what they were after. Instead of answering, they asked him where he was staying, implying that they would come see him later if he was too busy to talk right then. But Jesus invited them to spend the evening with him, since it was the tenth hour—about 4:00 p.m. No doubt he answered their questions and told them about his ministry.

what others say

William Barclay

"Come and see!" The Jewish Rabbis had a way of using that phrase in their teaching. They would say: "Do you want to know the answer to this question? Do you want to know the solution to this problem? Come and see, and we will think about it together." When Jesus said: "Come and see!" he was inviting them, not only to come and talk, but to come and find the things that he alone could open out to them.[10]

John didn't mind taking second place after he had enjoyed first place for a while. Instead of holding on to first, he encouraged his disciples to leave him and go follow Jesus. John wasn't the possessive or jealous type.

Two-for-One Special

go to

Peter
Matthew 16:17–19

Gospels
Matthew, Mark,
Luke, John

JOHN 1:40–42 *One of the two who heard John speak, and followed Him, was Andrew, Simon Peter's brother. He first found his own brother Simon, and said to him, "We have found the Messiah" (which is translated, the Christ). And he brought him to Jesus. Now when Jesus looked at him, He said, "You are Simon the son of Jonah. You shall be called Cephas" (which is translated, A Stone). (NKJV)*

Andrew was so impressed with Jesus that he hunted up his brother, Simon <u>Peter</u>, to tell him who Jesus was—the Messiah they were looking for. They weren't expecting God's Son, but rather a king who would free them from Roman rule and set up God's kingdom of peace.

Andrew, like John the Baptist, was a good second-place player. Throughout the **Gospels**, he lived in the shadow of his brother, Peter; only here did he come first. Starting with his brother, Andrew developed a reputation for bringing people to Jesus.

When Peter met Jesus, Jesus already knew who Peter was. He didn't just glance at Peter or look at his body; he read his heart. Then he changed Simon's name to Peter (in Greek), or Cephas (in Aramaic), which means a rock, someone steady and strong. Jewish people who lived in Palestine spoke Aramaic. However, most of those who lived outside of that land spoke Greek. That's why John translated the word "Messiah" and Simon's new name into other languages. It would take a few years for Peter to live up to that name change, but he did.

When Andrew heard what John the Baptist said about Jesus, he believed Jesus was the promised Messiah. Then he went to find his brother to tell him. If you had been there, what would you have done?

Jesus doesn't just see us how we are now. He saw us in our past. He also knows all our possibilities, what we can become if we trust him. And he will help us realize those possibilities to become all that God made us to be.

Say What?

JOHN 1:43–46 *The following day Jesus wanted to go to Galilee, and He found Philip and said to him, "Follow Me." Now Philip was from Bethsaida, the city of Andrew and Peter. Philip found Nathanael and said to him, "We have found Him of whom Moses in the law, and also the prophets, wrote—Jesus of Nazareth, the son of Joseph." And Nathanael said to him, "Can anything good come out of Nazareth?" Philip said to him, "Come and see." (NKJV)*

Nazareth
Acts 24:5

As Jesus continued recruiting disciples, he traveled north into the region called Galilee (see Appendix A). There he called Philip, who also followed him immediately. Philip in turn looked for his friend Nathanael to tell him about Jesus. Philip described Jesus in four ways. First, Philip said Jesus was the one whom Moses wrote about in the Law. Second, Philip said Jesus was the one whom the prophets wrote about. "Moses and the Prophets" is one way Jewish people referred to the whole of the Old Testament. Third, Philip said he was "Jesus of Nazareth," indicating the place where Jesus grew up. Fourth, Philip said Jesus was the "son of Joseph," indicating his humanity.

But Nathanael was doubtful because of where Jesus came from. People from <u>Nazareth</u> (see Appendix A) were looked down upon. They were considered to be from the other side of the tracks. Instead of trying to convince Nathanael with arguments, Philip echoed Jesus' words, "Come and see" for yourself.

When Jesus began his public ministry, he called a group of men to follow him. They spent time with him, watched him work, and told others about him. Jesus is still looking for people to do the same things today. Are you one of them?

You Ain't Seen Nothin' Yet

JOHN 1:47–51 *Jesus saw Nathanael coming toward Him, and said of him, "Behold, an Israelite indeed, in whom is no deceit!" Nathanael said to Him, "How do You know me?" Jesus answered and said to him, "Before Philip called you, when you were under the fig tree, I saw you." Nathanael answered and said to Him, "Rabbi, You are the Son of God! You are the King of Israel!" Jesus answered and said to him, "Because I said to you, 'I saw you under the fig tree,' do you believe? You will see greater things than these." And He said to him, "Most assuredly, I say to you, hereafter you shall see heaven open, and the angels of God ascending and descending upon the Son of Man." (NKJV)*

angels going
Genesis 28

fathers of Judaism
Abraham, Isaac, and
Jacob

Even before the introductions, Jesus saw Nathanael and knew who he was—just as he knew Simon Peter the day before. In calling Nathanael an "Israelite indeed, in whom is no deceit," Jesus was referring to one of the **fathers of Judaism**, Jacob. Jacob was a trickster, but after he met God, God changed his name to Israel, which means "prince with God." Jesus' knowledge of him, including the fact that deceit was not part of his lifestyle, convinced Nathanael that Jesus was who Philip claimed—God's Son, the King of Israel, or Messiah.

Jesus acknowledged Nathanael's belief in him and told him more revelations were to come. Following through on the reference to Jacob, who had a dream about <u>angels going</u> up and down a ladder between heaven and earth, Jesus told Nathanael that he too would see angels going up and down as the bridge between heaven and earth. Nathanael would witness Jesus as a ladder between man and God.

When was the last time you talked with someone who greeted you with a statement about your character? Nathanael's conversation with Jesus certainly wasn't one you hear every day. The fact that Jesus knew the kind of person he was, where he was, and what he had been doing drew Nathanael to him. Nathaniel immediately recognized Jesus as God's Son, the promised Messiah. And he followed Jesus.

Chapter Wrap-Up

- Jesus existed before he was born in Bethlehem (see Appendix A). He created the world and everything that is in it. (John 1:1–5)

- John the Baptist's ministry was to introduce people to Jesus, to testify to who he is. (John 1:6–9)

- Jesus came to offer eternal life to people, but many of his own Jewish people didn't recognize who he was and consequently rejected him. (John 1:10–13)

- Jesus, who is God, became a man to show us what God is like. (John 1:14–18)

- John the Baptist introduced Jesus to the Jewish people as the Lamb of God, who would later die to take away their sins. (John 1:19–34)

- Jesus recruited the first of twelve disciples to be with him, learn from him, and tell others about him. (John 1:35–51)

Study Questions

1. How did John describe Jesus?

2. What does this passage teach about John the Baptist?

3. How do we become God's children?

4. What did John do to encourage people to focus on Jesus instead of himself?

5. How did Andrew, John, Simon, Philip, and Nathanael respond to John the Baptist's testimony about Jesus?

John 2: Jesus the Authority

Chapter Highlights:
• Water with a Kick
• Cleaning Frenzy
  in the Temple
• Seeing to the Heart

Let's Get Started

So many people have the wrong idea of what Jesus is like. For example, some see him as a cosmic killjoy who wouldn't know a good time if he walked into one, a scowling fanatic who thumps the Bible and preaches a down-with-good-times message. In fact, they think he spends his days—and especially his nights—looking for people who are having fun in order to make them stop.

Others think of him as gentle Jesus, meek and mild. He's the Christmas baby who grew up with that same docile demeanor, who doesn't have the guts to stand up to anyone. He's a God of love who agrees with everyone, who passes out hugs like they were candy.

Surprise! Jesus fits neither of these perceptions. John blew away these misconceptions in chapter 2 of his book by describing two events Jesus was involved in—changing water to wine and cleaning out the Temple.

The first event was also the first of seven miracles in this book. They were like road signs pointing to Jesus as God, not just a man.

The Partygoer

JOHN 2:1–2 *On the third day there was a wedding in Cana of Galilee, and the mother of Jesus was there. Now both Jesus and His disciples were invited to the wedding.* (NKJV)

Jesus wasn't a stuffy religious leader who didn't know how to have fun. Instead, people wanted him at their parties, and he accepted their invitations. On this particular day, three days after he called Nathanael to follow him, Jesus attended a wedding in Cana (see Appendix A) with his mother, Mary, and his six new disciples. Since his earthly father, Joseph, is not mentioned here or in other events recorded after Jesus began his ministry, we assume he died before Jesus entered his ministry.

Some Christians come across as party poopers who think having a

apply it

his hour
Jesus' death and
resurrection

good time is a sin. Other Christians go all out to enjoy themselves and help others do the same but fail to use self-control. Mature Christians know how to have a good time without compromising their convictions. Christians should not be people who are so focused on "religious" activities that they don't have time to socialize with people who need to hear about Jesus.

Empty Jugs

> JOHN 2:3–5 *And when they ran out of wine, the mother of Jesus said to Him, "They have no wine." Jesus said to her, "Woman, what does your concern have to do with Me? My hour has not yet come." His mother said to the servants, "Whatever He says to you, do it." (NKJV)*

When the wine ran out, Jesus' mother knew who to go to for help: her son. Although his answer sounds harsh in English, he was not being rude or talking back to his mother. Rather, "woman" was a respectful form of address in his culture—like calling a woman "ma'am" today. Since it wasn't normal to use this name with one's own mother, Jesus was putting distance between himself and Mary. He was helping her understand his transition from being her child to becoming her Lord.

By saying **his hour** had not yet come, Jesus made it clear that he didn't do miracles on demand. However, Mary recognized his authority and had faith in his ability to remedy the problem when she told the servants to obey him.

what others say

Warren W. Wiersbe

Certainly [Mary] knew who He was, even though she did not declare this wonderful truth to others. She must have been very close to either the bride or the bridegroom to have such a personal concern for the success of the festivities, or even to know that the supply of wine was depleted. Perhaps Mary was assisting in the preparation and serving of the meal. Mary did not tell Jesus what to do; she simply reported the problem. . . . Jesus' reply seems a bit abrupt, [but] . . . His statement merely means, "Why are you getting Me involved in this matter?" He was making it clear to His mother that He was no longer under her supervision (it is likely that Joseph was dead), but that from now on, he would be doing what the Father wanted Him to do.[1]

Weddings typically lasted for seven days and included long guest lists. (Aren't you glad we don't celebrate weddings like that today, especially if you have to pay for it?) Although guests helped with the expenses, the host was responsible for providing enough wine for the whole week, as well as lodging for the guests. So running out of wine was a huge social embarrassment.

Watch This

JOHN 2:6–10 *Now there were set there six waterpots of stone, according to the manner of **purification** of the Jews, containing twenty or thirty gallons apiece. Jesus said to them, "Fill the waterpots with water." And they filled them up to the brim. And He said to them, "Draw some out now, and take it to the master of the feast." And they took it. When the master of the feast had tasted the water that was made wine, and did not know where it came from (but the servants who had drawn the water knew), the master of the feast called the bridegroom. And he said to him, "Every man at the beginning sets out the good wine, and when the guests have well drunk, then the inferior. You have kept the good wine until now!"* (NKJV)

These stone jars, filled with water, were common in Jewish houses. For this wedding, the family probably borrowed the best-looking ones they could find to make a better impression. Jewish people washed their hands by pouring water over them before and after eating. This ritual cleansed them from both physical dirt as well as symbolic dirt from touching people and objects that were considered bad influences or religiously unclean.

Although he didn't have to, Jesus responded to his mother's request. He told the servants to fill six jars with water all the way up to the brim (see Illustration #2). Doing so would leave no room to add wine or anything else to the water. When the servants ladled it out, the water had turned into wine with instant fermentation. This was no small miracle; Jesus created about 180 gallons of wine. That's 2,880 cups! Mary and the servants knew Jesus performed a miracle, but nobody else did. The servants delivered it to the banquet master, who tasted it before serving it to the guests. He discovered it wasn't ordinary or inferior wine; it was even better than what the bridegroom had served previously.

Normally the host served the best wine at the beginning of a social

Pharisees
religious leaders with
strict rules

gathering. Although Jewish people didn't promote or condone drunkenness, they saved inferior wine for later (in this case, later in the week), when guests' taste buds had been dulled from drinking. Thus the master of the banquet was surprised at the quality of the wine Jesus had made.

what others say

Craig S. Keener

The description of the stone jars indicates that they contained enough water to fill a Jewish immersion pool used for ceremonial purification. Although **Pharisees** forbade storing such water in jars, some Jews were less strict; thus these large jars were being reserved for ritual purposes. Stone jars were common because they were less likely to contract ritual uncleanness than those made of other substances. Using the jars for another purpose would temporarily defile them; Jesus shows more concern for his friend's wedding than for contemporary ritual.[2]

Illustration #2
Stone Water Jar—
Jews used large
stone water jars such
as this one to store
pure water meant for
ritual washing.

Jesus didn't need the servants' help to perform this miracle. He could have miraculously filled the jars with wine without their first filling them with water. But he chose to include people in his work then just as he does now. He uses us in small and large roles—when we obey him—to accomplish his purposes and demonstrate his power to the world.

The First of Many

JOHN 2:11 *This beginning of signs Jesus did in Cana of Galilee, and manifested His glory; and His disciples believed in Him. (NKJV)*

glory
John 1:14

John didn't record all the miracles Jesus performed while he was here on earth. Instead, he selected specific ones to teach specific truths: "Jesus did many other signs in the presence of His disciples, which are not written in this book; but these are written that you may believe that Jesus is the Christ, the Son of God, and that believing you may have life in His name" (John 20:30–31 NKJV).

believed
put confidence and trust in

Since turning the water into wine was Jesus' first miracle, it was important. (It also means that stories of Jesus performing miracles when he was a child and a teenager are false.) It "manifested His glory," showing that he is, indeed, God's Son. As a result, his disciples **believed** in him.

True to his focus on belief or unbelief in Jesus as God's Son, John was careful to give the results of each miracle. The chart below shows the miracles recounted in John.

Results of Jesus' Miracles

Jesus' Miracle	Result	Reference
Turned water into wine	Disciples believed	John 2:1–11
Healed official's son	Official and his household believed	John 4:46–53
Healed lame man	Jesus was persecuted by Pharisees	John 5:5–16
Fed five thousand	People wanted to make Jesus king	John 6:5–15
Walked on water	Jesus escaped and joined disciples	John 6:16–21
Healed the blind man	Pharisees were confused; healed man worshiped Jesus	John 9:1–38
Raised Lazarus from the dead	Pharisees plotted to kill Jesus	John 11:38–53

what others say

D. Edmond Hiebert

Six of the miracles are peculiar to this gospel.... In John these miracles are always designated as "signs," for they point to the deeper truth concerning Jesus as Messiah and Son of God.... The signs were intended to reveal the true nature of the person of Jesus and to awaken faith in Him. But the signs did not automatically produce conviction.[3]

Cleaning Frenzy in the Temple

go to

brothers
Matthew 13:55

synagogue
Luke 7:5

Passover
Exodus 12

pilgrim holidays
Deuteronomy 16:16

temple tax
Exodus 30:11–16;
Matthew 17:24–27

brothers
Jesus' half brothers,
children of Mary, his
mother, and Joseph

synagogue
gathering place for
religious instruction
and prayer

JOHN 2:12–17 *After this He went down to Capernaum, He, His mother, His brothers, and His disciples; and they did not stay there many days. Now the Passover of the Jews was at hand, and Jesus went up to Jerusalem. And He found in the temple those who sold oxen and sheep and doves, and the money changers doing business. When He had made a whip of cords, He drove them all out of the temple, with the sheep and the oxen, and poured out the changers' money and overturned the tables. And He said to those who sold doves, "Take these things away! Do not make My Father's house a house of merchandise!" Then His disciples remembered that it was written, "Zeal for Your house has eaten Me up." (NKJV)*

After the wedding, Jesus, his **brothers**, and his disciples went to Capernaum (see Appendix A), his headquarters for ministering in Galilee. Capernaum was an important city in that time since it was on a major trade route with a customs station and a Roman military post. It had a **synagogue** and was home to several of Jesus' disciples. Jesus did many miracles here and gave some of his most famous sermons in this area.

Passover is a Jewish holiday that comes in the spring, either March or April on our calendars. It commemorates the time when Moses freed the Jewish people from slavery in Egypt, and its meal is the basis for the Christian communion service. It was also one of three pilgrim holidays when Jewish males were required to travel to Jerusalem to celebrate it, most often taking their families with them. Thus the city was packed with pilgrims.

Since many of the people were from out of town and did not bring animals with them to sacrifice to God in the Temple, merchants sold animals in the temple area (see Illustration #3) at inflated prices. Imagine the noise of hundreds of creatures mooing, bleating, and cooing. And the stench! People probably had to hold their noses and watch where they walked in order to get inside the Temple to worship God.

All Jewish males over the age of nineteen, except for slaves, had to pay an annual temple tax of half a shekel to support their house of worship. A shekel equaled three days' wages in Jesus' time. Normally, worshipers paid this tax in person when they made the pilgrimage to Jerusalem if they didn't live there.

Since foreign coins were not acceptable for offerings or the annual temple tax, money changers made their living by exchanging foreign money for temple currency. They charged exorbitant exchange rates—much better than trying to make money from the stock market.

No wonder Jesus was angry! All those people came to worship God, and the merchants and money changers were trying to get rich at the people's expense. Their greed made it hard for others, especially the poor people, to worship. So Jesus expressed his anger at sin but did it without losing control like we so often do.

Annas
Jewish high priest

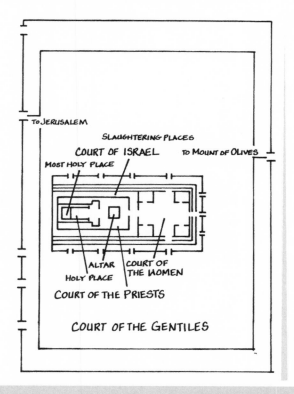

To JERUSALEM

SLAUGHTERING PLACES

COURT OF ISRAEL   TO MOUNT OF OLIVES

MOST HOLY PLACE

ALTAR   COURT OF
HOLY PLACE   THE WOMEN

COURT OF THE PRIESTS

COURT OF THE GENTILES

Illustration #3
Temple in Jesus' Day—The Temple was more than a building in which the Jewish people worshiped God. It was a gathering place. This diagram shows several courts that surrounded the main building. Animals were bought and sold in the Court of the Gentiles.

what others say

William Hendriksen

It is true, in the abstract, that each worshipper was allowed to bring to the temple an animal of his own selection. But let him try it! In all likelihood it would not be approved by the judges, the privileged venders who filled the moneychests of **Annas**! Hence, to save trouble and disappointment, animals for sacrifice were bought right here in the outer court, which was called the Court of the Gentiles because they were permitted to enter it. Of course, the dealers in cattle and sheep would be tempted to charge exorbitant prices for such animals. They would exploit the worshippers. And those who sold pigeons would do likewise, charging, perhaps, $4 for a pair of doves worth a nickel.[4]

Show Us the Proof

JOHN 2:18–22 *So the Jews answered and said to Him, "What sign do You show to us, since You do these things?" Jesus answered and said to them, "Destroy this temple, and in three days I will raise it up." Then the Jews said, "It has taken forty-six years to build this temple, and will You raise it up in three days?" But He was speaking of the temple of His body. Therefore, when He had risen from the dead, His disciples remembered that He had said this to them; and they believed the Scripture and the word which Jesus had said. (NKJV)*

After Jesus' cleaning frenzy, people wanted to know who he thought he was: "Show us the proof." Anybody who charged in and acted like he did, claiming the Temple was his Father's house, was suspect. Either he was nuts or he was the expected Messiah. They wanted proof for his claim to be Messiah.

Jesus, however, wasn't going to be manipulated into doing miracles on demand. Instead, he issued a counterchallenge, prophesying about his coming death and resurrection. But the people didn't get it. They thought he was talking about the temple building where they were standing. Three years later, after his resurrection from the dead, Jesus' disciples finally understood what he said.

what others say

D. A. Carson

As the legal authorities, these Jews had every right to question the credentials of someone who had taken such bold action in the temple complex. . . . But the way they cast their question betrays two critical deficiencies. First, they display no reflection or self-examination over whether Jesus' cleansing of the temple and related charges were foundationally just. They are therefore less concerned with pure worship and a right approach to God than they are with questions of precedent and authority. Second, if the authorities had been convinced that Jesus was merely some petty hooligan, or that he was emotionally unstable, there were adequate recourses; that they requested a miraculous sign demonstrates they harboured at least a suspicion that they were dealing with a heaven-sent prophet.[5]

Seeing to the Heart

JOHN 2:23–25 *Now when He was in Jerusalem at the Passover, during the feast, many believed in His name when they saw the signs which He did. But Jesus did not commit Himself to them, because He knew all men, and had no need that anyone should testify of man, for He knew what was in man. (NKJV)*

After the temple incident, Jesus did do some miracles. As a result, some people professed to believe in him. But he knew they didn't fully understand who he was. They were looking for a political king, and he fit the bill. Other people saw him only as a miracle worker, but he knew the depth—or shallowness—of their faith. He wasn't impressed by their words.

what others say

Warren W. Wiersbe

The word *believed* in John 2:23 and *commit* [entrust] in v. 24 are the same Greek word. These people believed in Jesus, but He did not believe in them! They were "unsaved believers"! It was one thing to respond to a miracle but quite something else to commit one's self to Jesus Christ and continue in His Word (8:30–31).[6]

Belief in Jesus comes in several varieties. Some people believe for the wrong reasons—because of what he has done for them or what they hope he'll do. Some believe with their minds; they agree he is God's Son, but that's it. Some believe with their emotions, but that initial belief fizzles when the emotional moment is gone. Others believe with their hearts; they commit their whole selves to Jesus as Savior from their sins and allow him to guide their lives. Which level of belief do you have?

Chapter Wrap-Up

- While attending a wedding, Jesus turned water into better wine than the host had already served. (John 2:1–10)
- The miracle of turning water to wine was the first of several signs that pointed to Jesus' deity. (John 2:11)
- Jesus drove the animal merchants and money changers out of the temple area, charging them with turning God's house of worship into a marketplace. (John 2:12–17)
- Jewish authorities demanded a sign from Jesus to prove his authority for cleansing the Temple. Instead of providing an immediate sign, he told them about his future death and resurrection. (John 2:18–25)

Study Questions

1. Why did Jesus' mother ask him to do something when the wine was gone?

2. How did he respond to her request?

3. Why did Jesus perform this miracle?

4. What did Jesus do when he saw the scene at the Temple? Why?

5. How did Jesus respond to the Jewish leaders' demand for a miracle after he cleansed the Temple?

6. How did the people respond to Jesus' miracles?

John 3: Jesus the Choice Giver

Chapter Highlights:
- Original Born Again
- An Old Object Lesson
- God's Great Big Love
- A New Star
- A Choice to Make

Let's Get Started

"Born again." How often have you seen this phrase in a news story or magazine feature? How many times have you heard it on TV and radio? It's a phrase that has been bandied about a lot in the last few years.

It seems like everything and everyone is born again. A restaurant changes its menu, and it's labeled born again. A man changes jobs, and his career is born again. A quick search for "born again" on the Internet produces hundreds of sites, many of them religious in nature. But there is an odd assortment of other uses for the term "born again":

- Born Again—a trademarked line of skin creams and oils
- Born-Again Boards—makers of surfboards and other hand-crafted wood products
- Born Again Used Books—a store in Colorado Springs, Colorado
- Born Again Records—the third biggest independent gospel record label in the United States
- Born Again—a CD title with explicit lyrics by the Notorious B.I.G.
- Born Again Card Recycling Program, which turns Christmas cards into ornaments
- Born Again Motorcycles, Inc.—a store that sells used parts for vintage cycles
- Born Again Creations—a company that produces one-of-akind dolls and other collectibles
- Born Again Bears—a company that recycles furs into teddy bears

The first time "born again" appears, however, is in John 3 when Jesus talks to Nicodemus. It's like a movie that generates a number of sequels. Today's phrase came from this original wording in John,

Nick at Night

JOHN 3:1–2 *There was a man of the Pharisees named Nicodemus, a ruler of the Jews. This man came to Jesus by night and said to Him, "Rabbi, we know that You are a teacher come from God; for no one can do these signs that You do unless God is with him." (NKJV)*

Many people witnessed Jesus' miracles, referred to at the end of chapter 2. One of them was Nicodemus, a religious leader. His credentials were impressive. He was both a Pharisee—a fundamentalist of his day who took Scripture seriously and taught it to the people—and a member of the Sanhedrin, the ruling body of the Jewish people.

Jesus' miracles had raised questions in his mind. He wanted to know more and probably had a hundred questions to ask. So he did the logical thing: he went directly to Jesus to get the facts. He started out by flattering Jesus: "Rabbi, we know that You are a teacher come from God." Lots of people in Nicodemus's day claimed they came from God, but the miracles proved Jesus did.

what others say

Manford George Gutzke

Nicodemus came to Jesus "by night." Some suggest that this was a cowardly thing to do, and criticize him because he did not come openly. Actually there is oftentimes more courage in quiet sincerity than in noisy approach. . . . It does not seem necessary to think that he was a furtive man, but rather his actions could show he was cautious and realistic. The night time was probably a time when Jesus was not besieged by hundreds of needy people, and so had time for the interview. Also it could be a mark of his urgent interest that he sought this interview at a time when Jesus was free to spend time in conversation with him.[1]

Philip Yancey

He [Nicodemus] comes to Jesus at night, in order to avoid detection. He risks his reputation and safety even by meeting with Jesus, whom his fellow Pharisees have sworn to kill. But Nicodemus has questions, burning questions, the most important questions anyone could ask: Who are you, Jesus? Have you really come from God?[2]

Happy Birthday, Happy Birthday

JOHN 3:3–8 Jesus answered and said to him, "Most assuredly, I say to you, unless one is born again, he cannot see the kingdom of God." Nicodemus said to Him, "How can a man be born when he is old? Can he enter a second time into his mother's womb and be born?" Jesus answered, "Most assuredly, I say to you, unless one is born of water and the Spirit, he cannot enter the kingdom of God. That which is born of the flesh is flesh, and that which is born of the Spirit is spirit. Do not marvel that I said to you, 'You must be born again.' The wind blows where it wishes, and you hear the sound of it, but cannot tell where it comes from and where it goes. So is everyone who is born of the Spirit." (NKJV)

God's Word
Ephesians 5:25–26

repent
turn away from sin

If Jesus' statements don't seem to follow Nicodemus's opening words and you feel like you missed part of the conversation, you're right. Jesus ignored his opening remarks and got right to the question that was on his mind: How can I get into God's kingdom? Because he's God, Jesus knew Nicodemus's problem—that even though Nicodemus knew the Bible, he'd missed the point. God doesn't care about how much Scripture we know; he wants everyone, including religious leaders, to have a heart relationship with him—to be born again.

But Nicodemus got stuck on the literal concept of birth. He couldn't understand how someone who is old could be born a second time physically. All he could think about was how silly it would be for a full-grown man to crawl back into his mother's womb. Even if he tried, he'd never fit. (And think how painful it would be to his mother!)

But Jesus camped on the spiritual meaning of "born again." He explained that the second birth comes from "water and the Spirit." Water may refer to <u>God's Word</u> or to John's baptism in water that symbolized repentance from sin. "The Spirit" is the Holy Spirit, God himself. The Holy Spirit uses the Bible to convict people of their sin. When they see their need for Jesus as Savior from that sin and **repent**, the result is the new birth. And without new birth, no one can get into heaven.

Being born again is a mysterious event—just like the wind blowing. Nobody can see the wind; we only see what it does. Similarly, nobody can see the Holy Spirit, only the effects of his work in a person's life.

lifted up
Numbers 21:4–9

An Old Object Lesson

JOHN 3:9–15 *Nicodemus answered and said to Him, "How can these things be?" Jesus answered and said to him, "Are you the teacher of Israel, and do not know these things? Most assuredly, I say to you, We speak what We know and testify what We have seen, and you do not receive Our witness. If I have told you earthly things and you do not believe, how will you believe if I tell you heavenly things? No one has ascended to heaven but He who came down from heaven, that is, the Son of Man who is in heaven. And as Moses <u>lifted up</u> the serpent in the wilderness, even so must the Son of Man be lifted up, that whoever believes in Him should not perish but have eternal life. (NKJV)*

For a Bible teacher, Nicodemus was dense. He didn't get what Jesus was telling him, even though it wasn't a new teaching. Although he knew the events and facts in the Old Testament, he didn't understand them. In spite of what Jesus had already taught, the religious leaders refused to submit to his authority. If Nicodemus couldn't understand Jesus' earthly illustrations, how could he possibly understand deeper spiritual truths?

But the same is true today. We live and think so much in the natural that we find God's supernatural a little confusing. We wind up looking at Christianity as a religious code, full of do's and don'ts, instead of a supernatural relationship and empowering by God. For most of us, trying to understand this relationship and empowering is like being blind and trying to understand the concept of color. If you've never had sight, how can you understand, say, the color blue?[4]

To further help Nicodemus understand the new birth, Jesus used another illustration, this one from the Law Nicodemus taught. Back in Moses' day, the Israelites were traveling through the wilderness from Egypt to the land God had promised them. God gave them food from heaven and water from rocks. Still they complained about having no real food or water. Then God sent them fiery snakes that bit them and made them die. So the people asked Moses to intercede with the Lord. When Moses prayed, God told him to make a bronze snake and put it on a pole. Then when the people were bitten, they would live if they looked at that snake.

The Israelites were given physical life as the result of believing and exercising faith in the cure God prescribed for the snakebites. So, too, people are saved from sin by exercising faith in Christ as their personal Savior from that sin. The cure for the Israelites was effective only for those who looked at the serpent; healing was not automatically given to everyone. Those who refused to look at the snake died. Similarly, God's gift of salvation is effective only for those who believe. People don't go to heaven automatically.

At this point, Nicodemus faded out of the narrative, so we don't have a record of his reaction to Jesus' invitation to be born again. Jesus is concerned with all persons, not just with Nicodemus, and addresses the following remarks to a wider audience. Although John did not record here how Nicodemus responded to this conversation, John 19:39 indicates he believed in Jesus. Nicodemus was probably a secret disciple until he helped Joseph of Arimathea bury Jesus' body.

JOHN 3:16–18 *For God so loved the world that He gave His only begotten Son, that whoever believes in Him should not perish but have everlasting life. For God did not send His Son into the world to condemn the world, but that the world through Him might be saved. He who believes in Him is not condemned; but*

perishing
spiritually lost

he who does not believe is condemned already, because he has not believed in the name of the only begotten Son of God. (NKJV)

Love in the Dark

In twenty-five English words, John 3:16 summarizes most of the Bible. It contains a number of profound—yet simple—truths. God loved the world so much that he took action. He sent his one and only Son, Jesus, on a rescue mission to save those who are **perishing**. Jesus made it clear that he came into the world to save people and give them eternal life, not to condemn them to hell.

God's greatest act of love divides humankind into two camps: the forgiven and the condemned. Everyone starts out life condemned in God's eyes. We all like to think we're pretty good—at least better than the next guy. We all think we're good enough to go to heaven. But God says, "No way. *Nada. Nyet.*" Only those who believe in the name of Jesus and trust him to save them from their sins will be able to go to heaven. Faith in Jesus changes our location after death. It also changes our life before death.

All the Greatest

God	The greatest Lover
So loved	The greatest degree
The world	The greatest number
That He gave	The greatest act
His only begotten Son,	The greatest gift
That whoever	The greatest invitation
Believes	The greatest simplicity
In Him	The greatest person
Should not perish	The greatest escape
But	The greatest difference
Have	The greatest certainty
Everlasting life	The greatest destiny

Light in the Dark

JOHN 3:19–21 *And this is the condemnation, that the light has come into the world, and men loved darkness rather than light, because their deeds were evil. For everyone practicing evil hates the light and does not come to the light, lest his deeds should be exposed. But he who does the truth comes to the light, that his* *deeds may be clearly seen, that they have been done in God."* (NKJV)

Light, in the form of Jesus' presence, came to earth and pierced the darkness of sin here. But people rejected him because they were comfortable in their sins and didn't want anyone to see them—like a burglar who works under cover of darkness so he won't be seen. The closer a person gets to the light of truth, the more exposed he or she is. People who live by God's truth and are trusting in Christ for their salvation are no longer afraid of God's light. They don't fear God's judgment. They know they have been saved from the penalty of sin. God's light draws them—like bugs to a light bulb.

Though some people teach that there are many ways to go to heaven, God makes it clear that there is only one way: through faith in his Son, Jesus. Jesus is God's gift to us, but not everyone takes the gift and unwraps it.

thrown into prison
Matthew 14:3–5

> ### what others say
>
> **Leon Morris**
>
> The very fact of salvation for all who believe implies judgment on all who do not. This is a solemn reality and John does not want us to escape it. Judgment is a recognized theme in contemporary Jewish thought, but it is the judgment of God, and it is thought of as taking place at the last day.[5]

God's welcome mat is always out. You can leave the darkness of sin and step into the light of God's love and eternal life at any time. But one day that opportunity will be gone without warning, either when you die or when Christ returns to take his children to heaven.

Battle of the Baptizers?

JOHN 3:22–26 *After these things Jesus and His disciples came into the land of Judea, and there He remained with them and baptized. Now John also was baptizing in Aenon near Salim, because there was much water there. And they came and were baptized. For John had not yet been <u>thrown into prison</u>. Then there arose a dispute between some of John's disciples and the Jews about purification. And they came to John and said to him, "Rabbi, He who was with you beyond the Jordan, to whom you have testified—behold, He is baptizing, and all are coming to Him!"* (NKJV)

No Room for the Green-Eyed Monster

JOHN 3:27–30 *John answered and said, "A man can receive nothing unless it has been given to him from heaven. You yourselves bear me witness, that I said, 'I am not the Christ,' but, 'I have been sent before Him.' He who has the bride is the bridegroom; but the friend of the bridegroom, who stands and hears him, rejoices greatly because of the bridegroom's voice. Therefore this joy of mine is fulfilled. He must increase, but I must decrease. (NKJV)*

John wasn't drawn into his disciples' resentment against Jesus. He knew that everything he had, including his ministry, was from God. There is no room for the green-eyed monster of jealousy or competition in God's work. Jesus wants his followers to be humble. Knowing this, John was happy for Jesus' popularity, like the best man is happy for the bridegroom. John shows an amazing level of humility in saying, "He must increase, but I must decrease." John recognized that, because Jesus had walked on the stage, it was time for him to exit stage left. Just a few months earlier, John had top billing. Now Jesus was the new star, and John was happy about it.

> **what others say**
>
> **William Barclay**
>
> Part of the aim of the writer of the Fourth Gospel is to ensure that John the Baptist received his proper place as the forerunner of Jesus, but no higher place than that. There were those who were still ready to call John master and lord; the writer of the Fourth Gospel wishes to show that John has a high place, but that the highest place was reserved for Jesus alone; and he also wishes to show that John himself had never any other idea than that Jesus was supreme.[6]

apply it

John the Baptist wasn't jealous of Jesus. Instead, he pointed his listeners to Jesus, saying, "Jesus is the main attraction; I'm just the warm-up band." How can you have the same attitude as John and give Jesus prominence in your life this week?

God's Seal of Approval

JOHN 3:31–33 *He who comes from above is above all; he who is of the earth is earthly and speaks of the earth. He who comes from heaven is above all. And what He has seen and heard, that He testifies; and no one receives His testimony. He who has received His testimony has certified that God is true. (NKJV)*

John the Baptist was through talking about himself. Instead, he focused on Jesus, who voluntarily brought the reality of heaven to earth. The fact that John said Jesus came from heaven was a claim that Jesus was God. Though the Jewish people understood this declaration, most of them rejected it. But a few people believed what Jesus had to say about God and his experiences in heaven. Those who accepted his testimony that he is the true God <u>certified</u> God's truthfulness.

go to

certified
John 6:27

eternal choice
Deuteronomy
30:15–20

The Choice Is Yours

JOHN 3:34–36 *For He whom God has sent speaks the words of God, for God does not give the Spirit by measure. The Father loves the Son, and has given all things into His hand. He who believes in the Son has everlasting life; and he who does not believe the Son shall not see life, but the wrath of God abides on him." (NKJV)*

The Gospel writer John concluded this section with a challenge. Since Jesus spoke God's words and came to show us what God is like, we all face an <u>eternal choice</u>: believe him or reject him. Take eternal life or God's wrath. If this conclusion sounds familiar, it is. This is the same place John brought us to with the story about Nicodemus. Jesus' life on earth means we must make a choice.

what others say

R. V. G. Tasker

Belief or disbelief in the Son of God is a matter of life or death; for, while to the believer His coming is the supreme revelation of God's love bringing the assurance of eternal life, to the unbeliever it is the sign that he remains the object of God's displeasure.[7]

Chapter Wrap-Up

- Jesus told Nicodemus he had to be born again to enter God's kingdom. (John 3:1–8)

- Jesus used the object lesson of the Israelites being saved from death by looking at the bronze snake to teach that spiritual salvation is the result of an individual decision to believe Jesus, who died for our sins. (John 3:9–15)

- God loved the world so much that he sent his Son to save men and women, not condemn them. (John 3:16–21)

- Although John the Baptist's disciples were upset that Jesus was more popular than their leader, John acknowledged that Jesus must become greater while his own ministry diminished. (John 3:22–30)

- Jesus' appearance on earth brought an eternal choice every person must make: receive him or reject him. (John 3:31–36)

Study Questions

1. Why did Nicodemus go to see Jesus?

2. What does it mean to be born again?

3. How did Jesus' illustrations help to explain the new birth?

4. Why did God send his Son, Jesus, to earth?

5. How did John view Jesus?

John 4: Jesus the Giver of Spiritual Life

Chapter Highlights:
- Contact with a Castoff
- Talking on Two Levels
- Spreading the Good News
- Long-Distance Healing

Let's Get Started

Think of the worst people you know—the kind of people you can't stand. Dirty politicians, religious bigots, murderers, groups who persecute or enslave others, drug dealers, rapists. We all categorize some groups as the scum of the earth.

The same was true in Jesus' day. Back then, Jewish people would have given the award for the worst ethnic/religious group in the world to the Samaritans. In fact, Jews hated Samaritans so much that they traveled miles out of the way to avoid them. But not Jesus—as John pointed out in chapter 4 of his book. Once again, Jesus broke the mold to meet someone's need, a Samaritan woman who came alone to a well to draw water.

through Samaria
Luke 9:51–56;
10:25–37

The Comparison Game

JOHN 4:1–3 *Therefore, when the Lord knew that the Pharisees had heard that Jesus made and baptized more disciples than John (though Jesus Himself did not baptize, but His disciples), He left Judea and departed again to Galilee. (NKJV)*

And the score is: Jesus, 103; John, 45. Okay, so we don't know the exact score. But the Pharisees were keeping it, trying to stir up trouble for Jesus. So Jesus left town to go north to Galilee (see Appendix A).

A Direct Detour

JOHN 4:4–6 *But He needed to go through Samaria. So He came to a city of Samaria which is called Sychar, near the plot of ground that Jacob gave to his son Joseph. Now Jacob's well was there. Jesus therefore, being wearied from His journey, sat thus by the well. It was about the sixth hour. (NKJV)*

Instead of taking the normal roundabout, avoid-Samaria route, Jesus opted for the direct route <u>through Samaria</u> (see Appendix A).

go to

Jacob
Genesis 33:18–20;
48:22

Jacob
grandson of
Abraham, founder of
Jewish nation

Most Jewish people didn't want anything to do with Samaritans, and that included going through their territory. But then Jesus wasn't most people, as you've probably noticed.

When he reached Sychar about noon, Jesus sat to rest at **Jacob**'s well. He'd been walking for about two days. The fact that Jesus was tired indicates he is a real man in addition to being God.

"You're Asking Me?"

JOHN 4:7–9 A woman of Samaria came to draw water. Jesus said to her, "Give Me a drink." For His disciples had gone away into the city to buy food. Then the woman of Samaria said to Him, "How is it that You, being a Jew, ask a drink from me, a Samaritan woman?" For Jews have no dealings with Samaritans. (NKJV)

Jesus was so unlike other people. Not only did he deliberately go through Samaria instead of around it, but he also broke all the social rules. He struck up a conversation with this woman—not just a Samaritan but a woman! This kind of action was totally unheard of. In fact, asking for water from a woman alone was like flirting today. But Jesus wasn't an ordinary Jew.

That this woman was alone at the well at noon speaks volumes about her reputation. Women didn't normally go to the well to get water at the hottest time of the day. But she didn't go with the rest of the village women because they shunned her or ridiculed her for her immoral lifestyle.

Since he was thirsty and didn't have a bucket or jar, Jesus asked this woman for a drink. His request surprised her since Jews and Samaritans didn't associate with one another.

what others say

Bruce Milne

On the issue of gender prejudice, male Jewish attitudes at the time are reflected in the following rabbinic citations: "One should not talk with a woman on the street, not even with his own wife, and certainly not with somebody else's wife, because of the gossip of men," and "It is forbidden to give a woman any greeting."[4]

The Gift of Life

JOHN 4:10–12 *Jesus answered and said to her, "If you knew the gift of God, and who it is who says to you, 'Give Me a drink,' you would have asked Him, and He would have given you living water." The woman said to Him, "Sir, You have nothing to draw with, and the well is deep. Where then do You get that living water? Are You greater than our father Jacob, who gave us the well, and drank from it himself, as well as his sons and his livestock?" (NKJV)*

Jesus began a conversation with this woman about water on two levels. The woman talked about literal water, and Jesus offered her God's gift of spiritual water, which is eternal life. When Jesus mentioned living water, the woman took him literally. She associated it with the water at the bottom of the well. It was obvious that Jesus didn't have a bucket to draw it up with.

That fact raised more questions in her mind about this Jewish stranger. Maybe she thought Jesus was putting down their ancestor who dug the well. Or maybe she was beginning to realize he was different.

Internal Spring

JOHN 4:13–15 *Jesus answered and said to her, "Whoever drinks of this water will thirst again, but whoever drinks of the water that I shall give him will never thirst. But the water that I shall give him will become in him a fountain of water springing up into everlasting life." The woman said to Him, "Sir, give me this water, that I may not thirst, nor come here to draw." (NKJV)*

We keep drinking water because we keep getting thirsty. The water from Jacob's well would quench the woman's thirst—temporarily.

thirst for God
Psalm 42:1–2;
Isaiah 55:1

She'd need to drink again in an hour or so. Jesus offered her an internal spring of water that would satisfy all her spiritual thirsts.

In the literal sense, "living water" is fresh or flowing water or the water at the bottom of a well that's fed from a spring. But Jesus used the term here to represent the spiritual water of life that permanently quenches our inner <u>thirst for God</u>. By accepting Jesus' words as God's words and believing in him as the Messiah, the woman could receive eternal life from the Holy Spirit. But the woman didn't get Jesus' meaning—not yet. She still took Jesus' words literally and wanted the water he offered, so she wouldn't have to return to the well.

The Samaritan woman almost didn't hear what Jesus had to tell her. She was too focused on the differences between them— Jew/Samaritan, man/woman, rabbi/layperson. How have you let racial, cultural, denominational, gender, or religious ritual differences get in the way of your hearing God?

Serial Wife with a Serious Thirst

> JOHN 4:16–18 *Jesus said to her, "Go, call your husband, and come here." The woman answered and said, "I have no husband." Jesus said to her, "You have well said, 'I have no husband,' for you have had five husbands, and the one whom you now have is not your husband; in that you spoke truly." (NKJV)*

It may seem that Jesus threw a curve into the conversation when he abruptly switched from talking about water to talking about husbands. But he really didn't. Although Jesus was a stranger, he knew all about this woman's past and present—her five husbands and the fact that she was living with a sixth man. He knew she had been trying to fill up the emptiness inside with a series of relationships with men, but she still hadn't found Mr. Right. Jesus knew she thirsted for love, acceptance, and security, but she'd been looking for it in the wrong men. Instead of condemning her for her sin of immorality, he offered her the only satisfying thirst quencher for her soul—eternal life through a relationship with himself, the real Mr. Right.

prophet
one who speaks
God's message and
future events

Paul N. Tassell

A person must understand he is lost before he will desire to be found. He must realize he is alienated from God before he sees the need to be reconciled to God. Jesus exposed the wickedness of the woman. . . . Jesus could have given her a lecture on the sins of divorce and adultery and sexual promiscuity. He could have railed on her for trying to evade the truth. He did instead get to the heart of the problem by getting to the problem of her heart. She was thirsty. She knew her sin did not satisfy. She knew that peace was not to be found in her sinful life-style. And Jesus tactfully brought all of that into focus for her.[4]

No matter what sins we've committed, we can still talk to Jesus. Although he hates sin, he loves us very much. He's always ready to listen to us whenever we want to talk to him about those sins. He offers us forgiveness, eternal life, and power to change.

key point

Where Do We Worship This Week?

JOHN 4:19–24 *The woman said to Him, "Sir, I perceive that You are a prophet. Our fathers worshiped on this mountain, and you Jews say that in Jerusalem is the place where one ought to worship." Jesus said to her, "Woman, believe Me, the hour is coming when you will neither on this mountain, nor in Jerusalem, worship the Father. You worship what you do not know; we know what we worship, for salvation is of the Jews. But the hour is coming, and now is, when the true worshipers will worship the Father in spirit and truth; for the Father is seeking such to worship Him. God is Spirit, and those who worship Him must worship in spirit and truth." (NKJV)*

The woman admitted that Jesus was right and that his knowledge of her was supernatural by calling him a **prophet**.

When Jesus got too close to the truth, what did she do? Like many of us, she changed the subject. She asked the question of her day: Where is the place to worship? The Samaritans had their own temple on Mount Gerizim, partly because they had mixed their own teachings with scriptural teachings and partly because of the feud between the Samaritans and Jews. If she believed Jesus, she wouldn't be accepted in the Jewish Temple in Jerusalem. But where she worshiped wasn't the real issue. Worshiping God "in spirit and truth" is the issue. It is more than showing up at the right time in the right place. Real worship begins with the right heart attitude that comes from a right relationship with God.

what others say

Anne Graham Lotz

We must worship God as He prescribes or He won't accept it. We can't worship Him any way we choose as long as we're sincere and not hurting anyone else. We can't worship Him the way we want while Muslims worship Him the way they want and Jews worship Him the way they want and Buddhists worship Him the way they want. Jesus said we must worship God as He wants.[4]

Answers Are Coming

JOHN 4:25–26 *The woman said to Him, "I know that Messiah is coming" (who is called Christ). "When He comes, He will tell us all things." Jesus said to her, "I who speak to you am He."* (NKJV)

The Samaritan woman wasn't quite ready to process the truth of what real worship is. Instead, she brought up another religious issue: Who is the **Messiah**? She knew that when he came—and she was expecting him—he would have all the answers. Jesus declared forthrightly that he is the expected Messiah.

what others say

Max Lucado

Remarkable. . . . It wasn't within the colonnades of a Roman court that he announced his identity. No, it was in the shade of a well in a rejected land to an ostracized woman. His eyes must have danced as he whispered the secret. "I am the Messiah." . . . Don't miss the drama of the moment. Look at her eyes, wide with amazement. Listen to her as she struggles for words. "Y-y-y-you a-a-a-are the M-m-m-messiah!" . . . Suddenly the insignificance of her life was swallowed by the significance of the moment. "God is here! God has come! God cares . . . for me!"[5]

Spreading the Good News

JOHN 4:27–30 *And at this point His disciples came, and they marveled that He talked with a woman; yet no one said, "What do You seek?" or, "Why are You talking with her?" The woman then left her waterpot, went her way into the city, and said to the men, "Come, see a Man who told me all things that I ever did. Could this be the **Christ**?" Then they went out of the city and came to Him.* (NKJV)

No wonder Jesus' disciples were surprised when they returned with lunch. He had crossed religious, ethnic, social, moral, and gender boundaries in force at the time. Jewish rabbis didn't speak to women in public. But none of the disciples were brave enough to ask Jesus why he would do such a "horrible" thing.

Notice that the woman left her water jar. She probably did so for a number of reasons. First, she wasn't focused on physical water anymore; she had found a spiritual <u>thirst</u> quencher. Second, she was expecting to return, since water pots were not disposable items back then. Finally, she may have left it so Jesus could get a drink of water while she was gone.

Imagine being in Sychar and hearing an outcast woman crying in the streets, "Come, see Jesus, who knows all about me and wants me anyway!" They certainly knew about her immoral lifestyle and didn't want her. Although she was the least likely person in town to be saved, God used her to introduce many in the town to himself.

Leaving behind her water jar was symbolic of the woman's leaving behind her former life and inner thirst for acceptance and satisfaction. Besides, carrying it would have slowed her down when she went back to town to tell others about Jesus. Are there things in your life that you need to leave with Jesus so you can enjoy what he offers you?

thirst
Isaiah 55:1–5

Christ
Greek word for Messiah

Solid Soul Food

JOHN 4:31–38 *In the meantime His disciples urged Him, saying, "Rabbi, eat." But He said to them, "I have food to eat of which you do not know." Therefore the disciples said to one another, "Has anyone brought Him anything to eat?" Jesus said to them, "My food is to do the will of Him who sent Me, and to*

God's work
Psalm 40:8

harvest
Matthew 9:37

John the Baptist
John 3:23

finish His work. Do you not say, 'There are still four months and then comes the harvest'? Behold, I say to you, lift up your eyes and look at the fields, for they are already white for harvest! And he who reaps receives wages, and gathers fruit for eternal life, that both he who sows and he who reaps may rejoice together. For in this the saying is true: 'One sows and another reaps.' I sent you to reap that for which you have not labored; others have labored, and you have entered into their labors." (NKJV)

When his disciples tried to get him to eat, Jesus wasn't interested. Instead, he focused on doing <u>God's work</u>, which was far more satisfying than physical food. God's work for him then was talking to people like the Samaritan woman about God. That satisfied him more than food satisfies physical hunger.

Then Jesus took the subject of food back a step to the harvest, the source of food. He compared the people coming from town to fields that were ready to <u>harvest</u>. In other words, these people were ready to be told about God's gift of salvation. The disciples probably didn't think of Samaritans as being "ripe" to hear this message, because they despised the Samaritans. But the woman told them her faith story, and others before her (probably <u>John the Baptist</u>) had sown seeds of knowledge about Jesus. The disciples were there to "harvest" those seeds, to introduce the people to Jesus and a right relationship with God through him.

When we hear—or read about—people's relationships with God, our own faith grows. The Bible is full of people's faith stories—honest accounts of their failures and successes in walking with him. So reading the Bible, as well as listening to others relate what God has taught them, encourages us to trust him more. And when we tell about our faith journeys, we motivate others to get to know God better.

Real satisfaction comes from doing God's will, not from accumulating more stuff or going from relationship to relationship like the Samaritan woman did. If you're trying to fill your life with anything other than God in order to feel full and satisfied, you'll never be truly happy.

<u>Ear Belief</u>

JOHN 4:39–42 *And many of the Samaritans of that city believed in Him because of the word of the woman who testified,*

"He told me all that I ever did." So when the Samaritans had come to Him, they urged Him to stay with them; and He stayed there two days. And many more believed because of His own word. Then they said to the woman, "Now we believe, not because of what you said, for we ourselves have heard Him and we know that this is indeed the Christ, the Savior of the world." *(NKJV)*

Many of those Samaritans believed in Jesus because of what the woman had told them. Others believed when they heard him teach.

At their urging, he stayed a couple of days to teach them and help them grow spiritually. As a result, they understood that Jesus is the Savior <u>of the whole world</u>, not just of Samaritans and Jews. Their perspective was broader than the disciples' view had been a couple of days earlier.

of the whole world
John 3:16

no honor
Matthew 13:57

feast
(Passover) spring
celebration of God's
delivering the
Israelites from
Egypt

what others say

Craig S. Keener

For Jesus to lodge there, eating Samaritan food and teaching Samaritans (v. 40) would be roughly equivalent to defying segregation in the United States during the 1950s or apartheid in South Africa in the 1980s—shocking, extremely difficult, somewhat dangerous. The Jesus of the Gospels is more concerned with people than with custom.[6]

Henry Blackaby

Knowledge of God comes through experience. We come to know God as we experience Him in and around our lives.[7]

Back in Cana

JOHN 4:43–47 *Now after the two days He departed from there and went to Galilee. For Jesus Himself testified that a prophet has <u>no honor</u> in his own country. So when He came to Galilee, the Galileans received Him, having seen all the things He did in Jerusalem at the **feast**; for they also had gone to the feast.*

So Jesus came again to Cana of Galilee where He had made the water wine. And there was a certain nobleman whose son was sick at Capernaum. When he heard that Jesus had come out of Judea into Galilee, he went to Him and implored Him to come down and heal his son, for he was at the point of death. (NKJV)

go to

first miracle
turning water to
wine

Herod
Roman governor of
Palestine

seventh hour
about 1:00 p.m.

After a brief stopover in Samaria, Jesus continued on to Galilee, where people welcomed him. He returned to Cana (see Appendix A), the place of his first miracle.

This royal official served in **Herod**'s court. He would have been wealthy but probably not religious. However, he had heard about Jesus and his first miracle. So he trekked twenty miles—almost a day's walk—to where Jesus was and begged him to heal his dying son. This official was desperate! But he went to the right person for help.

what others say

Matthew Henry

[The official showed] his great respect to our Lord Jesus, that he would come himself to wait upon him, when he might have sent a servant; and that he besought him, when, as a man in authority, some would think he might have ordered his attendance. The greatest men, when they come to God, must become beggars.[8]

A Master of Distance

JOHN 4:48–54 *Then Jesus said to him, "Unless you people see signs and wonders, you will by no means believe." The nobleman said to Him, "Sir, come down before my child dies!" Jesus said to him, "Go your way; your son lives." So the man believed the word that Jesus spoke to him, and he went his way. And as he was now going down, his servants met him and told him, saying, "Your son lives!" Then he inquired of them the hour when he got better. And they said to him, "Yesterday at the **seventh hour** the fever left him." So the father knew that it was at the same hour in which Jesus said to him, "Your son lives." And he himself believed, and his whole household. This again is the second sign Jesus did when He had come out of Judea into Galilee. (NKJV)*

Jesus lamented the fact that the Galileans subscribed to the seeing-is-believing philosophy. The official didn't get sidetracked with a philosophical or religious discussion. Instead, he kept after Jesus to go to Capernaum (see Appendix A) to heal his son. Jesus told him to go home, and his son would live.

Amazingly, the man did just that! He believed Jesus and acted on his faith. On the way, his servants met him to tell him that his son was healed—at the exact time Jesus said the boy would live. This fact convinced the official that Jesus was the Son of God, and he shared his faith with the rest of his household, who also believed.

The boy's healing became the second miracle Jesus performed in Cana, demonstrating his power over distance.

Although the royal official had never met Jesus and wasn't a religious man, he demonstrated unconditional trust in Jesus. When Jesus told him to go home, he obeyed, realizing Jesus didn't need to be present to heal his son. Do you have that kind of trust in Jesus? Or are you enrolled in the seeing-is-believing school of faith?

something to ponder

Chapter Wrap-Up

- Jesus made a detour through Samaria to talk with a woman at a well about himself and to offer her eternal life. (John 4:1–9)
- Jesus told the woman about her past and taught her about true worship. As a result, she believed he is the Messiah. (John 4:10–26)
- The Samaritan woman went back to her village to tell the people she had met the Messiah. In the meantime, Jesus explained to his disciples the principle of sowing and reaping in relation to faith. (John 4:27–42)
- Jesus demonstrated power over distance by healing an official's dying son from twenty miles away. (John 4:43–54)

Study Questions

1. What was unusual about Jesus' stop in Samaria?
2. What did Jesus teach the Samaritan woman in their conversation?
3. How did the woman respond to Jesus' teaching?
4. What lessons did Jesus teach his disciples when they returned after his conversation with the woman?
5. How did the Samaritan woman influence others after she believed in Jesus?
6. How did Jesus respond to the official's request to heal his son?
7. What do you learn about Jesus from the miracle he performed for the official's son?

John 5: Jesus the Healer

Chapter Highlights:
• Lame Man Walks
• Jewish Judgment
• The Defense Speaks
• Witnesses for the
  Defense

Let's Get Started

Desperate for healing, sick people will flock to any site that purports to offer a miracle cure.

For example, several years ago in Tlacote, Mexico, five thousand to ten thousand people a day stood in line for over a mile to get water from Jesus Chahin's well to cure their illnesses. When a sick farm dog recovered swiftly after lapping some of the water, Chahin started giving it away. Once the word got out, people traveled from as far away as Europe and Russia. The health department tested the water and found it to be normal. But Chahin said it weighs less than normal water, a fact to which he attributed its healing properties. It is supposed to have cured AIDS, blindness, lameness, cancer, obesity, high cholesterol, and a number of other diseases.

The following year, a spring of healing water was discovered in a cave in Germany, east of Dusseldorf. People claimed it healed blindness, bad backs, rheumatism, and high blood pressure.

A few months later, water began gushing out of a deserted well north of Delhi, India. People who bathed in it said they were healed of skin diseases, polio, and other illnesses.

The sites and healings go on and on.

But this phenomenon is not new. Even back in Jesus' day, sick people gathered at a pool in hopes of being healed, as John reported in chapter 5. When Jesus healed a lame man at that pool, the miracle led to a lot of trouble for Jesus. But he ably defended himself.

Lame Man Walks

JOHN 5:1–5 *After this there was a feast of the Jews, and Jesus went up to Jerusalem. Now there is in Jerusalem by the Sheep Gate a pool, which is called in Hebrew, Bethesda, having five porches. In these lay a great multitude of sick people, blind, lame, paralyzed, waiting for the moving of the water. For an angel went down at a certain time into the pool and stirred up the water; then whoever stepped in first, after the stirring of the water, was made well of whatever disease he had. Now a certain man was there who had an infirmity thirty-eight years. (NKJV)*

As an observant Jew, Jesus went to Jerusalem to celebrate a feast. But that wasn't the only reason he went. He made a stop at the Pool of Bethesda (see Illustration #4). Whether healing actually occurred here each year, we don't know. People were desperate to try anything that might work. So they gathered around the pool, hoping, waiting, and praying for healing.

what others say

Anne Graham Lotz

Most passersby would have been hardpressed to notice the bubbling water of the pool because the scene surrounding it was surely so heart-wrenching. Every reject in the city must have gathered at the pool of Bethesda, the "House of Mercy." The emaciated bodies, the pale faces, the pain-deadened eyes, the hollow cheeks all gave silent witness to the helplessness and hopelessness of the diseased and disfigured and dying who lay, crumpled and sprawled, like discarded refuse on the terrace that led to the water's edge.[1]

R. Kent Hughes

The Pool of Bethesda was a sort of shrine. The pool periodically rippled because of a subterranean spring. Long before, a sick person had been in the pool when it rippled and he had concluded that he was healed by the water. News of the "miracle" spread over the city and surrounding countryside and a legend was born: At certain seasons an angel of the Lord went down into the pool, and stirred up the water. The first person to go into the pool after the stirring would be healed (v. 4). As a result, hundreds of people from the countryside came to the Pool of Bethesda to be healed. Five porticoes were built so that the sick could be shaded from the sun as they waited for the stirring of the waters.[2]

Imagine living by the side of a pool with a lot of other sick people, hoping to be the first one in when the water is stirred up. Imagine knowing that, even if you are the first to see the water bubbling, there's no hope of your being healed because you can't get in by yourself and there's no one to help you. Imagine straining day in and day out to keep your arm, or some part of your body, as close to the water's edge as the hordes of people around you will tolerate as they push and shove to stake out a spot for themselves. Imagine calling out to the healthy people who walked by and begging them to give you, not the person beside you, some food or money. That's what this man's life was like—for thirty-eight years. Talk about depressing.

Who Wants to Be Healed?

JOHN 5:6–8 *When Jesus saw him lying there, and knew that he already had been in that condition a long time, He said to him, "Do you want to be made well?" The sick man answered Him, "Sir, I have no man to put me into the pool when the water is stirred up; but while I am coming, another steps down before me." Jesus said to him, "Rise, take up your bed and walk." (NKJV)*

The man Jesus picked out from the crowd to heal was a man who had been lame for almost four decades. When he asked the man if he wanted to be healed, the man made an excuse. He didn't give the straight answer—yes—that we would expect. Jesus ignored his excuse and told him to get up and walk, which was a ridiculous command. If the man could do that, he wouldn't be lying around waiting for someone to help him into the pool!

Instant Cure

JOHN 5:9 *And immediately the man was made well, took up his bed, and walked. And that day was the Sabbath. (NKJV)*

law to rest
Exodus 20:10

Sabbath
Saturday, Jewish day
of worship

the Jews
Pharisees, religious
leaders

Amazingly, the man obeyed Jesus, a stranger. As a result, he was cured immediately and walked away on that **Sabbath**. You would think the people watching would have cheered and hoisted Jesus on their shoulders like a hero. But that's not what happened. The strict religious leaders pitched a fit about two things: (1) that Jesus did "work" by healing on the Sabbath; and (2) that the sick man did "work" by picking up his mat and carrying it.

For this lame man to get up and walk at Jesus' command was impossible. Yet he did it. What is there in your life that seems impossible? Getting a job? Paying your bills? Finding a husband or wife? Having children? Getting healed? If it's in line with God's Word and will, it's possible with Jesus when you obey him.

The Mystery Healer

JOHN 5:10–13 *The Jews therefore said to him who was cured, "It is the Sabbath; it is not lawful for you to carry your bed." He answered them, "He who made me well said to me, 'Take up your bed and walk.'" Then they asked him, "Who is the Man who said to you, 'Take up your bed and walk'?" But the one who was healed did not know who it was, for Jesus had withdrawn, a multitude being in that place. (NKJV)*

The Jewish leaders didn't care that this man was miraculously healed. They cared that the healing had taken place on the Sabbath, the day of rest, the day of no work. They had added a lot of regulations to God's <u>law to rest</u> on the Sabbath day and so had distorted its meaning. According to these leaders, carrying a bed mat on the Sabbath was a sin, and healing on the Sabbath was outlawed as well.

As a result, they grilled the man to find out who had healed him. But he didn't know. He must have been so busy celebrating his healing that he forgot to thank Jesus. Or maybe the healed man was just too selfish to think of anyone but himself. Anyway, Jesus had disappeared before he could find out who he was.

Down with Jesus

JOHN 5:14–18 *Afterward Jesus found him in the temple, and said to him, "See, you have been made well. Sin no more, lest a worse thing come upon you." The man departed and told the Jews that it was Jesus who had made him well.*

For this reason the Jews persecuted Jesus, and sought to kill Him, because He had done these things on the Sabbath. But Jesus answered them, "My Father has been working until now, and I have been working." Therefore the Jews sought all the more to kill Him, because He not only broke the Sabbath, but also said that God was His Father, making Himself equal with God. (NKJV)

death penalty
Leviticus 24:16

blasphemy
insulting and disrespecting God

Later Jesus looked up the man he had healed to identify himself. Logically, the Jewish leaders should have prosecuted the healed man for breaking the law instead of going after Jesus. But they were on a mission to destroy this man who claimed to be God and who pointed out that God doesn't quit working on the Sabbath. After all, God keeps on holding the universe together, sending rain and sunshine, answering prayers, giving life, and taking life regardless of what day it is.

Although the Jews didn't believe in Jesus as the Messiah, they understood his claim to deity. Because they didn't believe Jesus was the Messiah, they regarded his claim as **blasphemy**, an offense that carried the <u>death penalty</u>. This is the first of many recorded persecutions of Jesus in the book of John.

what others say

Dana Gould

To the Jewish mind, Jesus' claim to be God was blasphemous because it suggested the idea of two Gods. Of course, nothing of the sort was in mind with Jesus' self-declaration as the Son of God. Rather, Jesus proclaimed that He was God in human form, the second person of the Trinity.[3]

Leon Morris

The expression "My Father" is noteworthy. It was not the way Jews usually referred to God. Usually they spoke of "our Father," and while they might use "My Father" in prayer they would qualify it with "in heaven" or some other expression to remove the suggestion of familiarity. Jesus did no such thing, here or elsewhere. He habitually thought of God as in the closest relationship to Himself. The expression implies a claim which the Jews did not miss.[4]

The Defense Speaks

JOHN 5:19–23 *Then Jesus answered and said to them, "Most assuredly, I say to you, the Son can do nothing of Himself, but what He sees the Father do; for whatever He does, the Son also does in like manner. For the Father loves the Son, and shows Him all things that He Himself does; and He will show Him greater works than these, that you may marvel. For as the Father raises the dead and gives life to them, even so the Son gives life to whom He will. For the Father judges no one, but has committed all judgment to the Son, that all should honor the Son just as they honor the Father. He who does not honor the Son does not honor the Father who sent Him.* (NKJV)

Instead of denying the leaders' accusation of blasphemy, Jesus gave them a lot of ammunition to use against him. (He doesn't act like we would expect, does he?) He and the Father know each other intimately and love each other very much. Because of this relationship, Jesus can do only what God does.

Jesus went on to shock his audience even more. These Jewish leaders knew only God can raise people from the dead and judge them at the final judgment. When Jesus claimed he could do the same things, he was clearly claiming to be God. As such, failure to honor him equaled failure to honor God. You can almost feel the anger rising from the leaders as they listened to Jesus' words.

what others say

Roger L. Fredrikson

The Father has given His power of life to the Son. The work of the Father is revealed in the works of the Son as He freely shares life with whomever He chooses. Every devout Jew knew that God was the Source of all life—not only in the act of creation, but even in raising the dead. They accepted the accounts of life being given to the dead in the Old Testament records, but for this itinerant preacher to claim that gift of life was an affront to their rigid orthodoxy. Yet, specific proof that the life of God was in Him was before them in the one who had been healed.[5]

When Jesus claimed to be equal with God, either he was joking (and it was a bad joke!), crazy (what sane person would give this much ammunition to the people who wanted to kill him?), lying (and therefore no one could trust him about anything), or telling the truth. What do you think?

No matter what anyone or any religion says, we can't have God without Jesus. They come as an indivisible set. If we reject Jesus, we also reject God. If we accept Jesus, we also accept God. There isn't an either/or option.

go to

Son of Man
Daniel 7:13–14

Lazarus
John 11:1–44

Dead Men Hearing

JOHN 5:24–27 *"Most assuredly, I say to you, he who hears My word and believes in Him who sent Me has everlasting life, and shall not come into judgment, but has passed from death into life. Most assuredly, I say to you, the hour is coming, and now is, when the dead will hear the voice of the Son of God; and those who hear will live. For as the Father has life in Himself, so He has granted the Son to have life in Himself, and has given Him authority to execute judgment also, because He is the Son of Man. (NKJV)*

The Hebrew Scriptures teach that eternal life happens after people are raised from the dead at the last judgment. Jesus gave this concept a new spin by declaring that eternal life—a new quality of life—is available right now when people believe in him.

Jesus' second claim to being the Son of God was the fact that God gave him the authority to raise people from the dead. Later he would demonstrate that ability with Lazarus. Here he mentioned two resurrections: (1) people who are dead in sin made alive to eternal life, and (2) his own physical resurrection from the dead.

Grave-Cracking Lesson

JOHN 5:28–30 *Do not marvel at this; for the hour is coming in which all who are in the graves will hear His voice and come forth—those who have done good, to the resurrection of life, and those who have done evil, to the resurrection of condemnation. I can of Myself do nothing. As I hear, I judge; and My judgment is righteous, because I do not seek My own will but the will of the Father who sent Me. (NKJV)*

In spite of what some people teach, death is not the end. We don't just breathe our last and go into oblivion. Rather, death is the begin-

go to

resurrection of dead
believers
1 Thessalonians
4:13–18

judgment
Revelation 20:11–15

**another who bears
witness**
Deuteronomy 17:6;
19:15

John the Baptist
John 1:29

ning of a new life that will last forever either in heaven or in hell. Jesus continued his list of resurrections by referring to the future <u>resurrection of dead believers</u> to eternal life and the resurrection of dead unbelievers to <u>judgment</u>. Both of these will happen when he returns.

Although God the Father gave Jesus the job of judging people, he can't—and won't—do it on his own. After all, they are an inseparable team and Jesus wants to please the Father. Once more, Jesus drove home the point that he is God, which caused the Jewish leaders to accuse him of blasphemy.

Witnesses for the Defense

JOHN 5:31–35 *If I bear witness of Myself, My witness is not true. There is <u>another who bears witness</u> of Me, and I know that the witness which He witnesses of Me is true. You have sent to John, and he has borne witness to the truth. Yet I do not receive testimony from man, but I say these things that you may be saved. He was the burning and shining lamp, and you were willing for a time to rejoice in his light. (NKJV)*

Jesus' third claim to being God's Son was a roll call of witnesses. He started with his own testimony, though he realized that wasn't enough by itself. So he trotted out <u>John the Baptist</u>, whom the Jewish people listened to for a while. John brought God's light, but they didn't really understand his message and put their faith in Jesus, God's Son.

Miracle Defense

JOHN 5:36–40 *But I have a greater witness than John's; for the works which the Father has given Me to finish—the very works that I do—bear witness of Me, that the Father has sent Me. And the Father Himself, who sent Me, has testified of Me. You have neither heard His voice at any time, nor seen His form. But you do not have His word abiding in you, because whom He sent, Him you do not believe. You search the Scriptures, for in them you think you have eternal life; and these are they which testify of Me. But you are not willing to come to Me that you may have life. (NKJV)*

Jesus then brought out his miracles as a testimony to his deity. After all, who but God could change <u>water into wine</u> and <u>heal a dying boy</u> from a distance? The people involved in those miracles could testify convincingly about what Jesus had done for them.

In case these witnesses were not enough, Jesus next called God the Father and his Word as witnesses. The people to whom Jesus was speaking had not seen God or heard his voice, but they had his written Word. Both the religious leaders and the common people respected God's written Word, which testifies to Jesus and his deity. But the leaders who studied and taught the Scriptures didn't understand that the passages about the Messiah pointed to Jesus, who was finally living there among them.

water into wine
John 2:1–11

heal a dying boy
John 4:46–54

what others say

Paul Little

People often ask, "If Christianity is true, why do the majority of intelligent people not believe it?" The answer is precisely the same as the reason the majority of unintelligent people don't believe it. They don't want to![6]

We can know the Bible backward and forward like the Jewish leaders in Jesus' day and still not know God and his Son. God didn't give us Scripture just so we would have something to study. Instead, he gave us his Word so we can know he exists, what he is like, that he loves us, and that he wants a personal relationship with us through faith in his Son. Bible head knowledge is useless unless we act on it— first by believing in Jesus and then by practicing the truth God tells us, so we can become more and more like him.

Short in the Love Department

JOHN 5:41–44 *I do not receive honor from men. But I know you, that you do not have the love of God in you. I have come in My Father's name, and you do not receive Me; if another comes in his own name, him you will receive. How can you believe, who receive honor from one another, and do not seek the honor that comes from the only God? (NKJV)*

Jesus wasn't looking for praise from people. Instead, he was evaluating their love for God. This group came up short in that department although they would have sworn they did love him. In reality,

wrote about Jesus
Numbers 24:17
Deuteronomy 18:15, 18

they loved their religion more. That's why they didn't accept Jesus' claim to be sent by God. Sure, they would have accepted him if he had fit their preconceived notions of what the Messiah was supposed to do—like free them from the Roman rule. But Jesus didn't. So these leaders continued to seek one another's approval instead of God's.

Accusations As a Closing Statement

JOHN 5:45–47 *Do not think that I shall accuse you to the Father; there is one who accuses you—Moses, in whom you trust. For if you believed Moses, you would believe Me; for he wrote about Me. But if you do not believe his writings, how will you believe My words?" (NKJV)*

For his closing statement, Jesus pointed out that Moses, whom the people revered and quoted, would become their judge. <u>He wrote about Jesus</u>, whom they wanted to kill. But they didn't believe either Moses or Jesus. Case closed.

Chapter Wrap-Up

- Jesus instantly healed a man who had been lame for thirty-eight years. (John 5:1–9)
- Because Jesus healed on the Sabbath and claimed to be God, the Jewish leaders tried to kill him. (John 5:10–18)
- Jesus claimed to be able to give life like God does. (John 5:19–30)
- Jesus called five witnesses to prove his deity: himself, John the Baptist, his works, God the Father, and God's Word. (John 5:31–47)

Study Questions

1. Why was the crowd of sick people gathered at the Pool of Bethesda?

2. Why did Jesus ask the man at the pool if he wanted to be healed?

3. How did Jesus heal him?

4. Why were the Jewish leaders upset about this healing?

5. Why did Jesus later seek out the healed man?

6. What claims did Jesus make to support his deity?

7. What witnesses did Jesus call to support his claim to be God's Son?

8. How effective was Jesus' defense for himself as the Son of God?

John 6: Jesus the Miracle Worker

Chapter Highlights:
- Lunch Feeds a Crowd
- He Can Walk on Water
- He Is a New Brand of Bread

Let's Get Started

Take a minute for these fun food facts:

The world's largest lollipop weighed 1.01 tons.

The largest cookie ever made was a chocolate chip cookie 34 feet in diameter with nearly 4 million chocolate chips.

The longest meat loaf on record was 3,491 feet, 9 inches long.

The largest omelet was 1,324 square feet and was made in a frying pan 41 feet, 1 inch in diameter.

The largest pizza ever baked was 122 feet, 8 inches in diameter.

The largest crowd fed with five loaves and two small fish lived in Jesus' day and was five thousand men plus women and children. John—as well as the other three Gospel writers—recorded this event. It must have been important, since all four of them wrote it up. It also introduced the first of Jesus' "I AM" descriptions of himself. These statements point to the fact that he is God and will provide what we need for our spiritual lives.

Jesus' feeding of the more than five thousand was the peak of his popular career. Up until now, his popularity quotient had been increasing steadily. But after this miracle, he started teaching about his death. As a result, the number of his disciples began to dwindle.

One Lunch Feeds a Crowd

> JOHN 6:1–4 *After these things Jesus went over the Sea of Galilee, which is the Sea of Tiberias. Then a great multitude followed Him, because they saw His signs which He performed on those who were diseased. And Jesus went up on the mountain, and there He sat with His disciples. Now the Passover, a feast of the Jews, was near. (NKJV)*

Jesus had healed the lame man and sparred with the Jewish leaders over doing it on the Sabbath. He needed some R and R. So he crossed the Sea of Galilee (see Appendix A) to get away from the crowd. But they followed him anyway, hoping for more miracles.

Going for Broke

go to

five thousand
Matthew 14:21

JOHN 6:5–9 *Then Jesus lifted up His eyes, and seeing a great multitude coming toward Him, He said to Philip, "Where shall we buy bread, that these may eat?" But this He said to test him, for He Himself knew what He would do. Philip answered Him, "Two hundred denarii worth of bread is not sufficient for them, that every one of them may have a little." One of His disciples, Andrew, Simon Peter's brother, said to Him, "There is a lad here who has five barley loaves and two small fish, but what are they among so many?" (NKJV)*

You'd think Jesus' disciples, after spending time with him and watching him do miracles, would be primed for another one. Instead, they had no idea how they'd feed this huge crowd—at least fifteen to twenty thousand people, counting women and children—when Jesus asked them where they could buy enough bread.

Philip saw the problem clearly. It would take more than eight months' salary just to give everyone a bite, and they didn't have that kind of money.

Andrew was a bit more helpful. He rounded up five bagels and a couple of sardines from a young boy. But he knew that lunch wouldn't make a dent in the crowd's appetite.

Jesus, however, knew how they'd feed that crowd.

> **what others say**
>
> **Erwin W. Lutzer**
>
> Their [the disciples'] initial response, according to the account in Mark, was to say, "Send the people away so they can go to the surrounding countryside and villages and buy themselves something to eat" (Mark 6:36 NIV). They were not hard-hearted, just realistic. What were they to do? Like us watching refugees on television, they felt both compassion and helplessness; a willingness to do something, along with the futility of knowing that nothing (or very little) could be done.[1]

God and Son Catering

JOHN 6:10–13 *Then Jesus said, "Make the people sit down." Now there was much grass in the place. So the men sat down, in number about <u>five thousand</u>. And Jesus took the loaves, and when He had given thanks He distributed them to the disciples,* *and the disciples to those sitting down; and likewise of the fish, as much as they wanted. So when they were filled, He said to His disciples, "Gather up the fragments that remain, so that nothing is lost." Therefore they gathered them up, and filled twelve baskets with the fragments of the five barley loaves which were left over by those who had eaten. (NKJV)*

Since Jesus already had the problem solved, he instructed his disciples to have the people sit down on the grass for a picnic. From the other accounts of this event, we can assume the miracle took place in Jesus' hands as he gave the food to his disciples to distribute to the crowd.

As a result of a young boy's generosity, Jesus multiplied a lunch into plenty to eat for a crowd—with twelve baskets of leftovers. It's good to know that even Jesus believed in using leftovers. (That's good news for moms everywhere!) The amount of food gathered shows that Jesus supplied more than enough for every hungry person.

go to

the Prophet
Deuteronomy
18:15–18

GOD AT WORK

the Prophet
one like Moses

manna
breadlike wafers
that miraculously
appeared on the
ground

Disappearing Act

JOHN 6:14–15 *Then those men, when they had seen the sign that Jesus did, said, "This is truly **the Prophet** who is to come into the world." Therefore when Jesus perceived that they were about to come and take Him by force to make Him king, He departed again to the mountain by Himself alone. (NKJV)*

The people got all excited. They had visions of Moses feeding their ancestors with **manna** from heaven. As a result of this miracle, the people wanted to use Jesus—to make him a king to gain freedom from Roman rule. Before they could try to manipulate him, however, Jesus disappeared. After all, he had come to offer spiritual, not political, salvation.

> **what others say**
>
> **Erwin W. Lutzer**
>
> After the feeding of the five thousand, there was a clamor to crown Jesus king. . . . What a king He would be! He could feed the country without effort, rancor, or fanfare! Good-bye fishing and baking bread. Welcome leisure and prosperity![2]

Herschel H. Hobbs

From the **Synoptics** we know that He first sent the Twelve away and then dismissed the crowd (Matthew 14:22–23; Mark 6:45–46). The fact that He first sent the disciples away allows two possible interpretations. Some see in this Jesus' desire to get them out of this revolutionary atmosphere lest they be affected by it. The other and more plausible position is that they themselves were the cause of this abortive attempt at revolution. Jesus' veiled reference to Judas the next day (vv. 70–71) suggests that he may have been at the bottom of the entire thing. If this be a correct surmise then Jesus had to send the Twelve away before He could control the crowd. Afterward, He slipped away to pray.[3]

Jesus not only fed thousands of people enough food to satisfy them, but in addition he provided so much that there were leftovers. That's typical of Jesus. He often gives us more than enough, more than we ask for. (But not always, so we can't get in the habit of expecting an abundance of money or things.)

This young boy gave Jesus all he had even though it wasn't very much. He didn't keep it for himself or give Jesus only part of it. As a result, Jesus multiplied it to feed thousands. What do you have that you can give to Jesus? Money? Time? Possessions? Yourself? The more you give, the more he will give back to you. It's a guaranteed investment.

Sailing into a Storm

> JOHN 6:16–18 *Now when evening came, His disciples went down to the sea, got into the boat, and went over the sea toward Capernaum. And it was already dark, and Jesus had not come to them. Then the sea arose because a great wind was blowing. (NKJV)*

After the impromptu picnic, Jesus' disciples set sail without their leader across the Sea of Galilee toward Capernaum (see Appendix A). However, they hadn't counted on dealing with a storm after dark.

The Sea of Galilee is a lake in northern Israel that's eight miles wide at the widest point and thirteen miles long. It's six hundred feet below sea level and surrounded by hills. It is known for sudden, violent storms. The disciples were probably more than halfway across the water when the storm started, so going back wasn't an option.

He Can Walk on Water!

JOHN 6:19–21 *So when they had rowed about three or four miles, they saw Jesus walking on the sea and drawing near the boat; and they were afraid. But He said to them, "It is I; do not be afraid." Then they willingly received Him into the boat, and immediately the boat was at the land where they were going. (NKJV)*

By now, the disciples should have been ready for anything as far as Jesus was concerned. But when they saw him walking on the water in the middle of a storm, they freaked out. (Wouldn't you?) When Jesus introduced himself, they recognized his voice and welcomed him on board.

Then another miracle occurred: the boat came to shore instantly at the other side of the sea.

Seeking the Supplier

JOHN 6:22–24 *On the following day, when the people who were standing on the other side of the sea saw that there was no other boat there, except that one which His disciples had entered, and that Jesus had not entered the boat with His disciples, but His disciples had gone away alone—however, other boats came from Tiberias, near the place where they ate bread after the Lord had given thanks—when the people therefore saw that Jesus was not there, nor His disciples, they also got into boats and came to Capernaum, seeking Jesus. (NKJV)*

In the morning, the people who were still there looked for Jesus. Maybe they were expecting breakfast. Since they saw the disciples leave in the only boat available, and since they hadn't seen Jesus get in that boat, they naturally wondered where he was. After boats arrived from Tiberias, the people used them to get across the lake toward Capernaum (see Appendix A) to find Jesus.

Vain Reasons

JOHN 6:25–29 *And when they found Him on the other side of the sea, they said to Him, "Rabbi, when did You come here?" Jesus answered them and said, "Most assuredly, I say to you, you seek Me, not because you saw the signs, but because you ate of the loaves and were filled. Do not labor for the food which perishes, but for the food which endures to everlasting life, which the Son of Man will give you, because God the Father has set His seal on Him." Then they said to Him, "What shall we do, that we may work the works of God?" Jesus answered and said to them, "This is the work of God, that you believe in Him whom He sent." (NKJV)*

The people were looking for Jesus for all the wrong reasons. They didn't care that the miracles authenticated his claim to be God and that he offered eternal life instead of eternal death. They were interested in physical bread.

Like so many people today, this crowd was focused on what they could do to earn God's favor. They were confident that they could earn their way into God's club of preferred members. But God doesn't want our works; he wants our faith in his Son.

what others say

Lawrence O. Richards

So much in our relationship with Jesus remains rooted in materialism. We trust Him, hoping He'll keep us healthy. Or get us a job. We even pray for the Lord to give us the numbers so we can win Lotto! . . . It's not that God doesn't care about our material needs. God does. And He meets them, providing our "daily bread." The thing is that God cares most about our spiritual needs: the truly vital and important needs that every human being has.[5]

what others say

W. Graham Scroggie

These people loved Jesus for His bread, and therefore loved the bread more than Jesus. Mark the double paradox in verse 27. The people are told that they should not labour for the perishable food, which is the very thing they must get by working; and that they should labour for the heavenly food, which is not to be earned by labour.[6]

Jesus invites us to come to him with our needs, and he wants to spend time with us. But sometimes we seek him for selfish reasons like this crowd did. They only wanted more physical food, not eternal life. Sometimes we expect miracles on demand. Neither of these reasons will get us a relationship with Jesus.

Real Bread

JOHN 6:30–34 *Therefore they said to Him, "What sign will You perform then, that we may see it and believe You? What work will You do? Our fathers <u>ate the manna</u> in the desert; as it is written, 'He gave them bread from heaven to eat.'" Then Jesus said to them, "Most assuredly, I say to you, Moses did not give you the bread from heaven, but My Father gives you the true bread from heaven. For the bread of God is He who comes down from heaven and gives life to the world." Then they said to Him, "Lord, give us this bread always." (NKJV)*

As if Jesus had not shown these people enough miracles already, they asked for a sign so they could believe in him. After all, Moses had fed their ancestors with manna for forty years. Could Jesus top that?

Sure he could. Moses hadn't provided the manna; God had. Now God was giving them true bread from heaven—Jesus himself. Jesus was offering them spiritual food. Manna had to be gathered every day. Physical food must be eaten every day. Spiritual food from Jesus, once accepted and believed in faith, lasts forever. The crowd missed the point, however. They wanted physical bread delivered hot to the breakfast table, and they boldly asked for it.

No Mystery in This Will

I AM
Exodus 3:14

JOHN 6:35–40 *And Jesus said to them, "I am the bread of life. He who comes to Me shall never hunger, and he who believes in Me shall never thirst. But I said to you that you have seen Me and yet do not believe. All that the Father gives Me will come to Me, and the one who comes to Me I will by no means cast out. For I have come down from heaven, not to do My own will, but the will of Him who sent Me. This is the will of the Father who sent Me, that of all He has given Me I should lose nothing, but should raise it up at the last day. And this is the will of Him who sent Me, that everyone who sees the Son and believes in Him may have everlasting life; and I will raise him up at the last day."* (NKJV)

As someone who could top Moses, Jesus claimed to be "the bread of life." In doing so, he again pointed to his deity. When talking with Moses, God called himself "I AM." By using the same name, Jesus clearly said, "I am God." He had come from heaven to provide spiritual nourishment to those who would believe in him.

Jesus performed the miracle of feeding this huge crowd, then taught them that he is the bread of life in the context of Passover. This holiday celebrated God's delivering the Israelites from Egyptian slavery. The night before they left Egypt, they made unleavened bread because there wasn't time to let the dough rise. As God provided physically for his people back then, and as Jesus provided physical bread for this crowd, so Jesus, as the bread of life, provides spiritual nourishment.

key point

The crowd could only see the miracles, not the fact that Jesus is God. They lacked the personal belief that is necessary for eternal life. But just because they didn't believe, that doesn't mean God gave up. He is in the business of drawing people to Jesus—people who are spiritually hungry. When they come to him through faith, they can never lose their salvation.

what others say

Bruce B. Barton

What does it mean to believe? The first step is accepting Jesus' claim to be the Son of God. We declare in prayer to Jesus, "You are the Christ, the Son of the living God"

(Matthew 16:16 NKJV). Accepting Jesus means giving him control of every area of life. To believe means to yield our wills, our desires, our plans, our strengths and weaknesses to Christ's direction and safekeeping. It means moment-by-moment obedience. Believing is a relationship with the one who promises to live within, trusting him to guide and direct us to do his will.[7]

in the prophets
Isaiah 54:13

The Opposition Party

JOHN 6:41–42 *The Jews then complained about Him, because He said, "I am the bread which came down from heaven." And they said, "Is not this Jesus, the son of Joseph, whose father and mother we know? How is it then that He says, 'I have come down from heaven'?"* (NKJV)

"So, who does this Jesus think he is anyway?" the people wanted to know. After all, they knew his parents, Mary and Joseph, and maybe some of them had known him since he was a baby. So, how could he say he came from heaven?

what others say

Philip Yancey and Brenda Quinn

That response shows why Jesus distrusts sensation-seeking crowds: they care far more for physical spectacle than for spiritual truth. And what happens next certainly bears out his suspicion. As he is interpreting the spiritual meaning of the miracle, all the enthusiasm of the previous day melts away. The crowd grows downright restless when he openly avows his true identity as the one sent from God. They cannot reconcile such exalted claims ("I have come down from heaven") with their knowledge that he is a local man, whose mother and father they know.[8]

A New Brand of Bread

JOHN 6:43–51 *Jesus therefore answered and said to them, "Do not murmur among yourselves. No one can come to Me unless the Father who sent Me draws him; and I will raise him up at the last day. It is written <u>in the prophets</u>, 'And they shall all be taught by God.' Therefore everyone who has heard and learned from the Father comes to Me. Not that anyone has seen the Father, except He who is from God; He has seen the Father. Most assuredly, I say to you, he who believes in Me has everlasting life. I am the bread of life. Your fathers ate the manna in the* *wilderness, and are dead. This is the bread which comes down from heaven, that one may eat of it and not die. I am the living bread which came down from heaven. If anyone eats of this bread, he will live forever; and the bread that I shall give is My flesh, which I shall give for the life of the world." (NKJV)*

Note that Jesus didn't try to convince the crowd that he is God. Those who were seeking God would not need more proof; God would draw them. Those who believe in Jesus will receive eternal life. It's that easy. He offers spiritual food through himself.

Again Jesus explained that he is the bread of life in contrast to the manna, which their ancestors ate and which couldn't keep them from dying. (You'd think they'd get the point, but they didn't—not unlike a lot of people today.) This time he equated the bread to his body, which he would soon give up on the cross so the world could have life.

Is Jesus a Cannibal?

JOHN 6:52–59 *The Jews therefore quarreled among themselves, saying, "How can this Man give us His flesh to eat?" Then Jesus said to them, "Most assuredly, I say to you, unless you eat the flesh of the Son of Man and drink His blood, you have no life in you. Whoever eats My flesh and drinks My blood has eternal life, and I will raise him up at the last day. For My flesh is food indeed, and My blood is drink indeed. He who eats My flesh and drinks My blood abides in Me, and I in him. As the living Father sent Me, and I live because of the Father, so he who feeds on Me will live because of Me. This is the bread which came down from heaven—not as your fathers ate the manna, and are dead. He who eats this bread will live forever." These things He said in the synagogue as He taught in Capernaum. (NKJV)*

The Jews listening to Jesus were thinking literally. But Jesus was speaking figuratively; he was not promoting cannibalism. To make himself understood, Jesus added a new twist to the conversation: drinking his blood. This phrase, if taken literally, was even more disgusting to the Jewish people than the possibility of eating Jesus' flesh. <u>Drinking blood</u> was a gross sin forbidden by the Law of Moses.

go to

drinking blood
Leviticus 17:10–14

After getting his listeners' attention, Jesus explained what he meant. He was not changing the meaning of his teaching. Again he pointed out that to get the spiritual benefits he offered we must take him completely into our lives and rely on him for everything—just as to get the benefits of bread we must eat and digest it.

Christians down through the ages have participated in a service called communion to remind them of Christ's gift of his body and blood given on the cross for the forgiveness of their sins.

The Jewish leaders began this conversation by wondering how Jesus could be greater than Moses. Jesus climaxed his talk by reminding them that Moses and the Israelites who ate manna died, but those who eat Jesus' food will never die. Jesus is indeed greater than Moses, and he wasn't afraid to say so while in a synagogue.

> **what others say**
>
> **James Montgomery Boice**
>
> Is he [Jesus] as real to you spiritually as something you can taste or handle? Is He as much a part of you as that which you eat? Do not think me blasphemous when I say that He must be as real and as useful to you as a hamburger and french fries. I say this because, though He is obviously far more real and useful than these, the unfortunate thing is that for many people He is much less.[10]

Bread, to benefit us, must be taken into our lives and assimilated. By analogy, Jesus must be taken into our lives by faith and assimilated. It does no more good to look at Jesus and not take him into our lives than it does to look at a loaf of bread and not eat it.

apply it

All or Nothing

JOHN 6:60–65 *Therefore many of His disciples, when they heard this, said, "This is a hard saying; who can understand it?" When Jesus knew in Himself that His disciples complained about this, He said to them, "Does this offend you? What then if you should see the Son of Man ascend where He was before? It is the Spirit who gives life; the flesh profits nothing. The words that*

knew
John 2:23–25

I speak to you are spirit, and they are life. But there are some of you who do not believe." For Jesus <u>knew</u> from the beginning who they were who did not believe, and who would betray Him. And He said, "Therefore I have said to you that no one can come to Me unless it has been granted to him by My Father." (NKJV)

The crowd faced a huge decision. Jesus' miracles certainly were attractive. After all, who wouldn't want free food and whole bodies? But his teaching was hard and cost much to practice. It greatly offended them.

Jesus wasn't surprised by their reaction. He already knew which of his followers believed in him and which did not. He even knew who would later betray him. That's more proof that he is God.

No One Else

JOHN 6:66–71 *From that time many of His disciples went back and walked with Him no more. Then Jesus said to the twelve, "Do you also want to go away?" But Simon Peter answered Him, "Lord, to whom shall we go? You have the words of eternal life. Also we have come to believe and know that You are the Christ, the Son of the living God." Jesus answered them, "Did I not choose you, the twelve, and one of you is a devil?" He spoke of Judas Iscariot, the son of Simon, for it was he who would betray Him, being one of the twelve.* (NKJV)

As a result of Jesus' teaching, many who claimed to be his followers left. Looking at the disappearing crowd, Jesus turned to his twelve disciples and asked them if they were going to leave too. Peter had the right idea when he said to Jesus, "Lord, to whom shall we go?" There is no one else; Jesus is the only one who can give eternal life.

Not all the disciples agreed with Peter, however. Jesus knew that Judas would later betray him, although for now he didn't walk away with the crowd.

Jesus wasn't looking for numbers or spiritual scalps. He didn't care about fame or having a huge following. He didn't want disciples who followed him when it was convenient or when they didn't have anything better to do. He wanted followers who were committed to him wholeheartedly. It was either all or nothing. The same is true today. Jesus still wants followers who are sold out to him, not a lot of people who warm pews and play church.

How much are you like the grumbling disciples? When life gets hard and Jesus doesn't meet your expectations, do you want to walk away? Do you want him on your terms or his? Are you willing to follow Jesus no matter what?

Chapter Wrap-Up

- Jesus fed five thousand men plus women and children with five loaves and two fish. (John 6:1–15)
- Jesus walked on water to help his disciples during a storm. (John 6:16–21)
- Jesus taught the crowd the necessity of believing in him for eternal life by comparing himself to bread that gives physical nourishment. (John 6:22–59)
- Most of the crowd walked away from Jesus after his speech, but his twelve disciples stuck with him. (John 6:60–71)

Study Questions

1. Why were the people following Jesus?

2. How did Jesus react to them?

3. What did the miracle of feeding the crowd teach about Jesus?

4. How did the crowd respond to this miracle?

5. What happened on the Sea of Galilee?

6. What did this miracle teach about Jesus?

7. Summarize what Jesus taught the crowd.

8. How did people respond to his teaching? Why?

John 7: Jesus the Divider

Chapter Highlights:
- The Great Debate
- The Great Teaching
- The Great Mystery
- The Great Quencher
- The Great Divide

Let's Get Started

When the temperature soars to the nineties and above, a glass of cold lemonade or iced tea is refreshing.

When the heat is accompanied by thick humidity, an air-conditioned car or house is refreshing.

When you're feeling sluggish, a brisk walk or a dip in a pool is refreshing.

When the heat dehydrates you, a bottle of water is refreshing. When you're tired, a twenty-minute power nap is refreshing. When you crave chocolate, a candy bar is refreshing.

When your nerves are frazzled, a long, hot bath is refreshing. When you've worked hard for a long period, goofing off and doing nothing is refreshing.

Refreshment takes many forms, depending on the situation and our needs.

Jesus offered spiritual refreshment to the Jewish people, but their responses varied widely, as John recorded in chapter 7. Some people said he was a good man. Some thought he was a deceiver. Some said he was demon-possessed. The Pharisees wanted to arrest him. Others believed he was the promised Messiah. One thing was clear: Jesus' offer divided the people into different camps.

Unwanted Advice

JOHN 7:1–5 *After these things Jesus walked in Galilee; for He did not want to walk in Judea, because the Jews sought to kill Him. Now the Jews' Feast of Tabernacles was at hand. His brothers therefore said to Him, "Depart from here and go into Judea, that Your disciples also may see the works that You are doing. For no one does anything in secret while he himself seeks to be known openly. If You do these things, show Yourself to the world." For even His brothers did not believe in Him. (NKJV)*

Samaritan woman
John 4

kill him
John 5:18

brothers
Matthew 13:55

Instead of choosing the most direct route between places, Jesus often determined his route by whom he wanted to see (like the <u>Samaritan woman</u> at the well) or whom he wanted to avoid. In this case, he was avoiding the Jewish leaders who wanted to <u>kill him</u>. Ever since Jesus had healed the paralyzed man by the Pool of Bethesda on the Sabbath, the religious leaders had wanted to kill him. From this point on, John focuses more and more on the opposition Jesus faced.

When it was time to go to Jerusalem to celebrate the Feast of Tabernacles, Jesus' half <u>brothers</u> were after him to go there and show the world who he was. The Feast of Tabernacles is a week-long thanksgiving celebration for the harvest, a commemoration of the Israelites' wandering in the wilderness, and a time to look forward to God's coming messianic kingdom. It falls in September or October on our calendar. It also was one of the three pilgrim feasts for which Jewish men were required to go to Jerusalem. They lived in temporary booths to remind themselves of how God was faithful to their ancestors in the wilderness.

The average people were gathered like the crowd waiting outside the Academy Awards ceremony. Anybody who was anybody would want to make a grand entrance. All Jesus had to do was walk in and announce, "Hey, guys! The Messiah is here, and you're looking at him!"

At this point, Jesus' brothers didn't believe he was the Messiah. But, for whatever reasons, they were concerned that Jesus was missing a huge opportunity to become even more famous and powerful than he already was. Jesus didn't need this advice. Obviously, Jesus could have done anything he wanted, including calling a staff of angels from heaven to escort him on a cloud to the feast. But Jesus didn't want to do that.

I'm Sticking with My Plan

JOHN 7:6–9 *Then Jesus said to them, "My time has not yet come, but your time is always ready. The world cannot hate you, but it hates Me because I testify of it that its works are evil. You go up to this feast. I am not yet going up to this feast, for My time has not yet fully come." When He had said these things to them, He remained in Galilee. (NKJV)*

Jesus operated on his own timetable and his own terms. This wasn't the right opportunity to go to the feast to celebrate, because of the Jewish leaders' hatred toward him even though he loved them. Jesus wanted to avoid unwelcome publicity, so he stayed behind in Galilee. He had plans of his own and was sticking with them.

go to

deceiver
Deuteronomy 13

what others say

Vernon McGee

Notice the little word *yet* in "My time is not yet come." Jesus did not say that He would not go down to the feast, but He was not going down with them publicly to win public favor by something spectacular, or whatever they wanted Him to do. He would go at His Father's appointed time and in His Father's way.[1]

If your family members ridicule your faith in God, treat it as unimportant, mock it, or refuse to talk about it, you're not alone. Even Jesus' family members didn't understand his relationship with God. And they certainly didn't approve of how he lived out that relationship and what he taught about it.

The Talk of the Town

JOHN 7:10–13 *But when His brothers had gone up, then He also went up to the feast, not openly, but as it were in secret. Then the Jews sought Him at the feast, and said, "Where is He?" And there was much complaining among the people concerning Him. Some said, "He is good"; others said, "No, on the contrary, He deceives the people." However, no one spoke openly of Him for fear of the Jews.* (NKJV)

When the time was right, Jesus went to the feast without drawing attention to himself. The atmosphere there was tense. As usual, Jesus was the topic of conversations and whispers. The people called him a good man and a <u>deceiver</u>, anything and everything but who he said he was—God's Son, the Messiah. And no one talked about him openly because they feared what the Jewish authorities would do to them.

Smart Without Studying

JOHN 7:14–15 *Now about the middle of the feast Jesus went up into the temple and taught. And the Jews marveled, saying, "How does this Man know letters, having never studied?"* (NKJV)

Halfway through the celebration, Jesus showed up in the temple court—a very public place—and began to teach. The people were surprised at how much he knew about the Scriptures since he didn't have a theological degree or training with a rabbi. Advanced theological education didn't take place in seminaries or graduate schools in Jesus' day. Rather, recognized rabbis, who were authorities in Scripture and Jewish law, trained groups of disciples who memorized their interpretations of the Law and quoted them when teaching.

After all, he was a carpenter, an uneducated man who didn't even profess to be a rabbi by dressing like one. Jesus didn't need formal training because his teaching came straight from God. Everyone who wanted to do God's will would recognize his teaching as such.

Discerning Right Teaching

JOHN 7:16–19 *Jesus answered them and said, "My doctrine is not Mine, but His who sent Me. If anyone wills to do His will, he shall know concerning the doctrine, whether it is from God or whether I speak on My own authority. He who speaks from himself seeks his own glory; but He who seeks the glory of the One who sent Him is true, and no unrighteousness is in Him. Did not Moses give you the law, yet none of you keeps the law? Why do you seek to kill Me?"* (NKJV)

Instead of waiting for the people to challenge his credentials, Jesus took the offensive and told them to check him out. He even challenged their lack of keeping the Law although they professed to do so. Then he wanted to know why they were trying to kill him.

go to

one work
John 5:1–15

circumcised
performed a rite of Jewish identity by removing the foreskin

what others say

J. Carl Laney

Jesus states that a willingness to obey the truth is a prerequisite to an understanding of His message. If anyone purposes to do God's will, he will come to recognize . . . the divine origin of Jesus' teaching. [A.] Plummer remarks, "The mere mechanical performance of God's will is not enough; there must be an inclination towards Him, a wish to make our conduct agree with His will; and without this agreement Divine doctrine cannot be recognized as such." Experiential knowledge of God comes with a willingness to do His will.[3]

You Can't Judge a Book by Its Cover

JOHN 7:20–24 *The people answered and said, "You have a demon. Who is seeking to kill You?" Jesus answered and said to them, "I did <u>one work</u>, and you all marvel. Moses therefore gave you circumcision (not that it is from Moses, but from the fathers), and you circumcise a man on the Sabbath. If a man receives circumcision on the Sabbath, so that the law of Moses should not be broken, are you angry with Me because I made a man completely well on the Sabbath? Do not judge according to appearance, but judge with righteous judgment." (NKJV)*

You could almost see the fireworks between Jesus and the people. He certainly wasn't going to win friends and influence people the way today's politicians do.

Naturally, the people denied they were going to kill him. Accusing him of being possessed by a demon was a classic sidestep of the issue. Jesus wouldn't let them get away with it though. He brought them back to the real issue of their false judgment. How could they accuse him of breaking the Sabbath law by healing a man when they **circumcised** infants on the Sabbath? What hypocrites!

As Jesus pointed out, a doctorate in theology or Bible does not guarantee a right relationship with God or even accurate knowledge about him. God isn't looking for academic credentials. Rather, he wants people with right heart attitudes, people who realize they need him and aren't too proud to confess that.

something to ponder

F. F. Bruce

Jesus argues that if the sabbath law may rightly be suspended for the removal of a small piece of tissue from one part of the body, it cannot be wrong to heal a man's whole body on the sabbath day. This type of argument, in fact was used by some rabbis to justify medical treatment in a case of urgency on the sabbath, but Jesus uses it to justify an act of healing whether the case is urgent or not.[4]

How to Spot False Teachers

- Their words don't match what the Bible teaches.
- They focus on themselves, not God.
- They want the glory instead of giving it to God.
- They don't point people to Jesus.
- They don't challenge people to live out the commands and principles of Scripture.
- They rarely talk about sin and the need for repentance.

We Know This Man

JOHN 7:25–27 Now some of them from Jerusalem said, "Is this not He whom they seek to kill? But look! He speaks boldly, and they say nothing to Him. Do the rulers know indeed that this is truly the Christ? However, we know where this Man is from; but when the Christ comes, no one knows where He is from." (NKJV)

Finally, the people realized that the man called Jesus was the center of all this controversy. They didn't think he could possibly be the Christ, the Messiah, since they knew where he came from. He was the son of Joseph and Mary who grew up in Nazareth, wasn't he? However, they claimed no one would know where Messiah comes from. That was a lie—or at least a lack of scriptural knowledge. After all, one of their prophets predicted the Messiah would be born in Bethlehem (see Appendix A): "But you, Bethlehem Ephrathah, though you are little among the thousands of Judah, yet out of you shall come forth to Me the One to be Ruler in Israel, whose goings forth are from of old, from everlasting" (Micah 5:2 NKJV).

Half Right/Half Wrong

JOHN 7:28–29 *Then Jesus cried out, as He taught in the temple, saying, "You both know Me, and you know where I am from; and I have not come of Myself, but He who sent Me is true, whom you do not know. But I know Him, for I am from Him, and He sent Me." (NKJV)*

As usual, Jesus didn't mince words. He told the people they were only half right. Sure, they knew where he came from physically. But he wasn't interested in focusing on his life history. Instead, Jesus returned again to the main issue: They didn't know God.

Taking on the Jesus Movement

JOHN 7:30–32 *Therefore they sought to take Him; but no one laid a hand on Him, because His hour had not yet come. And many of the people believed in Him, and said, "When the Christ comes, will He do more signs than these which this Man has done?"*

The Pharisees heard the crowd murmuring these things concerning Him, and the Pharisees and the chief priests sent officers to take Him. (NKJV)

Jesus certainly wasn't Mr. Popularity. Telling this crowd of religious people that they didn't know God was an invitation to opposition. And the opposition from those who didn't believe in him came. They tried to grab him, and the Pharisees sent guards to arrest him, but all these attempts failed because it wasn't his time to die.

Not everyone opposed him, however. Many people put their faith in him, believing he was the Messiah because of the miracles he did.

There is no middle ground with Jesus. Sooner or later, everyone has to take a side—believe in him or not believe in him. Have eternal life or eternal death. Be for him or against him. Which side are you on?

The Last Word

JOHN 7:33–36 *Then Jesus said to them, "I shall be with you a little while longer, and then I go to Him who sent Me. You will seek Me and not find Me, and where I am you cannot come." Then the Jews said among themselves, "Where does He intend to go that we shall not find Him? Does He intend to go to the*

provided water
Exodus 17:1–6

water
Isaiah 44:3

Greeks
all non-Jews,
Gentiles

*Dispersion among the **Greeks** and teach the Greeks? What is this thing that He said, 'You will seek Me and not find Me, and where I am you cannot come'?" (NKJV)*

Jesus got in the last word. He told the crowd that he wouldn't always be with them. Soon he would go back to God, and they wouldn't be able to find him. In their denseness, they didn't understand what he said. They thought Jesus meant he was planning a trip into Gentile territory, since they didn't understand his true relationship with God.

The Great Thirst Quencher

JOHN 7:37–39 *On the last day, that great day of the feast, Jesus stood and cried out, saying, "If anyone thirsts, let him come to Me and drink. He who believes in Me, as the Scripture has said, out of his heart will flow rivers of living water." But this He spoke concerning the Spirit, whom those believing in Him would receive; for the Holy Spirit was not yet given, because Jesus was not yet glorified. (NKJV)*

On the first day of the Feast of Tabernacles, a priest read Zechariah 14:8: "In that day it shall be that living waters shall flow from Jerusalem" (NKJV). For seven days, the priests led a procession from the Pool of Siloam through the Water Gate to the Temple. One priest carried water from the pool in a golden pitcher. Once there, they circled the altar, and the priest with the pitcher poured the water in a basin at the side of the altar. This water offering by the priests helped the Israelites remember how God had <u>provided water</u> to their ancestors during their desert wanderings. The people waved palm branches and sang psalms. On the seventh day, they circled the altar seven times. This ceremony was more than a time of praying for rain so they would have good crops; it also illustrated the prediction in Zechariah 14 and Ezekiel 47 of living water flowing from the Temple.

During the last day of the celebration, Jesus got up and shouted that he was the source of a steady stream of living <u>water</u> that would quench their spiritual thirst. In doing so, he gave new meaning to the celebration, pointing to the Holy Spirit who was yet to come. Just as water quenches our physical thirst, so the Spirit satisfies people's inner thirst for God. Water also causes seeds and cuttings to grow and produce fruit. So, too, the Spirit produces <u>spiritual fruit</u> in our lives—like love, joy, and peace.

Jesus also announced that his coming was the beginning of God's promised **kingdom**, a time of forgiveness and right relationships with the Father.

spiritual fruit
Galatians 5:22–23

born in Bethlehem
Luke 2:4–7

kingdom
God's rule on earth

Prophet
the one Moses predicted would come

> ## what others say
>
> ### Mitch and Zhava Glaser
>
> Jesus invited the whole congregation of Israel to come and drink of living water, just as He had previously extended a similar invitation to the woman at the well. . . . To come to Jesus and drink is to believe in Him as the Savior and source of eternal life. The bubbling inner spring and the thundering flow of living water are references to the Holy Spirit and His ministry of indwelling all who believe.[5]

So, Who Is This Man?

> JOHN 7:40–44 *Therefore many from the crowd, when they heard this saying, said, "Truly this is the Prophet." Others said, "This is the Christ." But some said, "Will the Christ come out of Galilee? Has not the Scripture said that the Christ comes from the seed of David and from the town of Bethlehem, where David was?" So there was a division among the people because of Him. Now some of them wanted to take Him, but no one laid hands on Him. (NKJV)*

Jesus had a real knack for dividing people. Some thought he was the **Prophet**. Some thought he was the Messiah, while others said he couldn't possibly be. They argued over where the Messiah would come from. Jesus obviously didn't qualify, the people thought, since he came from Nazareth in Galilee. (Although Jesus had grown up there, he was <u>born in Bethlehem</u>, as the Scriptures predicted.) Some people wanted to grab him, but no one did.

Thinking in Circles

> JOHN 7:45–49 *Then the officers came to the chief priests and Pharisees, who said to them, "Why have you not brought Him?" The officers answered, "No man ever spoke like this Man!" Then the Pharisees answered them, "Are you also deceived? Have any of the rulers or the Pharisees believed in Him? But this crowd that does not know the law is accursed." (NKJV)*

Nicodemus
John 3:1–21

The guards left Jesus alone, then had to endure the wrath of the Pharisees who sent them to make the arrest. The guards were smart enough to know that publicly arresting Jesus would probably start a riot and bring out the Roman army.

The authorities' reluctance to squash Jesus' ministry caused even more doubt in the minds of the common people. On the one hand, if Jesus really was the troublemaker that the Pharisees said he was, why didn't they just arrest him? On the other hand, since the religious leaders seemed divided in their opinions of Jesus, then maybe Jesus was who he said he was. Maybe Jesus deserved a closer look.

The Pharisees' thinking about Jesus was circular and closeminded. Since none of them believed Jesus was the Messiah, then he couldn't be. Case closed. If any of these people in the crowd wanted to believe, it was because they didn't know the law. They were obviously too ignorant to make the right decision.

Nicodemus Speaks Up

> JOHN 7:50–53 *Nicodemus (he who came to Jesus by night, being one of them) said to them, "Does our law judge a man before it hears him and knows what he is doing?" They answered and said to him, "Are you also from Galilee? Search and look, for no prophet has arisen out of Galilee."*
> *And everyone went to his own house.* (NKJV)

Nicodemus stood up for Jesus before his fellow Pharisees. According to Deuteronomy 1:16, an accused person gets a hearing before being judged. These teachers of the Law were ignoring the Law. Nicodemus raised the question of a legal technicality, no doubt hoping the other Pharisees would say, "Oh, you're right. We forgot about that. Well, we'll have to give the man a fair hearing." For Nicodemus to risk his reputation to speak out for Jesus is a good indication that he was a secret believer in Jesus.

The Pharisees rejected Nicodemus and ridiculed him. To be called a Galilean was like being called stupid. And in the Pharisees' minds, only dumb Galileans believed this "idiot" from Galilee.

Without reaching a final decision about Jesus, they all went home.

Chapter Wrap-Up

- Jesus' brothers, who didn't believe in him, tried to get him to show himself publicly at the Feast of Tabernacles. But he didn't go until the time was right according to God's timetable. (John 7:1–13)

- Jesus claimed his teaching was from God and challenged the leaders' claims that they were following the Law when they accused him of breaking it. (John 7:14–29)

- As the people divided over Jesus' teaching, he told them he would be going back to God. (John 7:30–36)

- Jesus offered living water to spiritually thirsty people when they believed in him. (John 7:37–39)

- Jesus' teaching divided the people. Some believed; others wanted to kill him. (John 7:40–53)

Study Questions

1. What problem did Jesus have with his brothers? Why?

2. Who did people think Jesus was?

3. Why were the Jewish people so divided on who Jesus was?

4. How can we know that Jesus' teaching is true?

5. What is significant about Jesus' speech on the last day of Tabernacles?

6. Why did Nicodemus stand up for Jesus before the Pharisees?

John 8: Jesus the Freedom Giver

Chapter Highlights:
• Woman Caught
  in Adultery
• Light in the Darkness
• Free at Last

Let's Get Started

Freedom. We all want it. But it has different meanings for different people.

To a child, freedom is being grown up and not having to obey parents and teachers.

To a teen, freedom is having a driver's license and a car.

To a mother, freedom is an afternoon or evening with a babysitter to watch the kids.

To a businessperson, freedom is a weekend with no work. To a teacher, freedom is summer vacation with no classes.

To a person in jail, freedom is parole or the end of the sentence pronounced by a judge.

In this chapter, we learn that freedom runs deeper than a change in circumstances or location. A woman caught in adultery and brought to Jesus learns that freedom is forgiveness of her sin—instead of being stoned for it. Later Jesus taught that freedom begins with a relationship with him. As a result, we'll know the truth that will set us free spiritually.

An Early-Morning Class

JOHN 8:1–2 *But Jesus went to the Mount of Olives. Now early in the morning He came again into the temple, and all the people came to Him; and He sat down and taught them.* (NKJV)

One thing about Jesus—he never missed an opportunity to teach. He was up and at 'em early. When people gathered to listen, he always had something to say. This day was no exception.

Almost a Perfect Trap

JOHN 8:3–5 *Then the scribes and Pharisees brought to Him a woman caught in adultery. And when they had set her in the*

go to

stoning to death
Leviticus 20:10

midst, they said to Him, "Teacher, this woman was caught in adultery, in the very act. Now Moses, in the law, commanded us that such should be stoned. But what do You say?" (NKJV)

Imagine being the center of attention, teaching important stuff about God to people who are actually interested in what you have to say. Class is going along well when suddenly a group of religious leaders crash the group, dragging a woman with them. And not just any woman. They had caught her in bed with a man who wasn't her husband.

Their interruption raises some interesting questions. How did they know where to find someone who was committing adultery?

(Normally, Pharisees wouldn't have much contact with a common woman like her.) How were they able to catch her in the act of having sex? (The context implies that witnesses had seen that act.) Why didn't they bring the man too? (He was just as guilty as the woman.) Smells like a setup, doesn't it?

These were men with a mission. According to the law, <u>stoning to death</u> was the punishment for both parties for sleeping with someone else's spouse. There was no way Jesus could wriggle out of this dilemma. If he said to let her go, he'd be disobeying God's Word and would lose his credibility as a teacher. If he agreed to stone her, the religious leaders would accuse him of having none of the mercy or love he taught about.

Words in the Dirt

JOHN 8:6–8 *This they said, testing Him, that they might have something of which to accuse Him. But Jesus stooped down and wrote on the ground with His finger, as though He did not hear. So when they continued asking Him, He raised Himself up and said to them, "He who is without sin among you, let him throw a stone at her first." And again He stooped down and wrote on the ground.* (NKJV)

Those religious leaders had Jesus trapped. No matter which choice he took, he gave them ammunition to use against him. So Jesus chose option C; he ignored them. (He's hard to keep in a box!) No doubt about it—being ignored takes all the fun out of an execution. But these men weren't going to give up easily. "They continued asking Him," no doubt hoping to break down his resistance. When that didn't work, Jesus went to option D, pointing the finger at the accusers. "If you want to kill her, go ahead," he said. "But be sure the first one to throw a stone at her has never sinned." That remark wasn't what those self-righteous men wanted to hear.

Bill Myers

To this day no one's sure what Jesus wrote when He bent down and scribbled on the ground. Some think it was a list of each of the Pharisees' sins.[1]

Everett F. Harrison

In His own manner, Jesus matched their rudeness with deliberate preoccupation, as He wrote on the ground. He was ignoring them as a rebuke to their harsh spirit. In His method, He contrived to embarrass the intruders, turning the tables on them. Through it all He had in view an educative motive, showing that the touching of the conscience of men was more potent than the debating of the requirements of the Law.[2]

Caught in Their Own Trap

JOHN 8:9–11 *Then those who heard it, being convicted by their conscience, went out one by one, beginning with the oldest even to the last. And Jesus was left alone, and the woman standing in the midst. When Jesus had raised Himself up and saw no one but the woman, He said to her, "Woman, where are those accusers of yours? Has no one condemned you?" She said, "No one, Lord." And Jesus said to her, "Neither do I condemn you; go and sin no more."* (NKJV)

Naturally none of these men could confess to never having sinned. So they all went home. Jesus had caught them in their own trap. When only the woman was left, Jesus stood up, looked at her, and asked the obvious question: "Where is everybody?" Then Jesus showed her his love by forgiving her instead of condemning her. He didn't say she was innocent. Neither did he hammer home her guilt or read her a laundry list of sins. She knew she had sinned against God, and Jesus wanted her to quit making sin a habit. Jesus gave freedom to the woman caught in adultery and claimed to be God by using the Father's name, I am.

go to

light of the world
Isaiah 42:6

Yeshua
Hebrew for Jesus

Torah
first five tooks of the
Old Testament

apply it

what others say

David H. Stern

Yeshua's response showed four things: he was not against the **Torah**, he was merciful toward the woman, he opposed her sin (Exodus 20:13 [14]), and he could silence hecklers and put them to shame.[3]

Although Jesus and the adulterous woman did not exchange a lot of words—at least words that are recorded here—this was a significant conversation. She learned that no one is perfect except Jesus, and therefore we do not have the right to condemn others for their sin. Jesus offers forgiveness, not condemnation, when we bring that sin to him. Although we don't have a record of the woman after this event, I doubt she slept with someone else's husband again.

No matter what you've done wrong—even if the legal penalty is death—Jesus wants to forgive you. There is no sin that's so bad he can't forgive it, as he demonstrated with the woman caught in adultery.

A Shining Light

JOHN 8:12 *Then Jesus spoke to them again, saying, "I am the light of the world. He who follows Me shall not walk in darkness, but have the light of life." (NKJV)*

Intermission's over. The short drama with the woman caught in adultery had a happy ending. Now John picks up the dialogue from 7:52 between Jesus and the Jewish leaders during the Feast of Tabernacles.

Jesus uttered this bold statement of being "the light of the world" against the backdrop of the light in the Temple and the court around it. In the Temple, a menorah, or golden candlestick, burned constantly (see Illustration #5). During the Feast of Tabernacles, four huge menorahs lit up the outside court at night while men danced and sang praises to God. This light commemorated the pillar of fire that led the Israelites when they wandered in the wilderness in Moses' day. At the end of the celebration each night—or rather, early morning—two priests faced the Temple and proclaimed, "Our fathers who were in this place turned their backs to the Temple of God and their faces eastward and threw themselves down eastward before the sun, but we direct our eyes to Yahweh." It was in this context that Jesus declared, "I am the light of the world."

That short sentence set off fireworks as Jesus' use of "I am" made it clear that he is God. The Jewish people understood that <u>light</u> stood for God's holiness. As if that wasn't enough, Jesus claimed to be light for <u>all people</u>, not just Jews. As the light that pierces darkness, Jesus sheds light on God, showing people what he is like and what he does. Jesus' presence and teachings also shed light on the darkness of people's sin and separation from God. So people who follow Jesus don't walk blindly in sin anymore. Instead, they can see their sin and need for forgiveness.

go to

light
Psalm 27:1; 36:9

all people
Isaiah 49:6

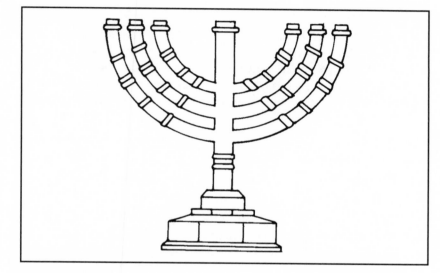

Illustration #5
Menorah—a seven-branched candlestick.

Time for Testimony

JOHN 8:13–18 *The Pharisees therefore said to Him, "You bear witness of Yourself; Your witness is not true." Jesus answered and said to them, "Even if I bear witness of Myself, My witness is true, for I know where I came from and where I am going; but you do not know where I come from and where I am going. You judge according to the flesh; I judge no one. And yet if I do judge, My judgment is true; for I am not alone, but I am with the Father who sent Me. It is also written in your law that the testimony of two men is true. I am One who bears witness of Myself, and the Father who sent Me bears witness of Me." (NKJV)*

go to

two witnesses
Deuteronomy 19:15

Instead of seeing Jesus' light, the Pharisees saw red. They understood what he was saying, but they didn't want to believe it. So they challenged him with the Law: For a valid testimony, <u>two witnesses</u> are needed.

Jesus didn't disagree. He pointed out that his testimony was true even without a second witness because he knew where he came from (eternity past with God) and where he was going (back to God). These leaders were judging him by their own standards as though he were another man. If they really needed a second witness, he had one—God the Father.

The Great Unknown

JOHN 8:19–20 *Then they said to Him, "Where is Your Father?" Jesus answered, "You know neither Me nor My Father. If you had known Me, you would have known My Father also." These words Jesus spoke in the treasury, as He taught in the temple; and no one laid hands on Him, for His hour had not yet come. (NKJV)*

Since Jesus said he had a second witness, the leaders asked him to produce this mystery man. They couldn't get out of their literal rut, refusing to consider that Jesus' Father was God. Obviously, they didn't know either Jesus or the Father.

This discussion took place out in the open in the Court of Women (see Illustration #3, page 27) outside the temple building near the offering boxes. These were thirteen trumpet-shaped collection boxes, inscribed with the use for money deposited in them. Seven were for the temple tax and six for offerings. The leaders could easily have grabbed Jesus there, but it wasn't time yet for his arrest.

what others say

Dana Gould

Jesus' assertion that if people knew Him, they would know His Father is one of the most striking in all the New Testament. He was speaking to some of the most educated, most religious people who have ever lived. They were confident they knew God and understood His ways. But their rejection of Jesus shows they didn't know God. They knew only their own ideas about God.[4]

Too Much Thinking Inside the Box

JOHN 8:21–24 *Then Jesus said to them again, "I am going away, and you will seek Me, and will die in your sin. Where I go you cannot come." So the Jews said, "Will He kill Himself, because He says, 'Where I go you cannot come'?" And He said to them, "You are from beneath; I am from above. You are of this world; I am not of this world. Therefore I said to you that you will die in your sins; for if you do not believe that I am He, you will die in your sins." (NKJV)*

If these religious leaders weren't going to believe in Jesus while he was there with them, they had no chance for salvation from their sins. As usual, they didn't have a clue as to what he was talking about. They thought he was going to commit suicide.

Instead of trying to correct their misinterpretation, Jesus told them why they didn't get it. They were tied to the earth with no understanding of spiritual truths; he was from heaven with a per-spective outside their closed box of thinking.

apply it

Not believing in Jesus equals spiritual death. It's only when we place our faith in him as Savior from our sin that we gain spiritual life.

Maximum Density

JOHN 8:25–26 *Then they said to Him, "Who are You?" And Jesus said to them, "Just what I have been saying to you from the beginning. I have many things to say and to judge concerning you, but He who sent Me is true; and I speak to the world those things which I heard from Him." (NKJV)*

This conversation was way over the heads of these leaders. Their direct approach—"Who are You?"—didn't get an answer they wanted. Jesus insisted he was exactly who he had said he was. Instead of continuing this fruitless discussion, Jesus took the high road and didn't say any more that would condemn them. Instead, he would speak what God told him to tell the world (not just the Jewish people).

The Ultimate Proof

JOHN 8:27–30 *They did not understand that He spoke to them of the Father. Then Jesus said to them, "When you lift up the Son of Man, then you will know that I am He, and that I do nothing of Myself; but as My Father taught Me, I speak these things. And He who sent Me is with Me. The Father has not left Me alone, for I always do those things that please Him." As He spoke these words, many believed in Him. (NKJV)*

The Pharisees still didn't understand what Jesus told them about his relationship with God the Father. So Jesus mentioned the ultimate proof: his resurrection after crucifixion. When that happened, they would know for sure that he was telling the truth and that he wasn't operating alone. Note that some of that hard-hearted, dense group finally believed in him.

Offended on the Defensive

JOHN 8:31–33 *Then Jesus said to those Jews who believed Him, "If you abide in My word, you are My disciples indeed. And you shall know the truth, and the truth shall make you free." They answered Him, "We are Abraham's descendants, and have never been in bondage to anyone. How can You say, 'You will be made free'?" (NKJV)*

Turning his attention to those who believed, Jesus urged them to continue in his teaching. As a result, they learned God's truth (Jesus himself as well as God's words), which would set them free from slavery to sin.

The Jewish leaders in the crowd took offense at Jesus' words. The very idea of telling them they needed to be set free was ridiculous! They weren't slaves and never had been.

What they conveniently forgot, however, was that their ancestors had been slaves in Egypt and later were taken into captivity by a couple of other countries. Furthermore, they currently lived under Roman rule.

what others say

Dana Gould

Hold to is a verb that means to "abide," "continue." Here it is used of holding to Jesus' teachings. Literally, "my teaching" is "my word." This is an active, not a passive, activity. To "hold to" the word means not only knowing the truth, but living it.[5]

go to

Charles U. Wagner

Abraham had never been a slave to any man, and because he was declared righteous by God, the Jews knew that he was not enslaved by sin. Since Abraham's descendants had been God's Chosen People from the beginning, how could anyone suggest that they needed to be made free? These people thought their family background and national heritage were enough to make them acceptable to God.[6]

slave of sin
Romans 6:14–23

Wrong Father, Wrong Family

JOHN 8:34–38 *Jesus answered them, "Most assuredly, I say to you, whoever commits sin is a slave of sin. And a slave does not abide in the house forever, but a son abides forever. Therefore if the Son makes you free, you shall be free indeed.*

"I know that you are Abraham's descendants, but you seek to kill Me, because My word has no place in you. I speak what I have seen with My Father, and you do what you have seen with your father." (NKJV)

So much for only the Pharisees squirming under Jesus' teaching. Jesus made everybody uncomfortable when he said, "Whoever commits sins is a <u>slave of sin</u>."(He doesn't play favorites.) While sin can be fun, it eventually controls us. We all know what it's like to want to do something right but instead do what we know is wrong. We don't have to let sin pull us down, however. Jesus can break the choke hold it puts on us and make us part of his family forever. Even though the Jews believed their family line from Abraham guaranteed them a place in God's family, they were wrong. The fact that they wanted to kill Jesus proved they had a different father—the devil.

Real freedom isn't being able to do what we want when we want. (Remember as a child knowing you'd have that kind of freedom when you grew up—and later discovering it doesn't exist even in adulthood?) Real freedom is getting out of the darkness of sin into the light of a relationship with Jesus.

something to ponder

Thinking in a Rut

JOHN 8:39–41 *They answered and said to Him, "Abraham is our father." Jesus said to them, "If you were Abraham's children, you would do the works of Abraham. But now you seek to*

parable
Luke 6:43–45

parable
a story that teaches
spiritual truth
through familiar
events or objects

kill Me, a Man who has told you the truth which I heard from God. Abraham did not do this. You do the deeds of your father." Then they said to Him, "We were not born of fornication; we have one Father—God." (NKJV)

No matter what Jesus said, the Jewish people couldn't get past their ingrained belief that they were fine because they were Abraham's children. The Jews relied on their own efforts to keep the Law and on the merits of Abraham to guarantee their salvation. Jewish theology held that, by obeying God's call, Abraham had accrued enough merit to cover the deficiencies of all his descendants throughout history. Thus to claim Abraham as father was to claim a special relationship with God that was guaranteed by physical descent from that patriarch. Their actions proved them wrong, and Jesus said so. Changing their tactic a bit, they claimed God as their only Father.

Jesus' arguments hinge on the principle that one's relationship with Abraham is dependent not on physical descent but on having a personal faith in God that is modeled on Abraham's faith. Jesus pointed out that relationship with God is indicated by belief in him. Abraham foresaw Christ's coming and believed in him, for Jesus is the I AM who spoke to Abraham in the first place.

The hatred that the religious elite showed toward Jesus mirrored the reaction of Satan to God, not the response of Abraham.

The Devil's Children

JOHN 8:42–44 *Jesus said to them, "If God were your Father, you would love Me, for I proceeded forth and came from God; nor have I come of Myself, but He sent Me. Why do you not understand My speech? Because you are not able to listen to My word. You are of your father the devil, and the desires of your* *father you want to do. He was a murderer from the beginning, and does not stand in the truth, because there is no truth in him. When he speaks a lie, he speaks from his own resources, for he is a <u>liar</u> and the father of it. (NKJV)*

liar
Genesis 3:4

For anyone who thinks Jesus is weak and mild, this encounter with the Jewish people blows away that image. He didn't mince words. If they really were God's children, they would love Jesus, not try to kill him. Their actions make it clear that they are of the family line of Satan rather than the family line of Abraham. It wasn't a matter of not understanding his words; it was a matter of the heart and will. Their hearts belonged to the devil, who is a murderer and a <u>liar</u>.

Deaf Ears

> JOHN 8:45–47 *But because I tell the truth, you do not believe Me. Which of you convicts Me of sin? And if I tell the truth, why do you not believe Me? He who is of God hears God's words; therefore you do not hear, because you are not of God." (NKJV)*

Unlike the devil, Jesus spoke the truth. But the people didn't believe him, nor could they point out any sin in his life. They were deaf to the truth because their hearts were hard and they were not God's children.

It's easy for God and his Word to get drowned out by the noise around us, by our busy schedules, by our selfishness, and by what we read, watch, and listen to. If you really want to hear God, find a quiet place without distractions, read the Bible with an open mind and heart, listen to what he says, then obey him.

Watch Where You're Looking

> JOHN 8:48–51 *Then the Jews answered and said to Him, "Do we not say rightly that You are a Samaritan and have a demon?" Jesus answered, "I do not have a demon; but I honor My Father, and you dishonor Me. And I do not seek My own glory; there is One who seeks and judges. Most assuredly, I say to you, if anyone keeps My word he shall never see death." (NKJV)*

Having run out of arguments, the leaders resorted to name-calling like children. They used the two worst insults they could think of—Samaritan and demon-possessed—likely in reaction to what Jesus

I AM
Exodus 3:14

had just said about them. In spite of what they thought and said about him, Jesus honored God. He wasn't seeking glory for himself; he was seeking to introduce people to the Father so they wouldn't spend eternity in hell.

When you have a choice to make, do you think about how the options will affect you and make you look good—or bad? Or do you consider how your actions will put God in the limelight? Jesus always chose the second option, seeking to bring glory to God the Father, not himself.

He Must Be a Madman

JOHN 8:52–56 *Then the Jews said to Him, "Now we know that You have a demon! Abraham is dead, and the prophets; and You say, 'If anyone keeps My word he shall never taste death.' Are You greater than our father Abraham, who is dead? And the prophets are dead. Who do You make Yourself out to be?" Jesus answered, "If I honor Myself, My honor is nothing. It is My Father who honors Me, of whom you say that He is your God. Yet you have not known Him, but I know Him. And if I say, 'I do not know Him,' I shall be a liar like you; but I do know Him and keep His word. Your father Abraham rejoiced to see My day, and he saw it and was glad." (NKJV)*

These Jews thought Jesus was crazy, claiming to be better than men of God like Abraham and the Old Testament prophets. They all died. Nobody could prevent death; it was inevitable.

The Jewish leaders stuck to their conviction that they were God's children by descent from Abraham. Likewise, Jesus never wavered in pointing them back to his relationship with God. God is the one who sent him and shows people his glory. Their physical ancestor Abraham saw the time when Jesus would be there on earth.

A Young Old Man

JOHN 8:57–59 *Then the Jews said to Him, "You are not yet fifty years old, and have You seen Abraham?" Jesus said to them, "Most assuredly, I say to you, before Abraham was, <u>I AM</u>." Then they took up stones to throw at Him; but Jesus hid Himself and went out of the temple, going through the midst of them, and so passed by. (NKJV)*

Abraham lived two thousand years before, and Jesus was only in his mid-thirties. How could Abraham have seen someone who wouldn't be born for a couple of millennia? All this talk was enough to drive anyone mad. But what Jesus meant was that he didn't have a beginning; he existed before Abraham.

The people understood exactly what Jesus was saying—that he is God. Consequently, they tried to stone Jesus for blasphemy. But Jesus was able to hide in the crowd and escape.

what others say

George R. Beasley-Murray

"Not yet fifty years" is not intended to suggest that Jesus was almost that age. . . . It simply indicates the common view of the end of a man's working life (see Numbers 4:2–3, 39; 8:24–25); Jesus has not yet reached seniority, and he claims to have seen Abraham![8]

Chapter Wrap-Up

- When the religious leaders brought a woman caught in adultery to Jesus, he forgave her sins instead of punishing her. (John 8:1–11)
- Jesus is the Light of the World who shows people their sins and what God is like. (John 8:12–20)
- People who don't believe in Jesus will die in their sins instead of gaining eternal life. (John 8:21–30)
- Freedom from slavery to sin comes from knowing Jesus and the truth of God's Word. (John 8:31–47)
- When Jesus claimed deity by saying he existed before Abraham, the religious leaders tried to stone him. (John 8:48–59)

Study Questions

1. Why did the religious leaders bring the adulterous woman to Jesus?

2. How did Jesus' attitude toward her differ from theirs?

3. What did Jesus mean when he said he is the "light of the world"?

4. What witnesses did Jesus offer to prove his words were true?

5. What does knowing the truth do for us?

6. Why did Jesus say the religious leaders weren't Abraham's children?

7. Who did he say their father was?

8. Why did the Jews try to stone Jesus?

John 9: Jesus the Sight Giver

Chapter Highlights:
- Sight for the Blind
- Seeing Men Go Blind
- Seeing the Messiah

Let's Get Started

When was the last time you noticed the fiery reds and oranges of a sunrise? Layers of blue in the sky? Shades of pink in a flower bed? Constellations in the night sky? Our world is full of color, yet too often we don't see it.

A man born blind in Jesus' day spent most of his life without being able to see colors or anything else. But when Jesus saw him and gave him sight, his world changed—in more than one way. He met the Messiah and stirred up even more controversy between the Jewish religious leaders and Jesus.

parent's sin
Exodus 34:7

Whose Fault Is It?

> JOHN 9:1–2 *Now as Jesus passed by, He saw a man who was blind from birth. And His disciples asked Him, saying, "Rabbi, who sinned, this man or his parents, that he was born blind?"* (NKJV)

He had never seen his parents' faces, nor his own in a reflection. He had never seen the beauty of a sunset, the red of a rose, the twinkling of stars, the greenness of grass. But when Jesus and his disciples met him, the disciples weren't concerned about helping this man. They were only curious about why he was blind, assuming his disability was punishment for someone's sin.

Light of the World

Since blind people could support themselves only by begging, they tended to hang out around the Temple. That was the best location because a lot of people would pass by them and because people would be more charitable when they came to worship.

According to Jewish teachers, a lot of suffering and physical deformities, like blindness and deafness, were caused by sin. Even a <u>parent's sin</u> could be passed on to a child in the form of suffering or sickness.

Roger L. Fredrikson

We humans persist in wanting to know who to blame. We discuss the matter endlessly, sometimes earnestly, but often foolishly. However, Jesus brushes this question aside. He does not focus on the past, nor is He interested in answering theological speculation, for He sets the needs of this man in the context of what God can do.[1]

Jesus' disciples had probably seen so many blind beggars that they were calloused to that man's situation. It's easy for us to have the same attitude today toward people who are sick, out of work, or homeless. Instead of viewing them with curiosity, ask God to show you ways to help them.

God on Display

JOHN 9:3–5 *Jesus answered, "Neither this man nor his parents sinned, but that the works of God should be revealed in him. I must work the works of Him who sent Me while it is day; the night is coming when no one can work. As long as I am in the world, I am the light of the world." (NKJV)*

The disciples were only concerned about the cause of the man's blindness. Jesus was concerned about the purpose for it. (He usually was on a different wavelength than other people.) According to Jesus, God allowed the blindness (he didn't deliberately inflict it) so Jesus could demonstrate his power in healing him. Jesus wasn't a grandstander, but he liked to put God's power on display. There wasn't a lot of time to do that. His time on earth was short, so there was an urgency to what he could do before his death.

A Real Eye-Opener

JOHN 9:6–7 *When He had said these things, He spat on the ground and made clay with the saliva; and He anointed the eyes of the blind man with the clay. And He said to him, "Go, wash in the pool of Siloam" (which is translated, Sent). So he went and washed, and came back seeing. (NKJV)*

Often Jesus used unconventional means to produce supernatural results. If a doctor today tried to restore sight with mud pies made with his saliva, he'd be laughed out of medicine—or sued for malpractice. But Jesus got away with it. In ancient days, people thought spit had the power to heal. Since it was linked to magical arts, Jewish people were suspicious of it. If this man knew what Jesus used to make the mud he put on his eyes, he would have been disgusted and uncomfortable.

The blind man must have been quite a sight, walking across town with mud pies on his eyes. He probably felt foolish. Certainly people would have stared at him, and he could have felt their stares even though he couldn't see them. Maybe he debated with himself about whether washing away the mud would work. Nevertheless, he went to the pool. That took a lot of faith! It also gave him his sight.

what others say

Anne Graham Lotz

It's another miracle that he ever even arrived home; each moment of discovery must have been distracting as well as thrilling! Surely the stupendous excitement that was welling up in his chest and spilling out in every pore of his being propelled him to seek out those who knew him that they might share in his incredible joy! But if he was expecting a neighborhood celebration, he was in for a rude awakening! Instead, he encountered hostile, incredulous interrogation.[2]

This blind man didn't know who Jesus was. Nor did he have any assurance that what Jesus asked would restore his sight. There was always the possibility that he would make a fool of himself. If you had been this blind man, would you have let Jesus put mud on your eyes and then obeyed his command to wash it off in the Pool of Siloam?

Even though it may seem hard to believe Jesus' miracles, they were easy for him to perform. After all, he invented the laws of nature. We serve a powerful God! So don't be afraid to ask for his help, no matter how big your problem seems.

Talk of the Town

JOHN 9:8–12 *Therefore the neighbors and those who previously had seen that he was blind said, "Is not this he who sat and begged?" Some said, "This is he." Others said, "He is like him." He said, "I am he." Therefore they said to him, "How were your eyes opened?" He answered and said, "A Man called Jesus made clay and anointed my eyes and said to me, 'Go to the pool of Siloam and wash.' So I went and washed, and I received sight." Then they said to him, "Where is He?" He said, "I do not know." (NKJV)*

This healing caused a lot of talk. Some people wondered if the man who could see was the same one who was blind. Some said he was. Others thought he was a look-alike. He cleared up the confusion by insisting he was that man. So then people wanted to know how he could see. He told them the story but couldn't tell them who the healer was.

Tell It Again

JOHN 9:13–15 They brought him who formerly was blind to the Pharisees. Now it was a Sabbath when Jesus made the clay and opened his eyes. Then the Pharisees also asked him again how he had received his sight. He said to them, "He put clay on my eyes, and I washed, and I see." (NKJV)

It was customary to involve the Pharisees, as keepers of the faith, in investigating questionable situations. The fact that Jesus healed the man on the Sabbath made this one worth looking into. So a group of people took the former blind man to the Pharisees for inspection. Once more the man had to tell his story.

Blind Man Sees; Seeing Men Don't

JOHN 9:16–17 Therefore some of the Pharisees said, "This Man is not from God, because He does not keep the Sabbath." Others said, "How can a man who is a sinner do such signs?" And there was a division among them. They said to the blind man again, "What do you say about Him because He opened your eyes?" He said, "He is a prophet." (NKJV)

As far as the Pharisees were concerned, evidence was irrelevant. They had already made up their minds about Jesus, and they weren't about to let the facts change their opinions. Instead of having the spiritual sight you'd expect from religious leaders, they were the ones who were blind. When Jesus gave the blind man sight on the Sabbath, the religious leaders refused to believe this miracle proved Jesus is God. After discussing the situation and failing to reach a verdict, they asked the former blind man who he thought the healer was. "A prophet" was all he could think to call him.

> **what others say**
>
> **Everett F. Harrison**
>
> These leaders could be expected to raise the issue of violation of the Sabbath rest. From the man's report they felt they had ample evidence for their complaint. The only catch was that the work was so humane and so unique. Could a sinner accomplish such a result? No wonder some of the Pharisees shook their heads. They were really perplexed.[3]

When in Doubt, Go to the Parents

JOHN 9:18–23 *But the Jews did not believe concerning him, that he had been blind and received his sight, until they called the parents of him who had received his sight. And they asked them, saying, "Is this your son, who you say was born blind? How then does he now see?" His parents answered them and said, "We know that this is our son, and that he was born blind; but by what means he now sees we do not know, or who opened his eyes we do not know. He is of age; ask him. He will speak for himself." His parents said these things because they feared the Jews, for the Jews had agreed already that if anyone confessed that He was Christ, he would be put out of the synagogue. Therefore his parents said, "He is of age; ask him." (NKJV)*

Since the Pharisees couldn't agree on the man's situation, they decided to review the case. First, they checked with the man's parents, hoping that he hadn't been born blind. If his blindness was the result of an illness or accident, they could probably come up with an explanation other than a miracle.

The parents were no help. They confirmed that the man had been born blind and now could see. Since they couldn't explain the miracle, they sent the Pharisees back to their son, who could speak for himself. In reality, they were afraid the religious leaders would kick them out of the **synagogue**.

Being "put out of the synagogue" equals excommunication. The whole family would be excluded from the community socially and religiously. Depending on the "crime," this punishment could be temporary or long-term. Sometimes it was accompanied by beatings.

One More Time

go to

give glory to God
Joshua 7:19

JOHN 9:24–25 *So they again called the man who was blind, and said to him, "Give God the glory! We know that this Man is a sinner." He answered and said, "Whether He is a sinner or not I do not know. One thing I know: that though I was blind, now I see." (NKJV)*

The Pharisees called the former blind man in for more cross-examination. They commanded him to admit the truth and tell them his healer was a sinner. The man hadn't gone to Bible school. He probably was not a great intellect. But he had an experience that no one could deny, and he repeated it—again.

> what others say
>
> **Gerald L. Borchert**
>
> The statement "Give glory to God" is not a praise statement but the equivalent of a Jewish oath, which the authorities employed to call the man to give an honest witness and confess any sinfulness in his testimony. . . . Then they defined the closed parameters in which further investigation was to take place.[4]

Give Us an Answer

JOHN 9:26–27 *Then they said to him again, "What did He do to you? How did He open your eyes?" He answered them, "I told you already, and you did not listen. Why do you want to hear it again? Do you also want to become His disciples?" (NKJV)*

The man must have been running out of patience. He had already told the Pharisees how he gained his sight. And here they were asking him again. They were worse than children who tune out their parents or teachers. Exasperated, the man asked them if they wanted to become Jesus' followers too. What a joke!

We're Moses' Men

JOHN 9:28–29 *Then they reviled him and said, "You are His disciple, but we are Moses' disciples. We know that God spoke to Moses; as for this fellow, we do not know where He is from." (NKJV)*

Not only did the Pharisees cross-examine the former blind man; they also insulted him when he didn't provide the answers they wanted. They accused him of being a disciple of an unknown man, which makes no sense. But when your mind is made up in spite of the facts, you grasp for anything. Once more the Pharisees trotted out their relationship with Moses, claiming to be his followers, as though that would settle the issue.

listen
Proverbs 15:29

A Thinking Man's Relationship

JOHN 9:30–34 *The man answered and said to them, "Why, this is a marvelous thing, that you do not know where He is from; yet He has opened my eyes! Now we know that God does not hear sinners; but if anyone is a worshiper of God and does His will, He hears him. Since the world began it has been unheard of that anyone opened the eyes of one who was born blind. If this Man were not from God, He could do nothing." They answered and said to him, "You were completely born in sins, and are you teaching us?" And they cast him out. (NKJV)*

Even this uneducated man figured out that the Pharisees' reasoning was illogical. Tired of being grilled and insulted, he tried teaching them. His logic made sense. The fact that the healer gave him sight proved he was from God. Since God doesn't <u>listen</u> to sinners, Jesus must not be one.

It doesn't take a great mind to put the facts together. But these teachers weren't teachable. They hated being taught by this common man, so they threw him out of the synagogue.

what others say

R. V. G. Tasker

By being content with the law that came by Moses and by shutting their eyes to the grace and truth which came by Jesus Christ, the Pharisees are being plunged into the darkness of unbelief as surely as the once-blind beggar is waking more and more towards the illumination of faith.[5]

20/20 Vision

JOHN 9:35–38 *Jesus heard that they had cast him out; and when He had found him, He said to him, "Do you believe in the Son of God?" He answered and said, "Who is He, Lord, that I may believe in Him?" And Jesus said to him, "You have both seen Him and it is He who is talking with you." Then he said, "Lord, I believe!" And he worshiped Him. (NKJV)*

One thing about Jesus—he doesn't abandon people when they are persecuted. When he heard the Pharisees had thrown the former blind man out of the synagogue, he looked him up. Jesus asked him if he believed in the "Son of God" (one of Jesus' names). When the man wanted to know more, Jesus introduced himself, and the man told him he believed.

What a day this had been for the blind man! He woke up seeing nothing, met Jesus, walked across town with mud pies on his eyes, got his sight, was grilled by the Pharisees, and ended up worshiping Jesus! Yes, it was a great day.

Faith is based on evidence. When the blind man found out who Jesus was, he believed he was the Messiah because of the miracle he had done in giving him sight.

No matter what trouble you're going through, Jesus will stick with you if you've put your trust in him. You might feel like you're alone, but you're not. He's always there with enough strength and hope to get you through the hard times.

Blind by Choice

JOHN 9:39–41 *And Jesus said, "For judgment I have come into this world, that those who do not see may see, and that those who see may be made blind." Then some of the Pharisees who were with Him heard these words, and said to Him, "Are we blind also?" Jesus said to them, "If you were blind, you would have no sin; but now you say, 'We see.' Therefore your sin remains."* (NKJV)

The blind man believed and gained physical and spiritual sight. The Pharisees, who supposedly had spiritual sight, were blind. To this latter group, Jesus preached a short sermon on blindness. Although Jesus came to earth to save people, those who do not believe in him will receive judgment. That judgment is the result of their choices.

In nature, the same sun that causes watered plants to grow also hardens dry clay. In the spiritual realm, Jesus brings salvation to spiritually blind people who see their need of a Savior. At the same time, he blinds religious people who think they know it all but reject him. The Pharisees got the point but wanted Jesus to exempt them. "You're not talking about us, are you?" they asked. They were sure they weren't part of that <u>blind group</u>. But they were. And they weren't willing to admit it, so they'd never see spiritually.

blind group
Matthew 15:14

Andreas J. Köstenberger

The Pharisees regard their own illumination as sufficient, so when the true light shines, they refuse to look closely. . . . Elsewhere, Jesus calls the Pharisees "blind guides" (Matt. 23:16; cf. 15:14; 23:26).[6]

Erwin W. Lutzer

Jesus used the blind man to illustrate His purpose for coming into the world. To put it simply, He came to give spiritual sight to those who admit that they are spiritually blind, and He came to confirm the blindness of those who self-righteously think they can see.... The self-righteous hate the light, withdrawing to their own secret deeds, more determined than ever that they will not be exposed.[7]

Giving sight to the blind without doing surgery should have convinced both the laypeople and the religious leaders that Jesus was God. Read the following verses.

- Exodus 4:11: "So the LORD said to him [Moses], 'Who has made man's mouth? Or who makes the mute, the deaf, the seeing, or the blind? Have not I, the LORD?'" (NKJV).

- Psalm 146:8: "The LORD opens the eyes of the blind" (NKJV).

- Isaiah 42:6–7, a passage spoken to the Messiah: "I [the Lord] will keep You and give You as a covenant to the people, as a light to the Gentiles, to open blind eyes" (NKJV).

Chapter Wrap-Up

- Jesus told his disciples that the man was born blind so Jesus could display God's power in healing him. Then he gave the man sight. (John 9:1–7)
- Some people didn't believe the man who could see was the same one who had been born blind. (John 9:8–12)
- The Pharisees grilled the man and his parents to determine who the healer was. When they didn't like the answers, they threw the man out of the synagogue. (John 9:13–34)
- Jesus looked up the man and introduced himself. As a result, the man believed in him. (John 9:35–38)
- Jesus told the Pharisees that they were spiritually blind and would stay that way unless they believed in him. (John 9:39–41)

Study Questions

1. What did Jesus' disciples want to know about the blind man?

2. How did Jesus view the man's blindness?

3. How did Jesus heal the man?

4. How did people react to the man's gaining his sight?

5. When the Pharisees questioned the man, how did he respond?

6. What convinced the man that Jesus was from God?

7. Why did Jesus look up the former blind man and introduce himself?

8. How did the man react to knowing who Jesus is?

9. What did Jesus tell the Pharisees about their blindness?

John 10: Jesus the Good Shepherd

Chapter Highlights:
- Jesus the Gate
- Jesus the Shepherd
- Jesus the Son

Let's Get Started

Sheep are such stupid animals that they can't fend for themselves. Even when standing within a few feet of grass to eat and water to drink, they can't find either. They need a shepherd to lead them to food and drink.

Sheep are directionally impaired. They get lost easily. When lost, they have no hope of finding their way back. They need a shepherd to look for them and guide them home.

Sheep are helpless, too. They can't defend themselves, so they are easy prey for wild animals. They need a shepherd to protect them.

People are a lot like sheep. We all do stupid things now and then. Some of us get lost just going up or down an escalator. And spiritually we are all lost and defenseless. We need a shepherd. Enter Jesus, the Good Shepherd who does for us what a shepherd does for short, woolly critters. This chapter of John describes Jesus' role as our shepherd.

go to

by name
Exodus 33:12, 17

Beware of Wall Climbers

> JOHN 10:1–3 *"Most assuredly, I say to you, he who does not enter the sheepfold by the door, but climbs up some other way, the same is a thief and a robber. But he who enters by the door is the shepherd of the sheep. To him the doorkeeper opens, and the sheep hear his voice; and he calls his own sheep <u>by name</u> and leads them out.* (NKJV)

When John wrote this book, he didn't divide it into chapters and verses. So there was no break between these verses and the ones that end chapter 9. Without missing a beat, Jesus switched topics from blindness to sheep tending as he sought to put the Pharisees in their place. As the religious leaders, they were supposed to shepherd God's people. But they flunked in this department. Instead, they were false shepherds, driving people away from God. To make his point, Jesus used this illustration.

Though shepherds and sheep may be unfamiliar to most of us today, Jesus' audience knew all about them. Sheep were like money in the bank. People raised them to earn a living. When in town, shepherds herded their sheep into pens with a gate (see Illustration #6). Often there was a community sheepfold that one man guarded while the other shepherds went home to sleep. The guard knew each shepherd and let him in through the gate, but unknown thieves couldn't get in that way. They'd have to climb over the wall and hoist lambs over it—a lot of work to steal some sheep. Since sheep know their shepherd's voice, all the shepherd had to do was call his sheep by name when he entered the pen, and the animals followed him out to the hillside to graze.

Trailing Behind the Shepherd

> JOHN 10:4–6 *And when he brings out his own sheep, he goes before them; and the sheep follow him, for they know his voice. Yet they will by no means follow a stranger, but will flee from him, for they do not know the voice of strangers." Jesus used this illustration, but they did not understand the things which He spoke to them. (NKJV)*

The sheep recognize their shepherd's voice and follow him anywhere and everywhere. They ignore everyone else. Although sheep appear to trail blindly behind the shepherd, people-sheep are a little different. They follow a shepherd deliberately. As sheep, we'll learn to tell God's voice from those of the religious crooks if we truly seek him.

In Jesus' day, these crooks, or "strangers," were the Pharisees who were leading the people astray. Even though the leaders understood sheep tending, they didn't understand the point Jesus was making with this illustration.

Illustration #6
Sheep Pen—A sheep pen is an area enclosed with high rock walls and a gate. Rural pens often had no gates.

Over My Dead Body

JOHN 10:7–8 Then Jesus said to them again, "Most assuredly, I say to you, I am the door of the sheep. All who ever came before Me are thieves and robbers, but the sheep did not hear them. (NKJV)

When the shepherd was out on the hillside with his sheep, he rounded them up at night in a sheepfold similar to the one in town. But it didn't have a gate or guard. To keep thieves out and sheep in, the shepherd lay down across the opening. Thus he literally was the gate. Since no one could get in or out unless the shepherd was dead, this action gives new meaning to the phrase "over my dead body."

As the Gate, Jesus is the only way to God and heaven. The religious leaders who claimed to lead people to God were, in reality, "thieves and robbers." They had added their own rules to God's— so many, in fact, that no one could keep them all. But God's sheep— those who belong to him—didn't listen to the false teachers.

key point

Through the Gate

JOHN 10:9–10 I am the door. If anyone enters by Me, he will be saved, and will go in and out and find pasture. The thief does not come except to steal, and to kill, and to destroy. I have come that they may have life, and that they may have it more abundantly. (NKJV)

To make his point, Jesus again claimed to be the Gate. Because he is the real Messiah, faith in him is the only way to salvation and eternal life. The religious thieves didn't care about the people's spiritual welfare. They only cared about themselves and taking what they could from the people. (Sound familiar? We have all kinds of religious "thieves" today.) They even killed and destroyed others.

Jesus, on the other hand, came to give life to his people—eternal life in the future and a satisfying, joyful, <u>full life</u> now.

full life
Psalm 23:5

good
Mark 10:17–18

what others say

Manford George Gutzke

Living in faith is like the marriage relationship. When a young couple gets married, they have a wedding day of much excitement and joyous celebration. But that day of celebration is not the last day! It is only the beginning. It would be a sad story if it were the last day. It is the days that follow, which are bright and rich with promise as they live with each other, and grow to know each other more deeply, that make the wedding day so important.

So it is with coming to the Lord Jesus Christ. The sinner receives forgiveness, is accepted as a child of God, and from then on puts his trust in the Lord Jesus. It is then that He can live as he goes in and out of that precious door and finds pasture.[2]

True happiness and fulfillment come from following Jesus, the Good Shepherd. They don't come from living by the bumper sticker that reads "He who dies with the most toys wins."

Jesus the Shepherd

JOHN 10:11 *I am the good shepherd. The good shepherd gives His life for the sheep.* (NKJV)

For people who want to know what a dedicated, loving leader looks like, they need only look at Jesus. He is the model for others to follow. As the "<u>good</u> shepherd," he is good from the inside out. Goodness is part of his character, not a veneer or mask he puts on. As the model shepherd, Jesus would voluntarily give his life so people could have eternal life.

what others say

Philip Yancey

"I am the gate," Jesus says in this chapter; "I am the good shepherd." Jews who hear those words undoubtedly think back to Old Testament kings like David, who are known as the shepherds of Israel. . . . As he [Jesus] explains, a truly good shepherd, unlike a hired hand, "lays down his life for the sheep." He is the only person in history who chooses to be born, chooses to die, and chooses to come back again. This chapter explains why he makes those choices.[3]

Jesus didn't dream up the image of shepherd and sheep. It's used throughout the Old Testament.

Old Testament References to Sheep

Image	Reference
God's actions as shepherd	Psalm 23
Israel as sheep	Psalm 74:1
David as shepherd	Psalm 78:70–72
People as the flock of God's pasture	Psalm 79:13
People as God's sheep	Psalm 95:7
God the Messiah as a shepherd	Isaiah 40:11
People like sheep going their own way	Isaiah 53:6
False and true shepherds contrasted	Ezekiel 34

Only for the Money

JOHN 10:12–13 *But a hireling, he who is not the shepherd, one who does not own the sheep, sees the wolf coming and leaves the sheep and flees; and the wolf catches the sheep and scatters them. The hireling flees because he is a hireling and does not care about the sheep. (NKJV)*

In contrast to the good shepherd, the hired hand is in the sheep business only for the money. He doesn't have any personal interest in the flock. So he flees instead of fights when a wolf or other wild animal comes around, leaving the flock defenseless. After all, why should he risk his own life for someone else's property? Without stating the obvious, Jesus was comparing the Pharisees to these hired hands. They were concerned about themselves and their reputations instead of caring about the people's spiritual well-being.

The Extended Flock

JOHN 10:14–16 *I am the good shepherd; and I know My sheep, and am known by My own. As the Father knows Me, even so I know the Father; and I lay down My life for the sheep. And other sheep I have which are not of this fold; them also I must bring,*

go to

the world
John 3:16

and they will hear My voice; and there will be one flock and one shepherd. (NKJV)

When the shepherd calls, his sheep follow because they know his voice. When Jesus the Shepherd calls, his people follow him because they know he is God. We have the same loving, trusting relationship with Jesus that he has with the Father. But it's not an exclusively Jewish family. There are people outside Judaism—the world of Gentiles—who believe in Jesus, too, and become part of the flock of God's family.

> what others say
>
> **Matthew Henry**
>
> It is the character of Christ's sheep that they know him; know him from all pretenders and intruders; they know his mind, know his voice, know by experience the power of his death.[4]
>
> **William Barclay**
>
> One of the hardest things in the world to unlearn is exclusiveness. Once a people, or a section of a people, gets the idea that they are specially privileged, it is very difficult for them to accept that the privileges which they believed belonged to them and to them only are in fact open to all men. That is what the Jews never learned. They believed that they were God's chosen people and that God had no use for any other nation. . . . But here Jesus is saying that there will come a day when all men will know him as their shepherd.[5]

Everyone is following someone or something. It might be self, Jesus, Satan, Muhammad, Buddha, atheism, agnosticism, family, money, materialism, horoscopes, the crowd, or any one of several hundred religions, people, philosophies, and things. The big question is, who are you following? If your answer is anyone or anything other than Jesus, you'll never have a full, satisfying life here and eternal life after you die unless you put your faith in God's only Son.

Life After Death

JOHN 10:17–18 *Therefore My Father loves Me, because I lay down My life that I may take it again. No one takes it from Me, but I lay it down of Myself. I have power to lay it down, and I have power to take it again. This command I have received from My Father." (NKJV)*

Few people volunteer to die. But Jesus did. When he was killed—as we will see later—it may have appeared that Jesus was powerless against the Roman soldiers who crucified him. In reality, Jesus chose to die. Only he wouldn't stay dead—he would rise again! That was a daring claim related to having the authority to control his death and life. But it wasn't an exaggeration. God gave him that authority.

When we think of power, it's usually in one of these contexts: having enough money to buy and do what we want, having political clout, being bigger than other people, or being in charge of a group or organization. Jesus gave power another definition. He taught that real power is choosing to give your life for others.

go to

having a demon
John 7:20; 8:48

blind man
John 9:1–9

Split Decision

JOHN 10:19–21 *Therefore there was a division again among the Jews because of these sayings. And many of them said, "He has a demon and is mad. Why do you listen to Him?" Others said, "These are not the words of one who has a demon. Can a demon open the eyes of the blind?" (NKJV)*

Jesus had a way of bringing out the best—and worst—in people. In this case, it was both. The unbelieving Jews in the crowd accused Jesus of <u>having a demon</u> and being insane. (Back then, people thought demon possession always drove people mad.) But others disagreed. They took Jesus' words seriously and remembered his healing of the <u>blind man</u>.

Do Tell

JOHN 10:22–24 *Now it was the Feast of Dedication in Jerusalem, and it was winter. And Jesus walked in the temple, in Solomon's porch. Then the Jews surrounded Him and said to Him, "How long do You keep us in doubt? If You are the Christ, tell us plainly." (NKJV)*

December is a festive month in the Jewish calendar. The big holiday is the Feast of Dedication, or Hanukkah, as it's called today. The Feast of Dedication celebrates the cleansing of the Temple in 164 BC after Antiochus Epiphanes, the king of Syria, sacrificed a pig on the altar. The event is recorded in the books of Maccabees, which are not part of Scripture but which record events that happened between the Old and New Testaments. It is also called the Feast of Lights since lighting the menorah is a central part of the celebration.

During this eight-day celebration, Jesus was in Jerusalem. One day, when he was walking on the east side of the Temple, a group of Jewish people surrounded him. They'd seen Jesus heal, do all kinds of other miracles, and say that he is God so many times that he must have sounded like a broken record. So, what comes out of their mouths? "Don't keep us in suspense. Just tell us who you really are."

> ### what others say
>
> **Louis Goldberg**
>
> Hanukkah commemorates a great and decisive victory over the Syrian king, preserving not only the land and the liberty of the Jewish people but, of far more significance, their religion and worship and the knowledge of the one true God.[6]
>
> **Victor Buksbazen**
>
> Hidden in one of the nooks of the Temple the Jews found a small jar of **consecrated** oil, used in former days for the per-petual light in the Temple. The oil was sufficient only for one night, but lo and behold the little cruse of oil lasted for eight days, until a new supply could be prepared and consecrated. In memory of the wonderful redemption from the hands of the wicked enemy, and the rededication of the Temple, it was decreed that for eight days eight candles should be lit in every Jewish household, beginning with one on the first day, two on the second, progressively until the eighth day.[7]

The Jewish people did not recognize Jesus as the Messiah because they were looking for a political leader. He didn't live up to their expectations, which got in the way of seeing who he really was. We have the same problem today. We put God in a box and expect him to act a certain way. When he doesn't, we're disappointed or disillusioned.

You Should Know Me

JOHN 10:25–26 *Jesus answered them, "I told you, and you do not believe. The works that I do in My Father's name, they bear witness of Me. But you do not believe, because you are not of My sheep, as I said to you. (NKJV)*

Jesus has to be the most patient person who ever lived on earth. He had told the Jewish people over and over who he was. In addition, he showed them by performing miracles. How much more proof did they need? Still, they didn't believe he was God. It wasn't a matter of having all the facts and understanding them; it was a matter of the heart. And their hearts did not belong to God.

> **what others say**
>
> **J. Carl Laney**
>
> In ancient times a person's name was believed to reflect something of his person. People were often named or renamed on the basis of a developing character trait.... The "Father's name" refers to all that God stands for in terms of His reputation and attributes. The miracles done "in my Father's name" were consistent with God's character and in accord with all that He stands for.[8]

Godly Security

JOHN 10:27–30 *My sheep hear My voice, and I know them, and they follow Me. And I give them eternal life, and they shall never perish; neither shall anyone snatch them out of My hand. My Father, who has given them to Me, is greater than all; and no one is able to snatch them out of My Father's hand. I and My Father are one." (NKJV)*

Jesus offers the best guarantee in the world: eternal life with God in heaven that will never end for those who follow him. This guarantee comes with an ironclad clause that we can never lose our salvation. No, never, ever, in no way. God the Father holds believers in his hand, and no one can pry open his fingers! Then, once again, Jesus tells the people he is God.

key point

When we sign up to follow Jesus, we get an unusual guarantee.

> **what others say**
>
> **Herschel H. Hobbs**
>
> Note that we do not hold on to Jesus or the Father. We are held by them. And before either man, thing, or devil can recapture to destroy us, such must overcome both the Son and the Father. And, of course, that is impossible.[9]

Promises for Following Jesus

Promise	Reference
Eternal life with God	1 John 5:11–12
Forgiveness of sin	Ephesians 1:7
Peace with God	Romans 5:1
Fellowship with God and with other believers	1 John 1:7
Protection from Satan	2 Thessalonians 3:3
Security	Romans 8:35–39
Suffering	1 Peter 4:12–13
Persecution	2 Timothy 3:12

stone Jesus
John 5:17–18;
8:58–59

A Stoning Obsession

> JOHN 10:31–33 *Then the Jews took up stones again to stone Him. Jesus answered them, "Many good works I have shown you from My Father. For which of those works do you stone Me?" The Jews answered Him, saying, "For a good work we do not stone You, but for blasphemy, and because You, being a Man, make Yourself God." (NKJV)*

For as many times as the Jewish leaders tried to stone Jesus, you'd think they were getting paid by the stone. The rocks weren't for any of the miracles Jesus had done. When Jesus taught that he is the Good Shepherd who cares for his people and claimed to be one with the Father, the religious leaders tried to seize him. They understood well that he was claiming to be God, and that was a sin punishable by stoning. Apparently it never occurred to them that Jesus could be who he said he was.

A Brilliant Defense

> JOHN 10:34–36 *Jesus answered them, "Is it not written in your law, 'I said, "You are gods"'? If He called them gods, to whom the word of God came (and the Scripture cannot be broken), do you say of Him whom the Father sanctified and sent into the world, 'You are blaspheming,' because I said, 'I am the Son of God'? (NKJV)*

In his defense, Jesus pulled out Psalm 82, a passage his stoners were acquainted with. Set in the context of a court, this psalm tells about God warning the gods, or judges, of the earth that they will be judged someday. Jesus' argument is that God calls humans "gods" because in serving as judges they participate in a function that is reserved for God. If Scripture gives human judges this honorary title, how much greater right to the title "God" does Jesus have, who is God by nature!

It was a brilliant defense. But Jesus didn't stop there. He boldly and plainly told them that God had sent him and that he was God's Son.

go to

John the Baptist
John 1:19–28

Whatever It Takes

JOHN 10:37–39 *If I do not do the works of My Father, do not believe Me; but if I do, though you do not believe Me, believe the works, that you may know and believe that the Father is in Me, and I in Him." Therefore they sought again to seize Him, but He escaped out of their hand.* (NKJV)

Once more, Jesus urged the people to believe in him. If they weren't going to believe his words, then he wanted them to believe on the basis of the miracles he performed. Whatever it took, he wanted them to look at the evidence so they'd know he really was God. But did they? No, they went into arrest mode. But Jesus slipped away from them. Jesus performed miracles so people would believe he is God, as well as a man, and put their faith in him.

what others say

Paul Little

There are only four possible conclusions about Jesus Christ and his claims. He was either a liar, a lunatic, a legend or the Truth. The person who doesn't believe he was the Truth must label him as a liar, a lunatic or a legend.[10]

Retreat to Regroup

JOHN 10:40–42 *And He went away again beyond the Jordan to the place where John was baptizing at first, and there He stayed. Then many came to Him and said, "John performed no sign, but all the things that John spoke about this Man were true." And many believed in Him there.* (NKJV)

Since the leaders were trying to arrest him, Jesus retreated from the area. He crossed the Jordan River (see Appendix A) to return to where John the Baptist had preached and baptized when Jesus first started his ministry. He didn't return to Jerusalem until Palm Sunday. But Jesus didn't retreat from people; he continued to teach. As a result, many people had a lightbulb moment. They realized that what John said about Jesus was true, and they believed in Jesus.

Chapter Wrap-Up

- Jesus compared people to sheep, and the religious leaders to thieves and robbers. (John 10:1–6)
- Jesus called himself the Gate who protects his people. (John 10:7–10)
- Jesus called himself the Good Shepherd who leads people to God, protects them, and gives his life for them. (John 10:11–18)
- The people were divided over who Jesus was. (John 10:19–21)
- During the Feast of Dedication, Jesus claimed again that he was God and challenged the Jews to believe in him. (John 10:22–30)
- The Jewish leaders tried to stone Jesus for blasphemy and arrest him, but he escaped. (John 10:31–42)

Study Questions

1. Who are the sheep?

2. Who is the shepherd?

3. Who are the thieves and robbers?

4. In what ways is Jesus the model shepherd?

5. How is Jesus the Gate?

6. Why do people-sheep follow Jesus?

7. At the Feast of Dedication, what did the Jewish leaders ask Jesus?

8. How did he answer them?

9. What was their response?

John 11: Jesus the Resurrection and the Life

Chapter Highlights:
- The Case of the Delayed Healer
- Back from the Dead
- The Plot Thickens

Let's Get Started

Death. It's the one sure thing we can count on in life. (Taxes are a close second.) We hate it, but we can't avoid it. We call it something else, like "passing away," so it doesn't sound so bad. But death still brings pain, grief, heartache, and years of loss.

In the history of the world, only two people (<u>Enoch</u> and <u>Elijah</u>) have ever escaped dying. That's because God took them to heaven before they quit breathing. And only a few people have ever come back from the grave. Lazarus is one of them.

In this chapter, John described Lazarus's death and how Jesus brought him back from the dead. This miracle is the turning point in the Book of John. It's the last of the seven sign miracles that pointed to Jesus' deity, proving that he has power over life and death. It also ended Jesus' public ministry.

go to

Enoch
Genesis 5:21–24

Elijah
2 Kings 2:1–11

Mary, Martha
Luke 10:38–42

poured perfume
John 12:1–3

The Bethany Trio

JOHN 11:1–2 *Now a certain man was sick, Lazarus of Bethany, the town of Mary and her sister Martha. It was that Mary who anointed the Lord with fragrant oil and wiped His feet with her hair, whose brother Lazarus was sick. (NKJV)*

<u>Mary, Martha</u>, and Lazarus, who lived in Bethany, a suburb of Jerusalem (see Appendix A), were all close friends of Jesus. He and his disciples often visited in the sisters' home. Although this is John's first mention of the trio, they were well known to his readers. John specifically identified Mary as the one who <u>poured perfume</u> on Jesus' feet, an event he didn't record until after this one. At this point, Lazarus was sick, but John leaves us with questions about what was wrong with him.

Plea to a Friend

JOHN 11:3–4 *Therefore the sisters sent to Him, saying, "Lord, behold, he whom You love is sick." When Jesus heard that, He*

go to

blind man
John 9:1–12

omnipotence
having all power

said, "This sickness is not unto death, but for the glory of God, that the Son of God may be glorified through it." (NKJV)

Lazarus must have been seriously ill for Mary and Martha to send word to Jesus, who was about twenty miles away. Certainly, they wouldn't have bothered if it were a cold or the flu. Whatever it was, Jesus wasn't concerned. Since he is God, he knew Lazarus was going to die but not stay dead—at least this time. Instead, he'd become another poster person for God's glory, like the <u>blind man</u> Jesus healed.

> **what others say**
>
> **James Montgomery Boice**
>
> To glorify God means to acknowledge Him as being who He truly is; and, since one of God's attributes is **omnipotence**, clearly the resurrection of Lazarus caused many to acknowledge that great power and so glorify Him.[1]

Two-Day Delay

JOHN 11:5–6 *Now Jesus loved Martha and her sister and Lazarus. So, when He heard that he was sick, He stayed two more days in the place where He was. (NKJV)*

Lest we think Jesus' delay was heartless, John states that Jesus loved Lazarus and his sisters. You'd expect your brother's friend to come when he heard your brother was sick, wouldn't you? Yet Jesus waited two days. Maybe Mary and Martha looked up the road every few hours, hoping to see him. Surely his disciples thought he was crazy for not dropping everything and trekking back to Jerusalem.

But Jesus wasn't indifferent to the sisters' plea to come. Nor was he preoccupied with a lot of other work and couldn't get away. Instead, he had his reasons for delaying. As always, he lived by his own timetable.

> **what others say**
>
> **Bruce Milne**
>
> This story teaches us two things about God's delays. The first is that they are inevitable. . . . The second point about God's delays is that they are not final. He will come, in his own time and way. No doubt that will frequently be later than we would have chosen. From his divine perspective, however, it will be

the right time. God is the best of time-keepers. He created time; he is never late for his appointments.[2]

Erwin W. Lutzer

Though Jesus loved Lazarus, that did not prevent his death. God's love toward us does not mean we will be spared that experience of passing through the iron gate of death. We might feel forsaken by God, but He is there; His love abides with us into eternity. Our suffering is not inconsistent with the love of God.[3]

God rarely operates on our timetable. We want things to happen right away and have no patience for waiting. God, on the other hand, usually doesn't work as fast as we want. But he's never late, and he's always worth waiting for.

Walking into the Face of Death

JOHN 11:7–10 *Then after this He said to the disciples, "Let us go to Judea again." The disciples said to Him, "Rabbi, lately the Jews sought to stone You, and are You going there again?" Jesus answered, "Are there not twelve hours in the day? If anyone walks in the day, he does not stumble, because he sees the light of this world. But if one walks in the night, he stumbles, because the light is not in him."* (NKJV)

Finally, after what must have seemed like an eternity to the disciples, it was God's time for Jesus to leave. Just in case Jesus forgot, his disciples reminded him about the leaders' plot to get rid of him that had been hatched back in Judea. But Jesus wasn't a bit concerned.

He didn't expect an answer to his question about daylight. It was obvious. Work and walking were done while there was daylight so people wouldn't run into obstacles. (Remember, there was no electricity back then.) Likewise, Jesus had only a limited amount of time to do God's work while he was here on earth. So, regardless of the death threat, he had to go back to Jerusalem. On another level, Jesus was reminding his disciples that, as the Light of the World, his presence would keep them from stumbling spiritually. But they had to stay close to him.

A Waking Plan

sleeps
1 Corinthians 15:51;
1 Thessalonians
4:13–15

doubter
John 20:24–25

JOHN 11:11–13 *These things He said, and after that He said to them, "Our friend Lazarus <u>sleeps</u>, but I go that I may wake him up." Then His disciples said, "Lord, if he sleeps he will get well." However, Jesus spoke of his death, but they thought that He was speaking about taking rest in sleep. (NKJV)*

When Jesus announced he was going to wake up Lazarus, his disciples took him literally. Naturally, they thought that sleep would help him get better. But Jesus used "sleep" to mean death. His plan was to go to Lazarus and raise him from the dead.

Let's Get Going

JOHN 11:14–16 *Then Jesus said to them plainly, "Lazarus is dead. And I am glad for your sakes that I was not there, that you may believe. Nevertheless let us go to him." Then Thomas, who is called the Twin, said to his fellow disciples, "Let us also go, that we may die with Him." (NKJV)*

Because his disciples missed the point, Jesus told them clearly that Lazarus was dead. In fact, it was likely Lazarus was dead by the time Jesus got the message about his illness. Jesus then went on to focus on the big picture. Lazarus's death wasn't a waste. God had allowed it so that Jesus could show his power over death and so that people would believe in him.

Although Thomas has a reputation as a <u>doubter</u> (you'll see why in John 20), here he showed loyalty and courage. This twin spoke up first and expressed the disciples' willingness to die with Jesus. They didn't have a clue as to what was ahead, but they were willing to follow Jesus anyway.

> **what others say**
>
> ### Charles H. Spurgeon
> Christ is not glad because of sorrow, but on account of the result of it. He knew that his temporary trial would help His disciples to a greater faith, and He so prizes their growth in faith that He is even glad of the sorrow which occasions it. . . . He sets so high a value upon His people's faith that He will not screen them from those trials by which faith is strengthened.[4]

When we suffer in some way, we tend to focus on the moment. We want the pain to be over quickly, to feel good, to have the problem solved immediately. But God is working from a bigger picture. He uses the pain and problems to glorify himself.

Dead and Buried

JOHN 11:17–20 *So when Jesus came, He found that he had already been in the tomb four days. Now Bethany was near Jerusalem, about two miles away. And many of the Jews had joined the women around Martha and Mary, to comfort them concerning their brother. Then Martha, as soon as she heard that Jesus was coming, went and met Him, but Mary was sitting in the house. (NKJV)*

Jesus didn't arrive until Lazarus had been buried for four days. After that length of time, everyone would be sure Lazarus was dead when Jesus raised him. No one could claim that Lazarus had a near-death experience or that he only seemed dead.

Back then in the Middle East, dead people were buried within twenty-four hours of their deaths. Bodies were not embalmed as they are today. Instead, they were covered with spices and perfumes and wrapped with long lengths of cloth. Mourning the loss of the dead was so important that the family hired professional mourners—at least one wailing woman and two flute players, many more if they were rich. After the burial, family members, friends, and neighbors came to the house to mourn with the bereaved for seven days. Jewish people still practice this custom; it's called "sitting shivah."

Jewish family members visited the tomb of a loved one for three days to make sure the person buried was really dead and not in a coma. In the hot climate a dead body would have begun to decay by that time.

When Mary and Martha heard that Jesus had finally come, Martha ran out to greet him while her sister continued mourning with the friends and neighbors who had come to grieve with them.

D. A. Carson

The implication is that the many Jews who came to comfort Martha and Mary were from Jerusalem, which in turn suggests that the family was rather prominent. Although comforting the bereaved was almost universally regarded as a religious and social responsibility . . . not every villager would have been consoled by "many" Jews from the nearby city.[6]

Faith That Didn't Waver

JOHN 11:21–22 *Now Martha said to Jesus, "Lord, if You had been here, my brother would not have died. But even now I know that whatever You ask of God, God will give You." (NKJV)*

Martha would never have said, "It's your fault, Jesus, that my brother died, because you didn't come when I asked." (People in the Middle East weren't as direct as Americans tend to be.) But that's what she meant. However, she was also sure that Jesus could bring Lazarus back to life if he chose to do so. She knew all about his other miracles, and she believed in him.

F. F. Bruce

This is not a complaint; it is an expression of her faith in Jesus' power. It is the same faith that finds voice in her assurance that God will grant Jesus whatever request he makes. She does not say, "If you ask God to restore my brother to life, he will grant your request"; but it is implied that she had this in her mind.[7]

Max Lucado

Something about death makes us accuse God of betrayal. "If God were here there would be no death!" we claim. You see, if God is God anywhere, he has to be God in the face of death. . . . Only God can deal with our ultimate dilemma—death. And only the God of the Bible has dared to stand on the canyon's edge and offer an answer. He has to be God in the face of death. If not, he is not God anywhere.[8]

The Source of Life

JOHN 11:23–27 *Jesus said to her, "Your brother will rise again." Martha said to Him, "I know that he will rise again in the resurrection at the last day." Jesus said to her, "I am the resurrection and the life. He who believes in Me, though he may die, he shall live. And whoever lives and believes in Me shall never die. Do you believe this?" She said to Him, "Yes, Lord, I believe that You are the Christ, the Son of God, who is to come into the world." (NKJV)*

future resurrection
Daniel 12:2–3

In response to Martha's plea, Jesus told her that Lazarus would rise from the dead. Jesus was talking about the present for a change; Martha thought he was talking about the <u>future resurrection</u> of believers. She may also have interpreted his statement as a common way of comforting the grieving, much as we say, "Your loved one is in a better place."

In the light of Lazarus's death, Jesus spoke his fifth "I am" statement: "I am the resurrection and the life." When we believe in him, he guarantees a future resurrection of our bodies from the grave and eternal life for our souls. Both of these come only through a relationship with him, since he is the source of resurrection and life. It was clearly a statement of deity, and Martha affirmed that fact and her belief in him.

what others say

Bruce B. Barton

Her statement of faith is exactly the response that Jesus wants from us. This confession presents a high point in John's Gospel, for here we see a believer acknowledging that Jesus is the Messiah, the Son of God. In recognizing Jesus as the Messiah, she saw him to be God's envoy appointed to deliver God's people; in recognizing Jesus as the Son of God, she saw his divinity.[9]

Faith in Jesus guarantees that, after death, our bodies will be raised from the dead and we will have eternal life. This is possible since Jesus is the source of resurrection and life.

Private Meeting

JOHN 11:28–32 *And when she had said these things, she went her way and secretly called Mary her sister, saying, "The Teacher has come and is calling for you." As soon as she heard that, she arose quickly and came to Him. Now Jesus had not yet come into the town, but was in the place where Martha met Him. Then the*

Jews who were with her in the house, and comforting her, when they saw that Mary rose up quickly and went out, followed her, saying, "She is going to the tomb to weep there." Then, when Mary came where Jesus was, and saw Him, she fell down at His feet, saying to Him, "Lord, if You had been here, my brother would not have died." (NKJV)

After the roadside chat with Jesus, Martha went back to her house to get Mary. She talked with her sister privately so the whole mourning crowd wouldn't follow. But when Mary disappeared, the mourners followed anyway, thinking she was going to the tomb. Martha and Mary must have talked about how Jesus could have saved Lazarus from dying, since they both gave him the same speech. Like Martha, Mary believed Jesus is God. She didn't say it like her sister, but she fell down at his feet—an act of worship reserved for God alone.

> **what others say**
>
> **Anne Graham Lotz**
>
> Just as a diamond seems to sparkle more brilliantly when displayed in a black velvet case, so the radiant beauty of Christlike character seems to shine more splendidly against the backdrop of suffering. Even in Martha's grief, the jewel of hope that seemed to have been birthed in her spirit sparkled. She eagerly went to Mary.[10]

Like Martha and Mary, we tend to deal in "if only's." If only this had happened. If only I hadn't done that. If only God had done what I asked. The next time you're tempted to say, "If only God . . . ," remember that God is bigger than your circumstance or problem. He's working even when you can't see him.

When God Cried

JOHN 11:33–35 *Therefore, when Jesus saw her weeping, and the Jews who came with her weeping, He groaned in the spirit and was troubled. And He said, "Where have you laid him?" They said to Him, "Lord, come and see." Jesus wept. (NKJV)*

These verses prove again that Jesus wasn't a wimpy, unfeeling man. Mary's and the people's grief affected him greatly. The Greek word for "deeply moved" is the same word used for a horse's snorting and an outburst of anger. Jesus was outraged at death—and he was going to do something about it. So he asked to see Lazarus's tomb. Verse 35, "Jesus wept," may be the shortest verse in the Bible, but it packs a powerful punch. Those two words tell us Jesus mourned his friend's death deeply. They also tell us that Jesus is like us and understands what we go through. When we hurt, God hurts.

A Crowd Splitter

JOHN 11:36–37 *Then the Jews said, "See how He loved him!" And some of them said, "Could not this Man, who opened the eyes of the blind, also have kept this man from dying?"* (NKJV)

It seems that whatever Jesus did he split the crowd. This time it was his emotions that divided the people. Some commented on how much Jesus loved Lazarus. Others complained because he didn't arrive in time to heal him. (Sound familiar?) They reasoned that since Jesus gave the blind man sight, surely he could heal a sick man before he died.

The Stench Will Knock You Out

JOHN 11:38–40 *Then Jesus, again groaning in Himself, came to the tomb. It was a cave, and a stone lay against it. Jesus said, "Take away the stone." Martha, the sister of him who was dead, said to Him, "Lord, by this time there is a stench, for he has been dead four days." Jesus said to her, "Did I not say to you that if you would believe you would see the glory of God?"* (NKJV)

Still angry, Jesus arrives at the tomb. So, what does he do? Something utterly ridiculous. He tells them to roll away the entrance stone.

Instead of burying dead bodies in holes in the ground, it was normal for people to be buried in caves. The body was wrapped tightly in long cloth strips, like covering someone with a roll of bathroom tissue. Faces were covered with square cloths. A huge round stone covered the entrance to the cave; it moved in a groove that was dug in the front of the opening. After a year, when the flesh had rotted off the bones, the family entered the tomb, put the bones in a box, and kept the box in a slot in the cave wall.

Confusion reigns. People must have been thinking, *What does he think he's doing? He must be crazy! The man's dead.* Dead is dead, whether it's one minute, one hour, one day, or four days after he takes his last breath.

Martha, the practical one, pointed out how bad the stench would be. After four days, it was probably strong enough to knock over the entire crowd. But it didn't keep Jesus from doing what he came to do: show them God's glory.

Return of the Living Dead

JOHN 11:41–44 *Then they took away the stone from the place where the dead man was lying. And Jesus lifted up His eyes and said, "Father, I thank You that You have heard Me. And I know that You always hear Me, but because of the people who are standing by I said this, that they may believe that You sent Me." Now when He had said these things, He cried with a loud voice, "Lazarus, come forth!" And he who had died came out bound hand and foot with graveclothes, and his face was wrapped with a cloth. Jesus said to them, "Loose him, and let him go." (NKJV)*

We don't know who moved the stone, but at least two people didn't hesitate. Maybe Mary and Martha. They weren't turned off by the prospect of a stench. They didn't consider the possibility of embarrassment if Jesus didn't come through. They weren't afraid they'd look like idiots. They just backed up their belief in him with obedience.

After the stone was moved, Jesus thanked God for hearing him. Most of us would have been holding our noses and keeping our mouths shut. But not Jesus. He prayed out loud so the people would hear him and know the source of the miracle he was about to perform.

Then Jesus called Lazarus to come out of the tomb. If he hadn't called him by name, he would have emptied the whole graveyard! And Lazarus waddled out the best he could (see Illustration #7). Jesus easily could have zapped the grave clothes and made them disintegrate. Instead, he involved people in the miracle, telling them to unwrap Lazarus. And somebody did. Jesus proved he is the resurrection and the life by raising Lazarus from the dead.

what others say

F. L. Godet

The Jews had said of the healing of the man born blind: As an infraction of the Sabbath, this cannot be a divine work. By rendering thanks to God on this day in presence of all the people, even before performing the miracle, Jesus positively calls upon God to grant or to refuse Him His cooperation. In the face of such a prayer God must be recognized either as the guarantor of His mission or as the accomplice in His imposture.[13]

Illustration #7
Lazarus in Grave Clothes—Lazarus was wrapped in strips of cloth. When Jesus commanded him to come out, he did so despite his wrappings.

Erwin W. Lutzer

This seventh miracle in John's gospel offers proof that Jesus is not just Lord of this world, but also Lord of the next. He is not just Lord of today, but also the Lord of the most distant tomorrows. He is there when we need Him the most.[14]

Panic Among the Pharisees

JOHN 11:45–48 *Then many of the Jews who had come to Mary, and had seen the things Jesus did, believed in Him. But some of them went away to the Pharisees and told them the things Jesus did. Then the chief priests and the Pharisees gathered a council and said, "What shall we do? For this Man works many signs. If we let Him alone like this, everyone will believe in Him, and the Romans will come and take away both our place and nation." (NKJV)*

Seeing a dead man live again ought to be enough to make anybody believe in Jesus. And many of the eyewitnesses to Lazarus's resurrection did believe. Some who didn't believe blabbed the event to the Pharisees, who called a meeting. (Isn't that how we try to solve a lot of problems?) The religious leaders had had trouble with Jesus all along, but now he proved he had the ultimate power—the power over death. How could they maintain control with him around? They panicked. They were afraid that Jesus would start a religious revolution—that everyone in the country would believe in him—and the Romans would take away their freedom.

Charles U. Wagner

All through the Lord's ministry, the Pharisees had tried to discredit the Lord Jesus on the basis of His humble origin, His home or His disregard for their legalistic restrictions. But here was a miracle they could not discount. Notice, they did not even deny that He had raised Lazarus (v. 47). They accepted the historical fact, but they rejected the One Who is the Resurrection and the Life because of the threat He posed to their position among men.[15]

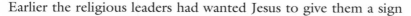

what others say

Alexander MacLaren

The holy things were, in their eyes, their special property. And so, at this supreme moment, big with the fate of themselves and of their nation, their whole anxiety is about personal interests. They hesitate, and are at a loss what to do.[16]

A variety of people gathered around Lazarus's tomb. Mary and Martha had believed in Jesus before they went there. After Jesus raised Lazarus from the dead, many more believed. Others refused to believe in spite of what they witnessed. Which group of people are you most like?

Out of the Mouths of Priests

JOHN 11:49–53 *And one of them, Caiaphas, being high priest that year, said to them, "You know nothing at all, nor do you consider that it is expedient for us that one man should die for the people, and not that the whole nation should perish." Now this he did not say on his own authority; but being high priest that year he prophesied that Jesus would die for the nation, and not for that nation only, but also that He would gather together in one the children of God who were scattered abroad. Then, from that day on, they plotted to put Him to death. (NKJV)*

That meeting must have been chaotic. Imagine seventy-one men talking among themselves, debating what to do with Jesus, arguing in loud voices. Finally, Caiaphas, the high priest, said, "You know nothing at all." In other words, he told them they didn't know what they were talking about. Tactful he wasn't. He had a reputation for being ruthless and proud. No one or nothing was going to get in his way. So naturally Jesus had to be eliminated—sacrifice the one for the good of the many.

Caiaphas was only thinking about how to save his position and the status quo in his own country when he said that. But John added a bigger perspective to the remark. In God's plan, Jesus was going to die for the sins of Israel as well as the whole world. One man's death would save them spiritually and bring all of God's children together in the future.

Earlier the religious leaders had wanted Jesus to give them a sign

key point

sign
John 6:30

Passover time
John 2:23; 6:4

ceremonial cleansing
Numbers 9:6

to prove that he was God. What better <u>sign</u> than raising Lazarus from the dead after four days? So, what do they do? Plot to kill Jesus.

Crowd Withdrawal

JOHN 11:54 *Therefore Jesus no longer walked openly among the Jews, but went from there into the country near the wilderness, to a city called Ephraim, and there remained with His disciples. (NKJV)*

Jesus was no dummy. He knew when it was wise to move on. With the religious leaders plotting to kill him with increasing intensity, he took his disciples to Ephraim (see Appendix A) for a private retreat. This town was close to the desert, and if necessary Jesus could run into the desert to get away from his enemies.

The Talk of the Town

JOHN 11:55–57 *And the Passover of the Jews was near, and many went from the country up to Jerusalem before the Passover, to purify themselves. Then they sought Jesus, and spoke among themselves as they stood in the temple, "What do you think—that He will not come to the feast?" Now both the chief priests and the Pharisees had given a command, that if anyone knew where He was, he should report it, that they might seize Him. (NKJV)*

John marked time in Jesus' ministry with the Jewish feasts. It was <u>Passover time</u> again—the third one mentioned in this book, making it the third year of Jesus' ministry. Since it was one of the three times when Jewish males were required to go to Jerusalem to celebrate, a huge crowd of people filled the city. One of the rituals of Passover was <u>ceremonial cleansing</u>, immersion in water to make people religiously clean after touching a dead body. This ceremony took place at the Temple. While people waited in line for their turn, naturally they talked to those around them. The number one topic of conversation was Jesus and whether or not he would show up for Passover.

Everybody knew the religious leaders had a warrant out for Jesus' arrest. It was as though WANTED posters were tacked to every tree in the country with a reward for turning him in to the religious leaders.

Chapter Wrap-Up

- When Lazarus was sick, his sisters asked Jesus to come, but he waited two days. (John 11:1–16)
- In light of Lazarus's death, Jesus told Martha that he is "the resurrection and the life." (John 11:17–27)
- Jesus joined the mourners in crying because Lazarus had died. (John 11:28–37)
- Jesus raised Lazarus from the dead. (John 11:38–44)
- As a result of this miracle, the religious leaders plotted to kill Jesus, so he withdrew from the city. (John 11:45–57)

Study Questions

1. Why didn't Jesus go to Lazarus as soon as he got word that his friend was sick?

2. What did Martha say to Jesus when he arrived after Lazarus died?

3. How is Jesus "the resurrection and the life"?

4. How did Jesus respond to Mary's mourning?

5. How did Jesus raise Lazarus from the dead?

6. What were the people's reactions to Jesus' raising Lazarus from the dead?

John 12: Jesus the King Who will Die

Chapter Highlights:
- Pour on the Perfume
- A Royal Welcome
- It's Time to Die
- The Danger of Unbelief

Let's Get Started

Even though we don't like to think about death, wouldn't it be great if we knew when we were going to die? We could write the date in the reference section of our schedule planners. Then we could take care of what needs to be done, like preparing our loved ones, writing a will, reconciling with estranged friends and relatives, and cleaning out the attic or basement. We could also schedule in the fun things we never seem to find time for—hiking in the Rockies, walking along the seashore, learning to hang glide, riding roller coasters.

Only one person has ever known when he would die. That's Jesus. As the time drew near, he returned to Jerusalem, and Mary, Lazarus's sister, anointed him for burial before he was welcomed back in a Palm Sunday parade. Once more he taught about the necessity of believing in him and explained why many of the Jewish people didn't.

Simon the Leper
Matthew 26:6

serving
Luke 10:40

Thanksgiving in April

> JOHN 12:1–2 *Then, six days before the Passover, Jesus came to Bethany, where Lazarus was who had been dead, whom He had raised from the dead. There they made Him a supper; and Martha served, but Lazarus was one of those who sat at the table with Him.* (NKJV)

Ignoring the death plot against him, Jesus and his disciples ended their retreat and headed back to Bethany, where Jesus raised Lazarus from the dead. To show their gratitude for this miracle, Martha and her siblings threw a dinner in Jesus' honor. Matthew tells us the party was in <u>Simon the Leper</u>'s home, although Martha did her usual job of <u>serving</u>.

Jesus Gets Smelly Feet

JOHN 12:3 *Then Mary took a pound of very costly oil of spikenard, anointed the feet of Jesus, and wiped His feet with her hair. And the house was filled with the fragrance of the oil. (NKJV)*

What a weird act of love Mary performed! Most of us would be extremely uncomfortable if we went to dinner and our friend's sister suddenly poured perfume on our feet and then wiped them dry with her hair.

The perfume Mary used was made from spikenard, an herb grown in the mountains of India and exported in alabaster bottles (see Illustration #8). It was so expensive that people bought it for an investment, not to be used every day to smell good.

Married women kept their hair covered in mixed company. Since Mary used her hair to wipe off Jesus' feet, she must have been single or widowed. Nevertheless, her action would have raised a lot of eyebrows among people of both genders.

But not with Jesus. He saw her heart of devotion and understood what she was doing. By kneeling at Jesus' feet, Mary also showed her humility.

Illustration #8
Alabaster Jar—
Perfume was typically kept in a jar with a long, narrow neck. Alabaster was commonly used because it was soft enough to be carved yet hard enough to be polished.

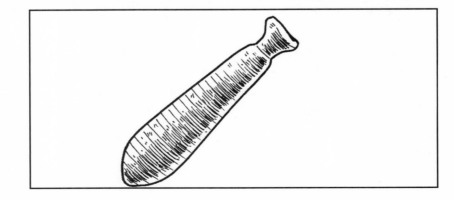

Follow the Money

> JOHN 12:4–6 But one of His disciples, Judas Iscariot, Simon's son, who would betray Him, said, "Why was this fragrant oil not sold for three hundred denarii and given to the poor?" This he said, not that he cared for the poor, but because he was a thief, and had the money box; and he used to take what was put in it. (NKJV)

supported
Luke 8:1–3

others
Mark 14:4

Since Jesus and his disciples weren't working at regular jobs, they had to have some means of buying food and paying for lodging between invitations to dinner and overnight stays. They were <u>supported</u>, at least in part, by several wealthy women. Judas was the treasurer of this group, and he was stealing from the money bag.

Judas's heart was on the money. He couldn't see Mary's love for Jesus because his eyes were blinded by dollar signs. He was only concerned about the fact that she wasted a whole year's salary on—of all things—foot perfume. If she had given that money to Jesus to help the poor, Judas would have had more to help himself to.

Mary was extravagant with her love, not stingy. She gave Jesus the best she had, although <u>others</u> at the party thought it was a waste of money—and probably an embarrassment in the way she gave it. Our best may not be something worth a year's salary. It may be a couple of hours a week teaching children the Bible; being a faithful, honest, hardworking employee; running errands for a shut-in; fixing cars for widows and single moms; or any of dozens of other acts of love and service. How can you give Jesus your best this week?

The Time Is Now

> JOHN 12:7–8 But Jesus said, "Let her alone; she has kept this for the day of My burial. For the poor you have with you always, but Me you do not have always." (NKJV)

Mary understood that Jesus would die; that's why she anointed him with her perfume. It was an act of preparing a body for burial. Jesus knew Judas's heart, but those around him did not. (John wrote his book after the true state of Judas's heart had been revealed—and after the disciples began realizing their money was disappearing.) But just in case those people in the group might misunderstand and think that Judas was sincere about wanting to help the poor, Jesus'

poor people
Deuteronomy 15:11

words would remind them of a sad truth. Even after Jesus was gone, there would still be plenty of <u>poor people</u> that Judas could help. Jesus was the one who would soon be leaving this earth.

what others say

James Montgomery Boice

How did Mary understand these things when the others, particularly the disciples, failed? The answer is: by being often in the place where we find her now. Where? She is at the feet of Jesus, anointing Him and wiping His feet with her hair. Where is she always? At the feet of Jesus! . . . Mary is at His feet worshiping Him and learning from Him.[2]

Jesus cares more about our hearts than our wallets. We can't buy off God by giving money to poor people or good causes. He doesn't even care if we have no money to give. He just wants our love and devotion.

Contract on Lazarus

JOHN 12:9–11 *Now a great many of the Jews knew that He was there; and they came, not for Jesus' sake only, but that they might also see Lazarus, whom He had raised from the dead. But the chief priests plotted to put Lazarus to death also, because on account of him many of the Jews went away and believed in Jesus. (NKJV)*

Jesus wasn't the only attraction in town. Large numbers of people came to see Lazarus. Any man who was raised from the dead would have become an immediate celebrity. With Lazarus running around as proof of Jesus' deity and causing more people to believe in Jesus, the chief priests decided they had to get rid of the evidence. They decided to kill Lazarus too.

what others say

Arthur W. Pink

It was not the Pharisees but the "chief priests," who were Sadducees, (cf. Acts 5:17), that "consulted that they might also put Lazarus to death": They would, if possible, kill him, because he was a striking witness against them, denying as they did the truth of resurrection. But how fearful the state of their hearts: they had rather commit murder than acknowledge they were wrong.[3]

Lazarus attracted people because he was walking evidence of Jesus' power at work in a person's life. The actions and words of those who believe in Jesus can either attract others or drive them away. We can carry with us the <u>smell</u> of eternal death or eternal life.

Palm Branch Parade

JOHN 12:12–13 *The next day a great multitude that had come to the feast, when they heard that Jesus was coming to Jerusalem, took branches of palm trees and went out to meet Him, and cried out:*
"Hosanna!
'Blessed is He who comes in the name of the LORD!'
The King of Israel!" (NKJV)

smell
2 Corinthians
2:14–16

Passover brought great crowds of people to Jerusalem, many of whom had seen Jesus perform miracles or at least heard about his ministry. Word of the raising of Lazarus spread quickly. Everyone wanted to see the man who had done this unbelievable thing. They lined the road into Jerusalem and waved palm branches and quoted Psalm 118:25–26.

Palm branches were used for several occasions: to celebrate military victories, to welcome out-of-towners for the Passover celebration, and as part of the observance of the Feast of Tabernacles.

During the Passover dinner, Jewish people sang Psalms 113–118, the first two before eating and the other four after the meal. They are called the Hallel, which means "praise," because most of these psalms begin or end with the sentence "Praise the LORD."

Hosanna is Hebrew for "save now." They thought Jesus was the king who would deliver them from Roman rule. Unfortunately, they had the wrong idea about who their Messiah-King would be.

what others say

David E. Garland

This staged arrival in Jerusalem . . . deviates from Jesus' previous attempts to avoid calling attention to himself. . . . Jesus encourages public rejoicing by his provocative entrance. [Ched] Myers goes so far as to call it "political street theater." His actions encourage the crowd to blazon his name jubilantly from street corners and rooftops. Passover crowds tended to be expectant during this season that celebrated Israel's deliverance from Egypt, but they will be sadly mistaken if they expect Jesus to mastermind some military coup.[4]

prophecy
Zechariah 9:9

Jesus' Grand Entrance

JOHN 12:14–15 *Then Jesus, when He had found a young donkey, sat on it; as it is written:*
"Fear not, daughter of Zion;
Behold, your King is coming,
Sitting on a donkey's colt." (NKJV)

The crowd treated Jesus as a military hero, but those great men rode on horses or in chariots. In contrast, Jesus rode a donkey to fulfill Old Testament <u>prophecy</u>. Israel's king would come on a donkey as a servant.

The way John states "Jesus found a young donkey" suggests that, after seeing the crowd and hearing the shouts of the people, Jesus deliberately chose to ride as he did. Jesus knew that most of the people were thinking of him as an earthly leader rather than a heavenly king. But he probably enjoyed this moment of triumph.

No Comprendo

JOHN 12:16 *His disciples did not understand these things at first; but when Jesus was glorified, then they remembered that these things were written about Him and that they had done these things to Him. (NKJV)*

The significance of Jesus' triumphal entry into Jerusalem was lost on the disciples. It wasn't until after his resurrection that they understood he was fulfilling prophecy in the way he entered the city.

John was honest as he wrote his Gospel. He often admitted that the true meaning of events had been beyond him and his friends. Just as is the case when we look back on events, John and the other disciples understood things much more clearly in hindsight.

key point

Curious Crowds Close In

JOHN 12:17–19 *Therefore the people, who were with Him when He called Lazarus out of his tomb and raised him from the dead, bore witness. For this reason the people also met Him, because they heard that He had done this sign. The Pharisees therefore said among themselves, "You see that you are accomplishing nothing. Look, the world has gone after Him!"* (NKJV)

As the news spread about Jesus' raising Lazarus from the dead, curious crowds closed around Jesus as he rode into Jerusalem. This situation disturbed the Pharisees to no end. How were they going to grab Jesus and get rid of him when he was surrounded by people who adored him? It may have looked like the whole Jewish world was following him, but most of the people didn't believe in Jesus. They were simply curiosity seekers, swept along by the excitement of the day.

Any More Appointments Available?

JOHN 12:20–22 *Now there were certain Greeks among those who came up to worship at the feast. Then they came to Philip, who was from Bethsaida of Galilee, and asked him, saying, "Sir, we wish to see Jesus." Philip came and told Andrew, and in turn Andrew and Philip told Jesus.* (NKJV)

Jesus was popular not only with the Jewish set; even Gentiles wanted to see him. Those Greeks were possibly God-fearers, people who attended Jewish worship services and celebrations but had not yet converted to Judaism. Or they may have been tourists. The Jerusalem Temple was one of the wonders of the ancient world, and many pagans came to see it.

One thing was for sure—they were brave. Either they didn't know the Pharisees were after Jesus because they were from out of town or else they didn't care. They just wanted to talk with Jesus. So they looked up Philip, who relayed the request to Andrew, who went with Philip to see if Jesus was taking appointments.

Dying to Live

JOHN 12:23–26 *But Jesus answered them, saying, "The hour has come that the Son of Man should be glorified. Most assuredly, I say to you, unless a grain of wheat falls into the ground and dies, it remains alone; but if it dies, it produces much grain. He who loves his life will lose it, and he who hates his life in this world will keep it for eternal life. If anyone serves Me, let him follow Me; and where I am, there My servant will be also. If anyone serves Me, him My Father will honor.* (NKJV)

All through this Gospel, John wrote that Jesus didn't do something because his time had not yet come. Finally, the time had come for Jesus' death when he would be honored as the Son of Man, the Messiah. To illustrate his death, he talked about wheat, which his listeners were familiar with. In order to have a wheat harvest, the kernels have to be planted, or die. Then they grow and multiply into a harvest of seed-producing grain. So, too, Jesus calls his followers to give up their own priorities, desires, and self-interests—to die to self or hate their lives. Then they will gain eternal life. Loving ourselves, focusing on our physical lives, and ignoring Jesus will result in spiritual death. True disciples follow Jesus even if it means physical death—and gain God's approval.

what others say

Bill Myers

When a grain of wheat falls and "dies" in the ground it eventually sprouts and bears more grain, which sprout and bear more, and so on and so forth until, before you know it, the initial "death" has led to life a thousand times greater.

When we give God our talents, our hopes, our lives—when we die to them (either emotionally or literally)—they too return in greater portion and abundance than we can possibly imagine.

Don't ask me how it happens, but it does . . . always.[7]

Follow the Leader is not a game for children only. If we're going to get anywhere spiritually and get anything done for God, Jesus has to be out in front. He doesn't follow us; we follow him. He leads; we don't.

A Word from Our Sponsor

JOHN 12:27–29 *"Now My soul is troubled, and what shall I say? 'Father, save Me from this hour'? But for this purpose I came to this hour. Father, glorify Your name." Then a voice came from heaven, saying, "I have both glorified it and will glorify it again." Therefore the people who stood by and heard it said that it had thundered. Others said, "An angel has spoken to Him." (NKJV)*

Jesus knew long before he was born here on earth that he would die. That's a heavy burden to live with all your life. As a man, he was not looking forward to being crucified—a painful way to die. No wonder he was troubled. Although he would have liked to be spared that death, that's why he came. So he asked the Father to glorify, or draw attention to, his name.

In response, God spoke audibly. He would glorify himself through his Son's death and resurrection. The people standing around Jesus heard God's voice. But they downplayed the supernatural, saying it was thunder or an angel speaking.

what others say

Bruce B. Barton

Glorify is one of those biblical terms we often use without understanding its true meaning. The Greek root word . . . refers to brightness, beauty, and even fame. One helpful way to think of the word is to substitute the word *spotlight*. Jesus was consciously giving God, the Father, permission to spotlight himself through what would happen to Christ, God's Son. The Father responded by affirming that he had already spotlighted his name in Jesus and would continue to do so.[8]

A Planned Death

JOHN 12:30–33 *Jesus answered and said, "This voice did not come because of Me, but for your sake. Now is the judgment of this world; now the ruler of this world will be cast out. And I, if*

I am lifted up from the earth, will draw all peoples to Myself."
This He said, signifying by what death He would die. (NKJV)

God the Father didn't need to speak from heaven for Jesus' sake. He did it for the benefit of the people standing there. His words were an introduction to Jesus' death, which would bring judgment on unbelievers, break Satan's stranglehold on the world, and eventually <u>drive him out</u> of the world altogether.

Jesus described his death as being "<u>lifted up</u>," meaning crucifixion. The religious leaders were trying to stone Jesus to death, but he knew that wouldn't be the method.

His death is the means by which he offers salvation from sin and eternal life in heaven. That offer is open to all people, not just the Jewish people.

Besides "prince of this world," Satan has a number of other descriptive names.

Names for Satan

Name	Reference
Tempter	Matthew 4:3
Beelzebub	Matthew 12:24
Wicked One	Matthew 13:19
Devil	Matthew 13:39
Murderer	John 8:44
Liar, father of lies	John 8:44
God of this age	2 Corinthians 4:4
Prince of the power of the air	Ephesians 2:2
Dragon	Revelation 12:7
Serpent	Revelation 12:9

Clarification, Please

JOHN 12:34 *The people answered Him, "We have heard from the law that the Christ remains forever; and how can You say, 'The Son of Man must be lifted up'? Who is this Son of Man?" (NKJV)*

Many of the Jewish people believed Jesus' claims to be the promised Messiah. Their palm-branch welcome was for a Messiah who would free them from Roman rule and set up a never-ending, earthly

drive him out
Revelation 20:10

lifted up
Psalm 102:10

kingdom. They knew from the Scriptures that Messiah would <u>reign forever</u>. They also knew the title Son of Man was another name for Messiah. One thing they weren't expecting was a Messiah who was going to die by crucifixion. So naturally they wanted to know if the Son of Man was someone else and, if so, who he was.

reign forever
Isaiah 9:6–7

Isaiah predicted
Isaiah 53:1

Take Advantage of the Light

JOHN 12:35–36 *Then Jesus said to them, "A little while longer the light is with you. Walk while you have the light, lest darkness overtake you; he who walks in darkness does not know where he is going. While you have the light, believe in the light, that you may become sons of light." These things Jesus spoke, and departed, and was hidden from them.* (NKJV)

Instead of debating theology, Jesus reminded the people that, as the Light of the World, he would be with them only a little while longer. Now was the time to believe in him, to walk in the light of his presence. If they did so, they would be able to live honestly and sincerely. After this warning, Jesus disappeared.

Ignoring the Evidence

JOHN 12:37–38 *But although He had done so many signs before them, they did not believe in Him, that the word of Isaiah the prophet might be fulfilled, which he spoke:*

> *"Lord, who has believed our report?*
> *And to whom has the arm of the LORD been revealed?"*
> (NKJV)

Jesus had done enough miracles, including raising a man from the dead, to convince the most hard-hearted person to believe in him. But still the religious leaders and most of the common people refused to do so. This response came as no surprise to Jesus or anyone else who understood the Old Testament Scriptures. Seven hundred years before, the prophet <u>Isaiah predicted</u> this reaction.

Eyes Wide Shut

JOHN 12:39–41 *Therefore they could not believe, because Isaiah said again:*

"He has blinded their eyes and hardened their hearts,
Lest they should see with their eyes,
Lest they should understand with their hearts and turn,
So that I should heal them."
These things Isaiah said when he saw His glory and spoke
of Him. (NKJV)

John explained the people's unbelief with another quote from Isaiah. Walking a path of unbelief is a dangerous route. The more people resist believing in Jesus, the closer they get to not being able to believe. Eventually they become so hardened in unbelief that God confirms their choices and they can't believe. Isaiah could predict the people's response because he saw what this crowd saw—Jesus' glory.

God expects us to believe and act on the truth of his Word as we read and hear it. If we don't, eventually we reach the point of no return and are unable to believe. None of us know where that point is.

what others say

J. Vernon McGee

They [the crowd] were like a man who wakes up in the morning and says to himself, "Today I won't see and I will keep my eyes closed all day." He is just as blind as the man who cannot see. . . . Jesus has presented Himself to them as the Messiah and as their King. They have rejected Jesus personally. Now He rejects them![9]

Everett F. Harrison

It was not arbitrary, but rather a judicial hardening. Opportunity long neglected evokes no responses. The conscience seared by repeated violation ceases to function. Thus the nation, steeled to resist the claims of Jesus, could not believe.[10]

Fear of Peers

JOHN 12:42–43 *Nevertheless even among the rulers many believed in Him, but because of the Pharisees they did not confess Him, lest they should be put out of the synagogue; for they loved the praise of men more than the praise of God.* (NKJV)

If we're honest, most of us will admit to wanting other people's approval. It was no different in Jesus' day. While most of the religious leaders had hardened their hearts against Jesus, some were secret believers. They were afraid of being excommunicated from the synagogue if they stood up for Jesus. We know from other passages that two of them were <u>Nicodemus and Joseph</u> of Arimathea, who finally showed their belief after Jesus died.

Nicodemus and Joseph
John 19:38–39

A Package Deal

> JOHN 12:44–46 *Then Jesus cried out and said, "He who believes in Me, believes not in Me but in Him who sent Me. And he who sees Me sees Him who sent Me. I have come as a light into the world, that whoever believes in Me should not abide in darkness.* (NKJV)

Many Bible scholars say the rest of this chapter is John's summary of Jesus' public ministry, pulling quotes from a variety of occasions. Others say Jesus returned from hiding to speak once more. Regardless of when Jesus said these words, they are a last appeal to believe in him.

Because Jesus is God with flesh, when people saw Jesus, they saw the Father. When people believe in him, they also believe in the Father. And when they believe, they step from the darkness of Satan's territory into the light of Jesus' kingdom.

Savior, Not Judge

> JOHN 12:47–50 *And if anyone hears My words and does not believe, I do not judge him; for I did not come to judge the world but to save the world. He who rejects Me, and does not receive My words, has that which judges him—the word that I have spoken will judge him in the last day. For I have not spoken on My own authority; but the Father who sent Me gave Me a command, what I should say and what I should speak. And I know that His command is everlasting life. Therefore, whatever I speak, just as the Father has told Me, so I speak."* (NKJV)

Three years before, when Jesus was talking with Nicodemus, he emphasized the fact that he came to save people from their sins, not condemn them. Here, before his final withdrawal from the public, he said the same thing. Someday, however, Jesus will return to judge people for rejecting him and his words. The message that either saves or condemns is not Jesus' alone; it came from the Father.

> **what others say**
>
> **F. F. Bruce**
>
> The message which proclaims life to the believer is the message which proclaims judgment to the disobedient. To bestow life, not to execute judgment, was the purpose of the Son's coming into the world; nevertheless, judgment is the inevitable effect of his coming for those who turn their backs on life.[11]

Chapter Wrap-Up

- Mary poured perfume on Jesus' feet to anoint him for burial, but Judas said it was a waste of money. (John 12:1–8)
- When Lazarus started attracting attention, the religious leaders plotted to kill him, too. (John 12:9–11)
- Jesus rode into Jerusalem on a donkey and was greeted by crowds waving palm branches. (John 12:12–19)
- Jesus taught that we must die to our own self-interests and put our trust in him in order to gain eternal life. (John 12:20–36)
- Many Jewish people did not believe in Jesus because they had hardened their hearts against God's truth. (John 12:37–43)
- Jesus made one last appeal to believe in him. (John 12:44–50)

Study Questions

1. What did Mary do for Jesus? Why?

2. How did Judas respond to her action? Why?

3. How did the crowd greet Jesus when he entered Jerusalem?

4. What was significant about how he entered the city?

5. What did Jesus teach about losing our lives?

6. Why didn't many of the Jewish people believe in Jesus?

Part Two
Jesus' Private Ministry

John 13: Jesus the Servant

Let's Get Started

When asked what we want to be when we grow up, nobody answers, "A servant." It's not on the list of preferred or popular occupations. Jesus had a different view of servanthood, however. (Isn't that just like him?)

His death on the cross was close. He had less than twenty-four hours left on earth. So, what did he do? He spent Thursday evening demonstrating servanthood and teaching his disciples in private. This chapter begins what Bible students have called the Upper Room discourse, which continues through chapter 17 and is named after the place where they were (a large upstairs room). Other Gospel writers recorded details of the Passover meal; John recorded Jesus' demonstration of servanthood and his teachings.

At this juncture, John slowed down in telling the story of Jesus' life. Chapters 1–12 cover three years; chapters 13–18, one night. In fact, John devoted about one-third of the book to Jesus' last two days, starting here.

the timing
Matthew 26:17;
Mark 14:12;
Luke 22:7

Picture of Love

> JOHN 13:1 *Now before the Feast of the Passover, when Jesus knew that His hour had come that He should depart from this world to the Father, having loved His own who were in the world, He loved them to the end.* (NKJV)

In the previous chapter, we saw how Jesus rode into Jerusalem on Sunday. John skipped the events of Monday through Wednesday and picked up the story on Thursday with the Passover dinner. Again he noted that Jesus operated on his own timetable, and it was time for him to die and go back to heaven with the Father. But he continued to show love to his disciples right up until the end.

Some commentators have disagreed about <u>the timing</u> of the meal John describes compared to the accounts in the other Gospels. Some believe that the four accounts refer to different meals. By closely examining all accounts, and by understanding that John's use of the word "before" does not mean twenty-four hours before, it is clear that John and the other disciples ate the Passover meal together on Thursday.

The Last Week of Jesus' Life Before the Last Supper

Day	Activity
Sunday	Triumphal entry into Jerusalem (John 12:12–19) Wept over Jerusalem (Luke 19:41–44)
Monday	Cursed the fig tree (Matthew 21:18–19) Cleansed the Temple (Matthew 21:12–13) Healed in the Temple (Matthew 21:14–17)
Tuesday	Teaching (Matthew 21:19–25:46) Anointed by Mary (John 12:2–8)
Wednesday	Nothing recorded

gospel harmony

Betrayal Ahead

JOHN 13:2 *And supper being ended, the devil having already put it into the heart of Judas Iscariot, Simon's son, to betray Him,* (NKJV)

The food was on the table and everyone reclined around it. This meal was the traditional Passover seder, or dinner, from which came the communion service that Christian churches celebrate. Although there was no outward indication yet that Judas would betray Jesus, Satan had already set that course of action.

what others say

Philip Yancey

Leonardo da Vinci immortalized the setting of the Last Supper in his famous painting, arranging the participants on one side of the table as if they were posing for the artist. John avoids physical details and presents instead the maelstrom of human emotions. He holds a light to the disciples' faces and you can almost see the awareness flickering in their eyes. All that Jesus has told them over the past three years is setting in.[1]

Real Greatness

who is greatest
Luke 22:24–30

JOHN 13:3–5 *Jesus, knowing that the Father had given all things into His hands, and that He had come from God and was going to God, rose from supper and laid aside His garments, took a towel and girded Himself. After that, He poured water into a basin and began to wash the disciples' feet, and to wipe them with the towel with which He was girded. (NKJV)*

Jesus always had a true sense of who he was. He knew where he came from, he knew where he was going, and he knew that God had given him power over everything. With that kind of confidence, he could do the unexpected.

Before the meal, the disciples had been arguing over <u>who is greatest</u>. When they arrived at the house and there was no servant to wash their feet, none of them volunteered to do this demeaning job. In Jesus' day, people wore sandals and walked on dusty, unpaved roads. So their feet were always dirty when they entered someone's house. A basin of water and a towel sat near the entrance, and a servant greeted guests with a foot washing. The lowliest servant in each household was given the job of foot washing—and didn't enjoy it.

Jesus may have gotten tired of waiting for one of them to volunteer. Finally, he did a shocking thing. He stripped down to his inner tunic and did the job himself. God, the Creator of the whole universe, stooped to wash stinky, dirty feet! What a powerful example of humility, which is true greatness!

> ### what others say
>
> **Fritz Ridenour**
>
> When Jesus did this most inferior of acts, He was certainly saying that humility is the absence of pride. Jesus was saying that humility is not only "putting pride in your pocket"; it is getting down on your knees—physically (if necessary) and psychologically (which is often hardest to do).[2]

When we think of great men and women, we don't put servants on our lists. But God does. From his viewpoint, real greatness is shown in serving others. As Jesus taught, "Whoever desires to become great among you, let him be your servant. And whoever desires to be first among you, let him be your slave" (Matthew 20:26–27 NKJV).

apply it

Don't Stop with the Feet

JOHN 13:6–9 *Then He came to Simon Peter. And Peter said to Him, "Lord, are You washing my feet?" Jesus answered and said to him, "What I am doing you do not understand now, but you will know after this." Peter said to Him, "You shall never wash my feet!" Jesus answered him, "If I do not wash you, you have no part with Me." Simon Peter said to Him, "Lord, not my feet only, but also my hands and my head!"* (NKJV)

Peter was so shocked that Jesus would want to wash his feet that he strongly protested against it. As usual, Jesus was teaching something beyond the surface meaning. If Peter didn't let Jesus wash him spiritually clean, he'd never be clean from his sins and would not be part of his kingdom. Peter didn't get it, though. His mind stayed on physical cleaning, so he asked for a bath.

Peter never did anything halfway. It was either all or nothing. He went from rejecting Jesus' foot washing to asking for a whole bath.

what others say

J. Carl Laney

Peter's refusal of His service was in essence a rejection of Christ's Person. Jesus was saying, "Peter, if you do not receive My ministry, of which this foot washing is a mere token, then you are guilty of rejecting my Person and cannot be My disciple."[3]

apply it

Like Peter, we usually find it hard to let others serve us, don't we? Most of us find it much easier—and less embarrassing—to be the one doing the serving. We can't be proud when another person does something nice for us. So the next time someone wants to do something for you, don't protest; accept it graciously.

Not Everyone Was Clean

JOHN 13:10–11 *Jesus said to him, "He who is bathed needs only to wash his feet, but is completely clean; and you are clean, but not all of you." For He knew who would betray Him; therefore He said, "You are not all clean."* (NKJV)

On a physical level, most people who take a bath in the morning don't take another one when their feet get dirty. They just wash their feet. On the spiritual level, when we believe in Jesus, he washes away our sins. We are saved forever. But when we sin after that—and we will—we don't need to get saved again. We just need to ask for <u>forgiveness</u> for that particular sin, like getting our feet washed, so we stay in fellowship with Jesus.

go to

forgiveness
1 John 1:9

Not all the disciples in that room had experienced the initial cleansing of salvation, however. Judas had hung around with the group for three years but had never believed in Jesus. It was no surprise to Jesus that Judas was going to betray him.

Love in Action

> JOHN 13:12–13 *So when He had washed their feet, taken His garments, and sat down again, He said to them, "Do you know what I have done to you? You call Me Teacher and Lord, and you say well, for so I am.* (NKJV)

With the salvation lesson over, Jesus returned to what he was doing. As Teacher and Lord, or Master, he was above the disciples on the social ladder. Yet he humbled himself and did the job of a servant, showing them in a practical way what love is all about.

In those days, out of respect for Jesus' teaching role, many called him both "Teacher" and "Lord." But here Jesus is hinting at the events to come when he would die for the sins of the world. After his death and resurrection, Christians would use the word "Lord" to mean the one whom God had raised from the dead and placed above every other name.

key point

Open Membership for the Towel Society

> JOHN 13:14–15 *If I then, your Lord and Teacher, have washed your feet, you also ought to wash one another's feet. For I have given you an example, that you should do as I have done to you.* (NKJV)

Notice that Jesus didn't scold them, saying, "Shame on you! You should have humbled yourselves and washed each other's feet." Although the disciples would have felt rebuked by his actions, Jesus was gentle and loving.

Now that Jesus had shown them how to serve, he expected them to follow his example. Some churches have taken Jesus' words literally and regularly perform foot-washing services. Whether or not we do that, we are to throw out our pride and humbly serve others as we can.

Foot washing can take many forms, such as cleaning up after a party, painting a house, walking a dog, providing a meal, or doing baby-sitting. The tasks may be menial. But if we do them out of love for Jesus, they'll be a lot easier. It's all in the attitude.

The Blessing's in the Doing

JOHN 13:16–17 *Most assuredly, I say to you, a servant is not greater than his master; nor is he who is sent greater than he who sent him. If you know these things, blessed are you if you do them.* (NKJV)

In the social order, servants are never above their masters, nor are messengers above their senders. Never. So if Jesus, the Master of the universe, could serve his disciples, then his disciples, in turn, can serve others. In the process, they will be blessed, or made happy.

This promise has two conditions: (1) we must remember as we serve that we will never be elevated to a position above our leader, Jesus; and (2) we must act on what we know and get busy serving. Sitting around talking about the great things we could do for Christ just doesn't cut it. To be blessed or made happy, we have to roll up our sleeves and get dirty.

Jesus' act of foot washing gave dignity to service. He made servants more important, rather than discounting their work. Then he threw in a bonus: real joy and satisfaction in serving other people.

An After-Dinner Kick

JOHN 13:18–20 *I do not speak concerning all of you. I know whom I have chosen; but that the Scripture may be fulfilled, 'He who eats bread with Me has lifted up his heel against Me.' Now I tell you before it comes, that when it does come to pass, you may believe that I am He. Most assuredly, I say to you, he who receives whomever I send receives Me; and he who receives Me receives Him who sent Me."* (NKJV)

lifting up the heel
Psalm 41:9

betrayal
2 Samuel 15:12; 16:23

Judas spent three years with Jesus, eating together, traveling together, seeing the miracles and Jesus' power, hearing his teaching, and watching him in private. Still, he didn't believe. However, Jesus wasn't surprised. He related what Judas was about to do in Scripture. <u>Lifting up the heel</u> in Hebrew means "has made his heel great against me." It was a phrase used to show the pain caused by a friend's betrayal. The Scripture portion Jesus quoted is in the context of David's <u>betrayal</u> by Ahithophel, his trusted advisor, making it more significant. Jesus warned the others, so they wouldn't be surprised when Judas betrayed him and would remember the prophecy from Scripture.

Once more Jesus emphasized that he comes as a package deal. When people received Jesus' representatives, they also received him. And when they accepted Jesus, they also accepted the Father.

A Traitor Among Us

JOHN 13:21–22 *When Jesus had said these things, He was troubled in spirit, and testified and said, "Most assuredly, I say to you, one of you will betray Me." Then the disciples looked at one another, perplexed about whom He spoke.* (NKJV)

Judas must have put on a good front, since only Jesus knew he was a hypocrite. He looked and talked like a believer. Most of us would have been mad and wanted to curse out Judas even if we didn't act on our feelings. But not Jesus. He was sad but told the group outright that one of them was the betrayer. The disciples could only look at one another, wondering who it was.

what others say

Herschel H. Hobbs

The **Synoptics** note that one after another they began to ask, "Lord, is it I?" (Matt. 26:22). Each question asked for a negative answer. Finally, Judas, lest his silence betray him, asked, "Rabbi, is it I?" (Matthew 26:25; "Rabbi," not "Lord"). Again inviting a negative answer. He still hoped that Jesus did not know of his purpose.[5]

Who's the Traitor?

JOHN 13:23–25 *Now there was leaning on Jesus' bosom one of His disciples, whom Jesus loved. Simon Peter therefore motioned to him to ask who it was of whom He spoke. Then, leaning back on Jesus' breast, he said to Him, "Lord, who is it?"* (NKJV)

Contrary to Leonardo da Vinci's famous painting of the Last Supper, Jesus and his disciples did not sit on chairs, all on the same side of the table. Although people sat for everyday meals, reclining at table was reserved for special occasions. For the Passover dinner, the men reclined on large floor pillows or backless couches (see illustration below). They leaned on their left elbows, eating with one hand. The seats of honor were on either side of the host. Since John was sitting to the right of Jesus, he could lean his head back against Jesus' chest.

Peter had a lot of practice speaking up. So it's not surprising that he said what was on everyone's mind. What is surprising is that he didn't ask Jesus directly instead of going through John. Maybe he didn't want everyone to hear him, so he asked John, "the disciple whom Jesus loved," who was sitting next to Jesus. Perhaps John whispered his question.

Illustration #9
Reclining at Passover—Special meals, such as the Passover, may have been eaten on backless couches like these. Guests reclined on one elbow and used the other hand for eating.

Bread for the Betrayer

JOHN 13:26–27 *Jesus answered, "It is he to whom I shall give a piece of bread when I have dipped it." And having dipped the bread, He gave it to Judas Iscariot, the son of Simon. Now after the piece of bread, Satan entered him. Then Jesus said to him, "What you do, do quickly." (NKJV)*

Jesus evidently answered John in a quiet voice and chose a discreet method of identifying his betrayer. Jesus gave Judas a piece of bread dipped in herbs. The bread Jesus gave Judas was *matzah*, a flat bread baked without yeast that is used in the Passover meal. Most of the food on the table represented something associated with the time the Israelites were slaves in Egypt and God brought them out. The *matzah* represents the bread the Israelites didn't have time to let rise when they escaped. Jesus dipped it in bitter herbs—horseradish, which reminded the diners of the misery of being slaves—and *charoset*, or *haroset*, a mixture of apples, wine, and nuts that represents the bricks the Israelites had to make.

This act was a sign of friendship and honor. The other disciples would not have thought it strange for Jesus to do this. Jesus showed his love for Judas. But Judas ignored the meaning. Judas chose to follow through with his plans, and at that moment Satan took control of him.

> **what others say**
>
> **David E. Garland**
>
> Table fellowship had more significance for Jews than simply a social gathering. Eating together was evidence of peace, trust, forgiveness, and brotherhood. To betray the one who had given you his bread was a horrendous act.[6]

Into the Night

JOHN 13:28–30 *But no one at the table knew for what reason He said this to him. For some thought, because Judas had the money box, that Jesus had said to him, "Buy those things we need for the feast," or that he should give something to the poor. Having received the piece of bread, he then went out immediately. And it was night. (NKJV)*

Now that Jesus had identified Judas as the betrayer, Jesus told him to do his job quickly. Jesus commanded Judas to do what he had planned. Jesus' words show that he was in control of the situation and willing to follow God's plan for him.

The rest of the disciples had no idea what Jesus was talking about. They thought Jesus was sending Judas to buy something for the Feast of Unleavened Bread, which began that night and would go on for seven days, or to give money to the poor. It was customary to make donations to the poor on Passover night. The temple gates were left open after midnight, and beggars gathered there. So the disciples assumed that Judas, the group's treasurer, was going to do some chore.

No doubt flustered by Jesus' earlier actions of love and his words now, Judas went out into the darkness of the night.

> **what others say**
>
> **Leon Morris**
>
> "Night" is more than a time note. In view of the teaching of this Gospel as a whole it must . . . point us to the strife between light and darkness and to the night, black night, that was in the soul of Judas (cf. 11:10). He had cut himself off from the light of the world and accordingly shut himself up to night.[7]

Turn on the Spotlight

JOHN 13:31–32 *So, when he had gone out, Jesus said, "Now the Son of Man is glorified, and God is glorified in Him. If God is glorified in Him, God will also glorify Him in Himself, and glorify Him immediately. (NKJV)*

If you knew that one of your closest friends was going to betray you and that his deeds would cost you your life, what would you do? Most of us would rebel. If you knew that your death would save millions, how would you feel? Most of us would be angry and say, "Why me?"

Not Jesus. Once Judas was gone, Jesus could get on with God's program for salvation. He knew what was coming and he was ready to get on with it. His death on the cross for our sins and resurrection would bring glory to, or spotlight attention on, both him and the Father. Jesus' act of obedience in telling Judas to do what he planned to do gave glory to Jesus now. And he would get even greater glory later.

Known by Your Love

JOHN 13:33–35 Little children, I shall be with you a little while longer. You will seek Me; and as I said to the Jews, 'Where I am going, you cannot come,' so now I say to you. A new commandment I give to you, that you love one another; as I have loved you, that you also love one another. By this all will know that you are My disciples, if you have love for one another." (NKJV)

love
Leviticus 19:18

The time of Jesus' death, of his return to heaven to be with the Father, was near. The disciples couldn't follow right away. They would go later when they died, however. At this time, Jesus began to prepare his disciples for being left behind without him.

When a man was dying or leaving for battle, he wrote out important teachings for his children, who, in turn, read them to their children, who passed them on to the next generation. Since Jesus knew he was dying, he left his disciples with final instructions, which John recorded in chapters 13–17.

He started by giving them a new command to "love one another." It wasn't really new in the sense of having been just issued; they already had a command to <u>love</u> their neighbors. But Jesus made it new in quality by adding a new twist: to love others as he loved them—unconditionally, humbly, and sacrificially. Love would become the mark that identified them as his followers.

key point

what others say

Bill Myers

Before He [Jesus] goes He gives His disciples a new commandment—a commandment to love one another. Not with the gushy, on-again-off-again, heart-flutter stuff we call love—but with a dedication and commitment so intense for our fellow brothers and sisters in Christ that, regardless of whether it makes us feel good or not, we would lay down our lives for them.[8]

Larry and Sue Richards

The night before he was crucified, Jesus issued a "new commandment" that his disciples love one another (John 13:34). The call to love others isn't new (Leviticus 19:18, 34). What then is "new" about this commandment?

A new relationship—Christians are family, not just neighbors.

A new standard—Christians love as Jesus loved.

A new outcome—when Christians love each other, people who are not yet believers realize these are Jesus' followers.[9]

go to

rooster crowed
John 18:27

Ready to Die

JOHN 13:36–38 *Simon Peter said to Him, "Lord, where are You going?" Jesus answered him, "Where I am going you cannot follow Me now, but you shall follow Me afterward." Peter said to Him, "Lord, why can I not follow You now? I will lay down my life for Your sake." Jesus answered him, "Will you lay down your life for My sake? Most assuredly, I say to you, the rooster shall not crow till you have denied Me three times." (NKJV)*

Once again Peter was the first to ask the question everyone else wanted to: "Where are You going?" Jesus repeated the fact that his disciples couldn't follow him; they would go later when they died. Peter was brave enough to volunteer to die for Jesus, but Jesus knew better. Peter was too cowardly to do that. Jesus predicted that Peter would deny knowing him three times before the <u>rooster crowed</u> at dawn.

what others say

W. E. Vine

Peter is occupied especially with the staggering fact that the Lord was going away. His answer elicits that disciple's impetuous but faithful assurance of the utmost loyalty.[10]

Jesus knew that Judas would betray him and that Peter would deny him. Yet he never stopped loving either one of them. Jesus went out of his way to reach them. That situation hasn't changed through the years. Jesus knows what we will do, but he keeps on loving us, too.

Chapter Wrap-Up

- Jesus gave his disciples an example of servanthood by washing their feet. (John 13:1–5)
- When Peter protested against the foot washing, Jesus taught him the importance of daily cleansing from sin. (John 13:6–11)
- Jesus taught that his disciples are to follow his example of serving others. (John 13:12–17)
- Jesus announced that Judas would betray him. (John 13:18–30)
- Jesus issued a new command to love one another. 256

John 14: Jesus the Comforter

Let's Get Started

It's hard to say good-bye to a close friend who's moving away. When that happens, we talk about the good times we had together, the tough times when we encouraged each other, and how lonely it'll be without that person around. We may cry, but even if we don't, we grieve the loss to some extent.

Jesus knows what it's like to say good-bye to friends. When he chose the disciples three years earlier, he knew he'd be saying good-bye at this point. It was hard for the disciples to deal with Jesus' leaving; they must have felt depressed and hopeless. So Jesus continued his final briefing by comforting them. He told them about their heavenly home to give them something to look forward to. He talked about the relationship they would have with a different person of the Godhead, the Holy Spirit, after he left them. And he promised them peace in spite of the turmoil that was coming with his arrest and crucifixion.

A Better Place Ahead

> JOHN 14:1–4 *"Let not your heart be troubled; you believe in God, believe also in Me. In My Father's house are many mansions; if it were not so, I would have told you. I go to prepare a place for you. And if I go and prepare a place for you, I will come again and receive you to Myself; that where I am, there you may be also. And where I go you know, and the way you know."* (NKJV)

Troubled hearts were the order of the day. A few minutes before, Jesus had announced that Judas was a betrayer. He told the disciples he was going away and they couldn't come with him. Then he told Peter he would deny him three times before morning. That was enough news to trouble anybody, and there were more bad times ahead for the disciples. Jesus' death would try their faith in him far beyond anything they had experienced so far.

To help calm their troubled hearts, and in light of the near future, Jesus told the disciples to keep trusting him and keep looking to what was ahead. He wouldn't let them down. After his death, he was going back to heaven to prepare places for them in the Father's house. One day he would return to take them home, which was a place they already knew how to get to.

John's readers would have pictured a first-century house when they read these words. Homes were built around a central courtyard (see Illustration #10) and designed for sons to bring their spouses to live there as well and raise their families there. Each household had its own room or apartment within the house that provided privacy. Members also had closeness to the father of the family by gathering in the courtyard.

what others say

James Montgomery Boice

Have you ever decorated a room for someone special? If you have, you know what it is like to make a room suit one particular personality. If it is a daughter, you make the room pretty. . . . If it is a son, the room might have airplanes or model cars. If it is for Grandma, the room might have her favorite books; and it might be far from the playroom or the children's bedrooms. We take care in such preparation. Are we to think that Jesus will take less care for those whom He loves, who are to spend eternity with Him?[1]

apply it

We all experience troubles, suffering, pain, anxiety, disappointment, and losses. These circumstances don't have to trouble us if we know Jesus. He is bigger than our needs and circumstances. So, when you're feeling anxious or disquieted, take your eyes off your troubles and put them on Jesus.

Illustration #10
First-Century House—This diagram shows how houses were built around an open courtyard. Ovens were usually located in the courtyard, which served as a kitchen.

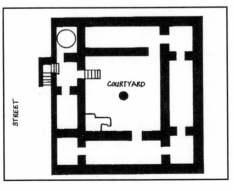

Jesus is in heaven right now, preparing rooms for those who believe in him. We like to imagine what those rooms will be like, but that's not the important issue. What we need to be concerned about is whether or not we have a room.

<u>One Way Only</u>

JOHN 14:5–6 *Thomas said to Him, "Lord, we do not know where You are going, and how can we know the way?" Jesus said to him, "I am the way, the truth, and the life. No one comes to the Father except through Me.* (NKJV)

Jesus' leaving was a blow to his disciples. Their goal for the last three years was to follow him, and now he was going away and telling them they couldn't follow. Naturally, they'd have questions. Even though Jesus thought they knew where he was going, they didn't think so.

In answer to Thomas's question about getting to God's house, Jesus made his sixth "I am" statement: "I am the way, the truth, and the life." He made it clear that not all religious roads lead to God and heaven. Only one does—Jesus himself. He bridges the gulf between sinful man and a holy God, with zero tolerance of other gods and religions.

key point

Not only is Jesus the way to God; he is also the truth, the source of all our knowledge about God. Everything he said is true and trustworthy.

In addition, Jesus is the source of life as opposed to death. He gives eternal life to those who believe in him.

what others say

Homer A. Kent Jr.

[Jesus] made it clear that the destination was the Father. He did not say that he came to show the way, but that he himself was the actual means for bringing men to God. An illustration might be a flowing river whose current actually conveys the boat to its destination, or the modern escalator which is not only the route but is also the conveyor from one level to another.[2]

C. S. Lewis

A man who was merely a man and said the sort of things Jesus said would not be a great moral teacher. He would either be a lunatic—on a level with the man who says he is a poached egg—or else he would be the Devil of Hell. You must make your choice. Either this man was, and is, the Son of God: or else a madman or something worse.[3]

All roads don't lead to God. Attending church, doing good works, trying to be a good person, or following another religious leader won't get you to God. Jesus is the only way. It might seem like a narrow way, but thank God there is a way to eternal life.

Show Us the Father

JOHN 14:7–9 *"If you had known Me, you would have known My Father also; and from now on you know Him and have seen Him." Philip said to Him, "Lord, show us the Father, and it is sufficient for us." Jesus said to him, "Have I been with you so long, and yet you have not known Me, Philip? He who has seen Me has seen the Father; so how can you say, 'Show us the Father'? (NKJV)*

Because Jesus came to earth, we don't have to wait until we get to heaven to know what God is like. Jesus is one with God the Father. Jesus is God with flesh and bones. The disciples should have known God because they knew his Son; they already had a relationship with the Father through Jesus.

Philip had the right desire—to know God. But his request to see the Father must have disappointed Jesus. All those years, he had been showing his disciples the Father through his words and works. You'd think Lazarus's resurrection would have shown them plenty about God.

Check Out My Record

JOHN 14:10–11 *Do you not believe that I am in the Father, and the Father in Me? The words that I speak to you I do not speak on My own authority; but the Father who dwells in Me does the works. Believe Me that I am in the Father and the Father in Me, or else believe Me for the sake of the works themselves. (NKJV)*

In response to Philip's question, Jesus, in essence, told him, "If you are having a hard time believing me now, remember what I've said and done in the past. My words and works aren't mine; they came from the Father. We are **one**. If that's too hard to believe, don't forget the miracles. They prove I'm God."

working in
Philippians 2:13

Is Jesus Handing Out Blank Checks?

one
same God, but with different functions

JOHN 14:12–14 *"Most assuredly, I say to you, he who believes in Me, the works that I do he will do also; and greater works than these he will do, because I go to My Father. And whatever you ask in My name, that I will do, that the Father may be glorified in the Son. If you ask anything in My name, I will do it.* (NKJV)

It is astonishing that Jesus said the disciples would do greater works than he had done. He was God. In addition Jesus worked in the power of the Holy Spirit. How much better could the work get?

The description "greater" doesn't mean better; it means greater in numbers and extent. That's possible because God the Holy Spirit would be living and <u>working in</u> believers. With faith in Jesus, his disciples (and we) would do even greater works than Jesus had done. What's so amazing is that all-powerful God chose to work through us—flawed and sinful humans—and was able to accomplish so much.

From only eleven disciples, Christianity spread to worldwide influence. They would take the good news about Jesus beyond Israel to the whole world. The book of Acts records some of these "greater works" in the first century.

Jesus' invitation to do what we ask in his name is not a blank check or magic formula to get what we want. Rather, he invites us to pray as he did—according to what God wants for us, for what will please him. When our requests are in line with his Word and will, Jesus will answer.

what others say

Gary M. Burge

Once Jesus departs, two promises will be realized in the community of faith: Great works will accompany those who believe (14:12) and prayer will be answered (14:13). Note that the promise of 14:12 does not simply point to miracles. What

love
John 13:35

Jesus has been doing includes deeds of humility, service, and love as well as miraculous signs. Jesus' followers will do works that are "greater" even than these.[4]

How Do You Love Me?

JOHN 14:15–17 *If you love Me, keep My commandments. And I will pray the Father, and He will give you another Helper, that He may abide with you forever—the Spirit of truth, whom the world cannot receive, because it neither sees Him nor knows Him; but you know Him, for He dwells with you and will be in you. (NKJV)*

Jesus talked with his disciples quite a bit about loving. He even called <u>love</u> the mark of a believer. One way we can know we love Jesus is by whether or not we obey him. Notice the order: Love first, obey second. First we establish a relationship with him, then we do what he says.

To help us obey him, Jesus told his disciples that God would send a Helper, the Holy Spirit. The title "Helper" for the Holy Spirit comes from a Greek word that means "one who is called alongside." It was used for a defense lawyer who stood alongside the accused person in court. A helper is someone who encourages—not from a distance but while standing right beside a person.

The description of the Helper as "another" uses the Greek word *allos*, which means another of the same kind—the same kind as Jesus. John did not use the word *heteros*, which means another of a different kind. The Holy Spirit is the same as God but with a distinct role. The Holy Spirit is a person—not an "it"—and a member of the Godhead.

No one fully understands the Trinity. What we know for sure is that God is three persons in one, each distinct and each God.

As a man, Jesus couldn't be in more than one place at a time. His leaving the earth was actually better for his followers because he sent the Holy Spirit to live in them. Therefore, he is with every believer all the time, no matter where they are. The Spirit comforts us when we need it and shows us truth about God. He gives us the same sort of intimate relationship with the Father that Jesus had.

key point

Verses to Check for Characteristics and Names of the Holy Spirit

Characteristics	Names
Nehemiah 9:20	John 16:13
Psalm 139:7	Ephesians 1:13
Luke 1:35	Romans 8:2
Romans 15:30	Hebrews 10:29
1 Corinthians 2:10–11	1 Peter 4:14
1 Corinthians 12:11	
Ephesians 4:30	
Hebrews 9:14	

Keeping God's commandments is not a substitute for loving him. Anybody can look and act like a Christian to a certain degree. But God wants our love. When we love him, we'll want to obey him. It won't be a chore to do so.

what others say

Henry Blackaby

When the Holy Spirit reveals Truth, He is not teaching you a concept to be thought about. He is leading you to a relationship with a Person.[5]

Spiritual Survival Kit

JOHN 14:18–21 *I will not leave you orphans; I will come to you. "A little while longer and the world will see Me no more, but you will see Me. Because I live, you will live also. At that day you will know that I am in My Father, and you in Me, and I in you. He who has My commandments and keeps them, it is he who loves Me. And he who loves Me will be loved by My Father, and I will love him and manifest Myself to him." (NKJV)*

Even though Jesus was going away, he wouldn't leave his disciples as orphans without families. He loved and cared for them as a father loves his children, so he would come back for them. After his death and resurrection, he met with the disciples and gave them the Holy Spirit to live in them when he returned to heaven. Because Jesus would live again after being crucified, his followers would also gain life after death—eternal life.

Then Jesus repeated himself. Whenever teachers repeat something, it must be important and they want their students to pay attention.

go to

Judas
Luke 6:16

appear
Matthew 25:32

apply it

So Jesus drove home the point that obeying his commands is proof that we love him. And when we love him, we receive his and the Father's love in return.

what others say

John Calvin

Orphans [are] exposed to every kind of fraud and injustice, incapable of governing themselves, and in short unable of themselves to do anything. The only remedy for such a great weakness is for Christ to rule us by his Spirit, which he promises to do.[6]

It's easy to say we love Jesus, but can others see it in the way we obey him? Two people can say they love each other, but if they don't show it with actions and commitment, it's hard to believe their words. The same is true in our relationship with Jesus. He showed his love for us by dying for our sins. How do you show your love for him?

Pay Attention

JOHN 14:22–24 *Judas (not Iscariot) said to Him, "Lord, how is it that You will manifest Yourself to us, and not to the world?" Jesus answered and said to him, "If anyone loves Me, he will keep My word; and My Father will love him, and We will come to him and make Our home with him. He who does not love Me does not keep My words; and the word which you hear is not Mine but the Father's who sent Me. (NKJV)*

Jesus' teaching created questions in the disciples' minds. Some of it would have been hard to understand before his death and resurrection. So Judas asked for a clarification. John was careful to note that this wasn't the same Judas who would betray Jesus and who had already left the group. Judas wanted to know why Jesus was going to show himself to them and not to the world. It was a good question since Jesus had told them previously that he would appear to all nations.

Someday, when Jesus comes back to earth again, everyone will see him. But that's still in the future. In the meantime, Jesus' answer took the disciples back to their relationship with him. If they love and obey him, Jesus and the Father will abide with them (in the person of the Holy Spirit). But the Spirit only lives in those who believe in Jesus. This teaching isn't something Jesus made up; it came from the Father.

Spiritual Memory Jog

JOHN 14:25–26 *"These things I have spoken to you while being present with you. But the Helper, the Holy Spirit, whom the Father will send in My name, He will teach you all things, and bring to your remembrance all things that I said to you.* (NKJV)

Most of us lament the fact that we can't remember everything. The disciples were probably the same way, especially since Jesus was giving them a lot of teaching in a short amount of time. No problem, according to Jesus. The Holy Spirit, whom he would send after his death and resurrection, would help them remember. Furthermore, the Spirit would continue Jesus' teaching ministry.

what others say

Lawrence O. Richards

The Holy Spirit reminds us of what we have learned. The person who has made no effort to study and understand what Jesus has said will have nothing to be reminded of![7]

Peace Instead of Fear

JOHN 14:27 *Peace I leave with you, My peace I give to you; not as the world gives do I give to you. Let not your heart be troubled, neither let it be afraid.* (NKJV)

Jesus started this section by telling his disciples, "Do not let your hearts be troubled." Now he came full circle with this concept. They didn't have to be troubled and afraid, because he was leaving them his peace—peace that the world of unbelievers would never receive. It's peace that comes from inside, not from calm outward circumstances. It's a peace we can have in the midst of suffering, trials, or persecution because it comes from our relationship with Jesus and is totally independent of what's happening to us or around us.

going away
John 13:3

incarnation
God becoming man

infinite
unending

jeers
insults

vilified
spoke evil of

Rejoice with Me

JOHN 14:28–29 *You have heard Me say to you, 'I am going away and coming back to you.' If you loved Me, you would rejoice because I said, 'I am going to the Father,' for My Father is greater than I. And now I have told you before it comes, that when it does come to pass, you may believe. (NKJV)*

Repeating what he had said earlier, Jesus reminded his disciples that he was <u>going away</u> (dying) and coming back (resurrecting). Knowing a friend is going to die makes us sad, but Jesus told those men it should make them happy. (You've probably noticed by now that often Jesus' teaching is the opposite of how we think or what we expect.) Jesus was glad to be going home to the Father. That's something to look forward to.

The End Is Near

JOHN 14:30–31 I will no longer talk much with you, for the ruler of this world is coming, and he has nothing in Me. But that the world may know that I love the Father, and as the Father gave Me commandment, so I do. Arise, let us go from here." (NKJV)

It was time to leave the Upper Room. This intimate fellowship between Jesus and his disciples was almost over, and it was time for Jesus to die. Satan, "the ruler of this world," was God's instrument behind Jesus' crucifixion. But Jesus' death would not be permanent. In spite of the fact that Satan kept trying to defeat Jesus and take his place as God, he didn't have that kind of power. Jesus was going to die because that was God's will, not because Satan had a hold over him.

what others say

Ben Witherington III

This first farewell discourse ends with the affirmation both that Jesus is going away and that in another sense he is coming to them. He tells this to the disciples in advance so they will be prepared when it happens. The ruler of this world is about to come and do his worst with Jesus, but he really has no ultimate power over Jesus, for Jesus has chosen to act in this fashion anyway. Jesus is acting as the Father commanded, not as Satan demanded.[10]

Chapter Wrap-Up

- Jesus claimed to be the only way to God. (John 14:1–6)
- Jesus reinforced the truth that he and the Father are one. His words and works prove that fact. (John 14:7–14)
- Jesus promised to send the Holy Spirit, who will live in believers. (John 14:8–21)
- Anyone who loves Jesus will obey him. (John 14:22–24)
- The Holy Spirit will remind Jesus' followers of what he said to them. (John 14:25–26)
- Jesus promised peace to his followers. (John 14:27–31)

Study Questions

1. What two things will Jesus do after he leaves this earth?
2. How did Jesus describe himself to Thomas?
3. In what ways will Jesus' followers do greater works than he did?
4. How do we prove that we love Jesus?
5. Who did Jesus say he would send when he went back to heaven?
6. What kind of peace does Jesus give his followers?

John 15: Jesus the Vine

Let's Get Started

Time was running out fast. Jesus was close to being arrested, tried, and crucified. And there was so much more to teach his disciples to prepare them for the time when he would no longer be with them. How do you cram a lot of information into tired minds? One way is to use pictures to help students remember. That's what Jesus did.

He and his disciples left the Upper Room in Jerusalem and walked through the Kidron Valley and up the Mount of Olives to the Garden of Gethsemane (see Illustration #11). Along the way, they probably passed through at least one vineyard, which may have prompted Jesus to compare himself to a vine and his disciples to the branches. Jesus taught that believers who abide in him will bear fruit, just like vine branches bear grapes.

After that lesson on fruitfulness, Jesus taught mini courses on love, friendship, persecution, and the Helper he'd send them after he left earth.

fruit of the Spirit
Galatians 5:22–23

Painful Pruning

JOHN 15:1–2 *"I am the true vine, and My Father is the vine-dresser. Every branch in Me that does not bear fruit He takes away; and every branch that bears fruit He prunes, that it may bear more fruit.* (NKJV)

In the vineyard comparison, Jesus called himself the vine and called his Father the vinedresser. Believers are the branches, and the fruit they bear is character, such as the character qualities Paul called the <u>fruit of the Spirit</u>—"love, joy, peace, patience, kindness, goodness, faithfulness, gentleness and self-control."

Vines exist to bring forth fruit—large, sweet, juicy grapes. In order to get a crop like that, the vinedresser has to cut back the vines, getting rid of unproductive and dead branches. Grapevines were pruned way back for the first three years to keep them from bearing fruit, so that they would produce quality grapes later on. Each year after the third, they were pruned in late winter so they would yield larger harvests of fruit in August and September. Gardeners pruned with a hook that had a sharp, curved blade. They cut off fruitless and dead branches to make the sap flow to fruit-bearing branches. If a vineyard wasn't pruned, it was useless.

As the vinedresser, God knows what we need—and don't need—to develop Christlike character. In order to get that kind of fruit and to keep us depending on him, he allows hard times to "prune" us. No matter how painful the pruning is, God does it to produce something better from the process.

God prunes his children in a variety of ways. He may allow financial hardship, sickness, family members or friends who refuse to talk to them, or the loss of a loved one. Whatever it is, it's designed to drive us to God so we'll depend on him and grow to be more like Jesus.

God's Green Thumb

JOHN 15:3–4 *You are already clean because of the word which I have spoken to you. Abide in Me, and I in you. As the branch cannot bear fruit of itself, unless it abides in the vine, neither can you, unless you abide in Me.* (NKJV)

God's Word had already cleaned, or pruned, the eleven men with Jesus. They were ready for bearing fruit. To do so, they needed to abide in Jesus. "Abide" means to stay with, be joined to, and spend time with someone. It's more than a casual relationship or a nodding acquaintance; it's an ongoing, deepening friendship.

Remaining in Jesus is not an automatic act. We have to work at the relationship through the following things:

- Praying
- Reading and studying the Bible
- Worshiping God alone and with other believers
- Being accountable to at least one other believer
- Serving others

apply it

The Vineyard Scene

> JOHN 15:5–6 *I am the vine, you are the branches. He who abides in Me, and I in him, bears much fruit; for without Me you can do nothing. If anyone does not abide in Me, he is cast out as a branch and is withered; and they gather them and throw them into the fire, and they are burned. (NKJV)*

Attachment to Jesus is the only way to produce fruit, since he is the source of our spiritual nourishment and strength. In the physical realm, the gardener cuts off dead branches and burns them like garbage. In the spiritual realm, God, the gardener, removes believers—sometimes through death—who don't bear fruit after he's pruned them.

Some Bible students believe the branches that are removed are believers who lost their salvation. Previously, Jesus taught that that isn't possible: "I give them eternal life, and they shall never perish; neither shall anyone snatch them out of My hand. My Father, who has given them to Me, is greater than all; and no one is able to snatch them out of My Father's hand" (John 10:28–29).

Others believe the dead branches are people who claim to be believers but were never saved, like Judas Iscariot. But dead branches on a grapevine started out being connected to the vine. People who have never believed in Jesus have never been connected to him. The subject of this passage is fruitfulness, not salvation.

A Bumper Crop

JOHN 15:7–8 *If you abide in Me, and My words abide in you, you will ask what you desire, and it shall be done for you. By this My Father is glorified, that you bear much fruit; so you will be My disciples. (NKJV)*

True followers of Jesus do more than believe in him. They remain in him and let Jesus' words change the way they live. When they're doing that, Jesus will answer their prayers that are in line with becoming more like him and glorifying the Father. What draws attention to God is bearing much fruit, becoming more and more like Jesus.

For Jesus' words to change the way we live, we need to know what his words are. The primary way to know them is to read the Bible. We can also get to know his words by listening to sermons based on Scripture and studying the Bible with other believers.

Love and Joy from the Vine

JOHN 15:9–11 *"As the Father loved Me, I also have loved you; abide in My love. If you keep My commandments, you will abide in My love, just as I have kept My Father's commandments and abide in His love. These things I have spoken to you, that My joy may remain in you, and that your joy may be full. (NKJV)*

One of the advantages of being connected to Jesus is experiencing his love—the same kind of love the Father has for him. His love is unconditional, constant, and never ending. We remain in Jesus' love by obeying his commands, just like Jesus obeyed the Father. As a result, we'll be full of joy.

go to

first fruit
Galatians 5:22–23

mark of believers
John 13:35

Henry Blackaby

God is far more interested in a love relationship with you than He is in what you can do for Him.[4]

John Calvin

"Remain in my love." Some people explain this as meaning that Christ demands a return of love from his disciples. Others better understand it as Christ's love to us. He means for us to enjoy continually the love he had for us, and so he warns us to be careful not to deprive ourselves of it.[5]

Loving the Branches

JOHN 15:12–13 *This is My commandment, that you love one another as I have loved you. Greater love has no one than this, than to lay down one's life for his friends. (NKJV)*

Loving other believers must be important since Jesus repeated this command several times. It's the <u>first fruit</u> of the Spirit that Paul listed in Galatians. It's also the <u>mark of believers</u>. The ultimate expression of love is dying for someone else like Jesus did, although our death could never save a person the way Jesus saved us. The kind of love that Jesus wants his followers to show toward others is a selfless love—one that always does what is best for others rather than for oneself.

We don't get many calls to be a hero and die for someone else. But we can lay down our lives for our friends in other ways: listening to someone who needs to talk, giving away money and other possessions, spending time with friends who are lonely, and helping out in a variety of ways.

apply it

Befriending the Branches

JOHN 15:14–15 *You are My friends if you do whatever I command you. No longer do I call you servants, for a servant does not know what his master is doing; but I have called you friends, for all things that I heard from My Father I have made known to you. (NKJV)*

So often Jesus operated in a way that was opposite to the way of everybody else. In his day, a teacher's followers were servants. But

Abraham
2 Chronicles 20:7

Moses
Exodus 33:11

Jesus called his followers friends. The master doesn't tell his servants about his business or share what he knows; he tells his friends. That's what Jesus did. He told his disciples what the Father told him.

Today we use the term "friend" in a much more casual way than Jesus and his disciples understood that word. For them, friendship included loyalty, equality, the sharing of possessions, and the intimacy of sharing secrets. The Greek word for "friend" means a friend in the court, someone who is part of the king's inner circle. To the Greeks of that time, the greatest expression of friendship was to die for a friend.

Only two people who lived before Jesus are called friends of God: <u>Abraham</u> and <u>Moses</u>. Jesus widened the friendship circle to include everyone who believes in him.

what others say

William Barclay

Jesus called us to be his friends and the friends of God. That is a tremendous offer. It means that no longer do we need to gaze longingly at God from afar off; we are not like slaves who have no right whatever to enter into the presence of the master; we are not like a crowd whose only glimpse of the king is in the passing on some state occasion. Jesus gave us this intimacy with God, so that he is no longer a distant stranger, but our close friend.[6]

Fruit Attraction

JOHN 15:16–17 *You did not choose Me, but I chose you and appointed you that you should go and bear fruit, and that your fruit should remain, that whatever you ask the Father in My name He may give you. These things I command you, that you love one another. (NKJV)*

Jesus' disciples were his friends because he chose them. That left no room for them to be proud because they were attached to Jesus. He chose them to be with him for three years and also to go out into the world and produce lasting fruit. As they became more like Jesus, they would attract people to put their faith in him, thus growing the fruit of more disciples. As they obeyed Jesus, God would answer their prayers.

Remember the principle of repetition indicating importance? Here it is again. Jesus commanded his disciples to love each other. It's the fruit that will make them most attractive to unbelievers.

go to

friend
James 4:4

what others say

Wayne Jacobson

Anyone who has ever waited in line only to be the last chosen for a team knows the terrifying humiliation of not being wanted. When we are grafted into Christ, we never have to know that humiliation again. There is no greater assurance than knowing that Jesus has chosen you and me to be grafted into him. Yet his choosing does not exclude anyone else. On this Vine there is room for everyone.[7]

Loving other believers doesn't depend on our feelings for them. We can love a person we don't even like. That's because love is an action, not a feeling. When we show love, the feelings generally follow the action.

This Is Good News?

JOHN 15:18–19 *"If the world hates you, you know that it hated Me before it hated you. If you were of the world, the world would love its own. Yet because you are not of the world, but I chose you out of the world, therefore the world hates you.* (NKJV)

Most of us would try to encourage our friends if we knew we were dying, but what Jesus told his friends was enough to depress any group. He had startling news: The world of unbelievers hated Jesus enough to kill him, and they could expect the same treatment because he had chosen them out of that group. Definitely not a selling point for following Jesus. (But he offers plenty of benefits to offset this drawback.) Jesus made it clear that we can't be a <u>friend</u> of both him and the world; they are mutually exclusive.

Unsaved people hated Jesus and his disciples almost two thousand years ago. They have hated Christians through the years since then and still hate them today. The reasons may change, but the reality of that relationship has not. God's values and absolutes always run counter to the world's.

something to ponder

Persecution Prophecy

kill him
Matthew 2:13–16

predicted
Psalm 69:4

JOHN 15:20–21 *Remember the word that I said to you, 'A servant is not greater than his master.' If they persecuted Me, they will also persecute you. If they kept My word, they will keep yours also. But all these things they will do to you for My name's sake, because they do not know Him who sent Me.* (NKJV)

Because believers are connected to Jesus, they will get the same treatment Jesus did. All his life, Jesus was hated—from King Herod's attempt to <u>kill him</u> as a young child to the religious leaders' convincing the ruling Romans to crucify him within twenty-four hours. So believers can expect persecution too.

> **what others say**
>
> **John MacArthur Jr.**
>
> The Jews of Jesus' day prided themselves on what they thought was an in-depth knowledge of God. When Jesus said that they did not know God, the religious leaders were infuriated. But in rejecting Christ they themselves proved that He was right. They claimed to know God, yet they hated Christ, who was God in human flesh. Their love for God was a façade.[8]

No Excuse for the World

JOHN 15:22–25 *If I had not come and spoken to them, they would have no sin, but now they have no excuse for their sin. He who hates Me hates My Father also. If I had not done among them the works which no one else did, they would have no sin; but now they have seen and also hated both Me and My Father. But this happened that the word might be fulfilled which is written in their law, 'They hated Me without a cause.'* (NKJV)

Jesus had given the people enough evidence to prove he is God. They heard his teaching and saw his miracles, but they rejected him anyway. Therefore, they were guilty of rejecting God and were without an excuse for that sin. Their unfounded hatred and rejection didn't surprise Jesus, though. God had already <u>predicted</u> it in the Scriptures.

what others say

Herschel H. Hobbs

Why did the world hate Jesus? Because in His ministry He had revealed to them their sin (v. 22). Under the searching gaze of His perfect life and teaching, they no longer could hide under cloaks of self-righteousness.[9]

Time for Testimonies

JOHN 15:26–27 *"But when the Helper comes, whom I shall send to you from the Father, the Spirit of truth who proceeds from the Father, He will testify of Me. And you also will bear witness, because you have been with Me from the beginning."* (NKJV)

Jesus was big on repetition, especially in those last hours before his death. In repeating the fact that the Holy Spirit would be coming, he added that he would be the one sending him, not the Father. It's a subtle way of saying again that he's God. Jesus also used a new name, "Spirit of truth." The Spirit will teach people God's truth and point to Jesus, the truth. The Spirit isn't the only one who will witness about Jesus; his followers will too.

Chapter Wrap-Up

- Jesus expects his disciples to remain in him, like branches on a vine, in order to be fruitful spiritually. (John 15:1–8)
- Jesus commanded his disciples to love one another, even to the point of dying. (John 15:9–14)
- Jesus called his disciples friends instead of servants and shared God's words with them. (John 15:15–17)
- Because the world hated Jesus, it would also hate his disciples. (John 15:18–25)
- When Jesus sent the Holy Spirit, he would tell people about Jesus, along with his disciples. (John 15:26–27)

Study Questions

1. What natural object did Jesus use to describe his relationship with his disciples?
2. When we abide in Jesus, what do we produce?
3. What does God do to be sure we are productive?
4. Why did Jesus call his disciples friends?
5. What did Jesus tell his disciples to expect after he was gone?

John 16: Jesus the Teacher

Chapter Highlights:
- Mission of Conviction
- Guide into Truth
- Joy for the Pain

Let's Get Started

Most of us like to know what's going to happen in the future, no matter how bad it is. At least that way we can prepare for it. The night before Jesus was crucified, he tried to prepare his disciples for the near future—some of which was going to be bad.

One more time, to be sure they understood before he went back to heaven, Jesus revisited several truths: he was going away; the disciples would be persecuted; he was sending the Holy Spirit in his place; they could pray in his name; he'd give them peace in the midst of trouble. Jesus fortified and encouraged those eleven men for the days ahead when they'd need his teaching most.

Coming Attractions

JOHN 16:1–3 *"These things I have spoken to you, that you should not be made to stumble. They will put you out of the synagogues; yes, the time is coming that whoever kills you will think that he offers God service. And these things they will do to you because they have not known the Father nor Me. (NKJV)*

Jesus' preview of coming attractions was not a pleasant one. He wanted to prepare his disciples for what was ahead so they wouldn't be taken by surprise and go AWOL. What was ahead was persecution. Unbelieving Jewish people would think they were doing God a favor by kicking them out of the synagogues and even killing them. When John wrote this book, Jesus' warning had already come true.

what others say

William Hendriksen

The followers of the Nazarene would be excommunicated from the religious and social life of Israel. They would be cut off from the hopes and prerogatives of the Jews. They would be viewed by their former friends as worse than pagans. They would lose their jobs, would be exiled by their families, and would even lose the privilege of honorable burial. Worse than this even, they would actually be killed.[1]

something to ponder

Believers today are not immune to persecution for their faith. Christians are still persecuted physically around the world. Others are persecuted verbally. No matter what form persecution takes, it's a compliment to be persecuted for our faith. It puts us in the same company with Jesus, and that's the best place to be.

Forewarning for the Future

JOHN 16:4–6 *But these things I have told you, that when the time comes, you may remember that I told you of them. And these things I did not say to you at the beginning, because I was with you. "But now I go away to Him who sent Me, and none of you asks Me, 'Where are You going?' But because I have said these things to you, sorrow has filled your heart. (NKJV)*

It must have been confusing and discouraging for Jesus to keep telling his disciples that he was going away, especially since he had just told them to remain in him. Even though they couldn't sort it all out that night, they would remember what he said when the events happened. So he repeated that he was going back to the Father, who had sent him. His departure would certainly cause the disciples grief. After all, they were about to lose their best friend.

what others say

Matthew Henry

Christ dealt faithfully with his disciples when he sent them forth on his errands, for he told them the worst of it, that they might sit down and count the cost.[2]

I'm Doing This for Your Own Good

JOHN 16:7 *Nevertheless I tell you the truth. It is to your advantage that I go away; for if I do not go away, the Helper will not come to you; but if I depart, I will send Him to you. (NKJV)*

How many times did your parents tell you they were doing something for your own good when it hurt you? This was the same kind of situation for the disciples. When Jesus went away, he would send the Helper, the Holy Spirit. The Holy Spirit can be everywhere at once; Jesus was limited to wherever his body was; so the disciples really were getting something better.

When John wrote "It is to your advantage," he used the Greek word *sumphero*, which means good in the sense of beneficial or profitable. He did not use the word *kalos*, which means good in the sense of beautiful or pleasant. It wasn't pleasant for the disciples to have Jesus leave, but it was beneficial.

sin
Romans 3:23

Conviction Report

> JOHN 16:8–11 *And when He has come, He will convict the world of sin, and of righteousness, and of judgment: of sin, because they do not believe in Me; of righteousness, because I go to My Father and you see Me no more; of judgment, because the ruler of this world is judged. (NKJV)*

The Spirit not only ministers to believers, but also has a mission. He is the prosecuting attorney in God's courtroom, charged with showing unsaved human beings their lost condition.

To "convict" means to show, to expose, to unmask. The Spirit's special ministry to the world is to convict of sin in three specific areas.

First, the Spirit convicts of sin "because they do not believe in Me." The issue is not the specific sins that human beings commit, but the one condemning <u>sin</u> of unbelief. No wonder we need to keep the focus on Jesus as we witness to unsaved friends.

Second, the Spirit convicts "of righteousness, because I go to My Father." Christ's return to heaven established a new standard of righteousness. No longer can righteousness be considered a matter of do's and don'ts. The issue is no longer one of keeping rules, but of living as perfect a life as Jesus did. Our friends might argue that "I kept that commandment." But no one can claim to have led as perfect a life as Jesus Christ.

Third, the Spirit convicts in regard to judgment, "because the ruler of this world is judged." Satan is the ruler of this world, and at times it may look as if he is getting away with evil. The cross is God's announcement that he does and will punish sins—Satan's and everyone else's. No longer can anyone scoff at the idea that those who do evil are doomed. God revealed his commitment to judge sin by sending his own innocent Son to a cross for our sakes.

Each convicting ministry of the Holy Spirit is focused on Jesus Christ. And he should be our focus as we cooperate with the Spirit in telling others the good news.

Sometimes those of us who believe in Jesus try to guilt-trip peo-

ple into believing too. Jesus said it's the Spirit's job to convict people of their sin, not ours. He's the only one who can change their hearts permanently.

You've Got Spirit

JOHN 16:12–13 *I still have many things to say to you, but you cannot bear them now. However, when He, the Spirit of truth, has come, He will guide you into all truth; for He will not speak on His own authority, but whatever He hears He will speak; and He will tell you things to come.* (NKJV)

In preparation for his dying, Jesus taught his disciples about the Holy Spirit and that he would rise from the dead.

Not only will the Spirit convict unbelievers of their sin; he will also guide believers into knowledge of the truth. Like a guide leads a stranger into an unknown place, the Spirit will guide Jesus' followers into an understanding of Jesus' death and resurrection. He works in tandem with the Son to tell them what Jesus didn't have time to teach, including what we now have as the New Testament.

key point

Passing Along Jesus' Words

JOHN 16:14–15 *He will glorify Me, for He will take of what is Mine and declare it to you. All things that the Father has are Mine. Therefore I said that He will take of Mine and declare it to you.* (NKJV)

While people in the world are busy rejecting Christ and persecuting Christians, the Holy Spirit is working in believers to glorify Christ. The harder the world works against Christians, the more God will pour into them his wisdom. But it won't happen to us painlessly while we sleep. We have to go through the hard times and be diligent to study the Bible.

Studying Scripture is not an exercise in filling our minds with information or stockpiling facts to win religious arguments. We study God's Word to get to know Jesus. That's what the Holy Spirit helps us do. He shines the spotlight on Jesus while helping us understand what he said and how to live victoriously.

A Short Leave

JOHN 16:16–18 *"A little while, and you will not see Me; and again a little while, and you will see Me, because I go to the Father." Then some of His disciples said among themselves, "What is this that He says to us, 'A little while, and you will not see Me; and again a little while, and you will see Me'; and, 'because I go to the Father'?" They said therefore, "What is this that He says, 'A little while'? We do not know what He is saying." (NKJV)*

Yes, the Holy Spirit was coming. But first Jesus had to die and rise again. This news was not something the disciples could process. Although Jesus had raised people, like Lazarus, from the dead, no one had risen by his own power before. They talked among themselves, trying to figure out what Jesus meant.

what others say

D. A. Carson

It is true that the Counselor, the blessed Spirit of truth, will be sent to the disciples; but first, the cross. It is true that the disciples will learn to serve as witnesses in a hostile world; but first, the cross. They will, of course, enter into deep, spiritual intimacy with the exalted Lord; but first, the cross. More revelation will be given by the coming Holy Spirit; but first, the cross. And so it is to the cross, this crucial saving appointment, that Jesus now turns his attention.[4]

Grieving Isn't Forever

JOHN 16:19–20 *Now Jesus knew that they desired to ask Him, and He said to them, "Are you inquiring among yourselves about what I said, 'A little while, and you will not see Me; and again a little while, and you will see Me'? Most assuredly, I say to you that you will weep and lament, but the world will rejoice; and you will be sorrowful, but your sorrow will be turned into joy. (NKJV)*

Nothing escaped Jesus. He knew the disciples wanted to question him but were probably afraid or embarrassed to. So he voiced their question—but didn't answer it directly. Instead, he talked about the emotions they would experience after his death. They would mourn his death, while unbelievers would rejoice that Jesus was no longer around to challenge them. The disciples' grief wouldn't last, however. It would "turn to joy" when they understood why Jesus died and when they saw him alive again.

> **what others say**
>
> **D. A. Carson**
>
> Jesus replies to their need, rather than to their question. Their question is phrased in terms of understanding what Jesus has said; but Jesus discerns that their deepest concern is his departure, not the meaning of a phrase. They are upset, confused; but above all they are still ill-prepared for the acute grief that will be theirs.[5]

Birth Pangs

JOHN 16:21–22 *A woman, when she is in labor, has sorrow because her hour has come; but as soon as she has given birth to the child, she no longer remembers the anguish, for joy that a human being has been born into the world. Therefore you now have sorrow; but I will see you again and your heart will rejoice, and your joy no one will take from you. (NKJV)*

When a woman is about to give birth, she experiences great pain. Then when she hears the baby cry, her pain becomes joy. The cross would affect Jesus' disciples in a similar way. Watching their friend and teacher die would bring great pain, but his resurrection would change their grief into everlasting joy.

It was common for women to die in childbirth in Jesus' day. In the Old Testament Scriptures, suffering was often described as birth pains, especially when it was the result of God's judgment on his people Israel. Hebrew words for mental and physical agony were used to explain that the spiritual birth pains were intense and that God's coming judgment was serious.

something to ponder

> ### what others say
>
> **Philip Yancey**
>
> Although childbirth may involve great pain, the pain is not a dead end, like pain caused by cancer. The effort of giving birth produces something—new life!—and results in joy. In the same way, the great sorrow he and the disciples are about to undergo will not be a dead end. His pain will bring about the salvation of the world; their grief will turn to joy.[6]

Direct Line to God

JOHN 16:23–24 *And in that day you will ask Me nothing. Most assuredly, I say to you, whatever you ask the Father in My name He will give you. Until now you have asked nothing in My name. Ask, and you will receive, that your joy may be full.* (NKJV)

After Jesus' resurrection, the disciples would have answers to all their questions about Jesus' leaving. His death would make sense. Then they could go directly to God in prayer and ask him for anything in Jesus' name. They wouldn't need a human priest as a go-between. To ask in Jesus' name does not mean bringing a shopping list of requests and expecting home delivery of everything. It does mean asking for the things Jesus desires, like more people believing in him and a Christlike character. Not only will God answer requests like that; he will also give great joy when the answers are received.

> ### what others say
>
> **Leon Morris**
>
> God is interested in the wellbeing and the happiness of His people. They will go through trials . . . but when their trust is in Him He puts a joy into their hearts that can never be removed. Notice that this is connected with prayer. They are to pray in order that their joy may be made complete.[7]

Although believers have a direct prayer line to God, we don't always use it. Sometimes we talk to everyone else but God about a situation or need. Sometimes we ignore him when he's the only one who can help. Sometimes we're too busy to talk to God. But he's waiting to hear from us.

The Situations Are Changing

> JOHN 16:25–26 *"These things I have spoken to you in figurative language; but the time is coming when I will no longer speak to you in figurative language, but I will tell you plainly about the Father. In that day you will ask in My name, and I do not say to you that I shall pray the Father for you;* (NKJV)

The Resurrection changed religion and history. It also changed the way Jesus would talk to his disciples. Afterward, he could talk plainly and they would understand. He wouldn't have to demonstrate truth by washing feet or explain relationships by comparing them to a vine and branches. At that time Jesus wouldn't have to be the go-between for the disciples and God. They could talk directly to the Father.

Father Love

> JOHN 16:27–28 *for the Father Himself loves you, because you have loved Me, and have believed that I came forth from God. I came forth from the Father and have come into the world. Again, I leave the world and go to the Father."* (NKJV)

Even though Jesus was going away, his disciples would not go unloved. The Father loved them because they loved Jesus and believed in him. Then, in one sentence, Jesus clearly summarized his life and mission.

Summary of Jesus' Life and Mission

Life and Mission	Reference
Jesus left heaven	"came forth from the Father"—Philippians 2:5
He became a man	"have come into the world"—Philippians 2:6–7
He would die for our sins	"leave the world"—Philippians 2:8
He would rise from the dead and return to heaven	"go to the Father"—Philippians 2:9; Acts 1:11

go to

scatter
Zechariah 13:7

triune
three parts or
aspects in one

what others say

Ruth Myers

Why is our love so important to God? Why does He care so much whether or not we love Him? I think it's because He has always been a relational God. He was never a lonely, solitary, figure somewhere out in eternity, all alone in the empty reaches of space. He has always been a **triune** God in intimate relationship—the Father, Son, and Holy Spirit in loving communion. And before time began God decided He wanted to include many others in that circle of love.[8]

Now We Get It

JOHN 16:29–30 *His disciples said to Him, "See, now You are speaking plainly, and using no figure of speech! Now we are sure that You know all things, and have no need that anyone should question You. By this we believe that You came forth from God."* (NKJV)

It took them a while, but the disciples finally understood what Jesus had been saying—that he was going to die, rise again, and go back to heaven. Once they understood that, they didn't have to ask any more questions (at least for the time being). Jesus' knowledge and prediction of the future persuaded them that Jesus knew everything and is truly God. You could almost see the light bulbs going on in everyone's mind.

Watch Out for the Curve Ball

JOHN 16:31–32 *Jesus answered them, "Do you now believe? Indeed the hour is coming, yes, has now come, that you will be scattered, each to his own, and will leave Me alone. And yet I am not alone, because the Father is with Me.* (NKJV)

Once the disciples understood what was going to happen to Jesus, he threw them a curve ball. Not only was he leaving them but in addition they would all <u>scatter</u>, leaving him alone. In only a couple of hours, that prediction would come true when Jesus was arrested. Even though Jesus would be alone physically, the Father would still be with him.

Defeating Deity

JOHN 16:33 *These things I have spoken to you, that in Me you may have peace. In the world you will have tribulation; but be of good cheer, I have overcome the world." (NKJV)*

Wrapping up his teaching, Jesus left the disciples with a word of encouragement. He promised them peace in times of trouble—and there would be plenty of troubled times ahead. But Jesus' death would break Satan's choke hold on the world system that causes trouble for believers. It was a sure thing, even though his death was still hours away.

what others say

J. Vernon McGee

He closes with peace. The child of God can have peace in this life because peace is found in Christ and in no other place. You won't find peace in the church. You won't find peace in Christian service. Peace is found in the person of Jesus Christ.[9]

Dana Gould

The verb John used here means to "conquer," "overcome." The force of this verb indicates a continuing victory. Jesus' words, "I have overcome the world," were not so much a promise as a statement of fact. His victory also applies to us today.[10]

apply it

All that Jesus promised his disciples that night—peace, a direct line to God, the power of God, the Holy Spirit living in them, spiritual fruit, a room in heaven, and his constant presence—is available to believers today.

Chapter Wrap-Up

- Jesus predicted the persecution of his disciples, including their deaths, which the Jewish people considered a favor to God. (John 16:1–4)
- Jesus repeated that when he went back to heaven, he would send the Helper, or Holy Spirit, in his place. (John 16:5–11)
- After Jesus left earth, the Spirit would teach believers further truth about him. (John 16:12–15)
- The disciples did not understand what Jesus meant when he said he was going away. (John 16:16–19)
- Jesus explained that the disciples' grief at his departure would turn to joy. (John 16:20–22)
- After Jesus' death, his followers could pray directly to God the Father. (John 16:23–28)
- The disciples finally understood what Jesus was saying about his death and resurrection. (John 16:29–33)

Study Questions

1. Why can people who believe in Jesus expect to be persecuted?

2. What will the Helper do for unbelievers?

3. What will the Spirit of truth do for believers after Jesus goes back to heaven?

4. How did the disciples react to Jesus' teaching about his going away?

5. What does it mean to ask in Jesus' name?

6. Why can Jesus' followers be sure of having peace?

John 17: Jesus the Pray-er

Chapter Highlights:
* Eavesdropping on Jesus
* Beseeching for Believers
* Including Us in
  His Prayers

Let's Get Started

The clock was counting down to Jesus' crucifixion. Before he was arrested, however, Jesus prayed. This was not an unusual occurrence, since prayer was a priority in his life. The other Gospel writers noted that Jesus often got up early in the morning to pray before his day was crowded with people and crises.

Earlier in his ministry, Jesus taught his disciples to pray. That prayer, which begins with "Our Father in heaven" and is repeated often in worship services, is called the Lord's Prayer. That one was a model to follow. This one is the real Lord's prayer.

In this chapter, we get to eavesdrop on Jesus talking to his Father. We don't know if he prayed in the presence of all eleven disciples or if only John overheard him, enabling him to record Jesus' words for us. In this prayer, we get a brief glimpse into a conversation between members of the Godhead. We learn that Jesus prayed for himself, for his disciples, and for future believers.

Glory Be

> JOHN 17:1–2 *Jesus spoke these words, lifted up His eyes to heaven, and said: "Father, the hour has come. Glorify Your Son, that Your Son also may glorify You, as You have given Him authority over all flesh, that He should give eternal life to as many as You have given Him. (NKJV)*

"I have overcome the world," Jesus declared to his disciples (John 16:33 NKJV), and this prayer illustrates that fact. As he prayed for himself, Jesus focused on glorifying the Father—turning the spotlight of attention on him. It was time for Jesus to die. His whole ministry on earth had led to this point in time. He left heaven to become a man for the sole purpose of dying for our sins, so we can have eternal life with God. Jesus' request was not a selfish one like many of our prayers for ourselves. Instead, he asked God to draw attention to the supreme sacrifice of himself so that he, in turn, could focus people's attention on the Father.

key point

go to

glory
John 1:1, 18;
Philippians 2:5–11

Serpent
Satan

woman's Seed
Jesus

what others say

Martin Luther

This is truly beyond measure a warm and hearty prayer. He opens the depths of His heart, both in reference to us and to His Father, and He pours them all out. It sounds so honest, so simple. It is so deep, so rich, so wide. No one can fathom it.[1]

Arthur W. Pink

It was the hour for fulfilling and accomplishing many prophecies, types and symbols which for hundreds and thousands of years had pointed forward to it. It was the hour when events took place which the history of the entire universe can supply no parallel: when the **Serpent** was permitted to bruise the heel of the **woman's Seed**.[2]

What people pray in private reveals what is uppermost on their minds and hearts. If someone could listen in on your private conversations with God for a week or two, what would they learn about you?

Giving God Glory

JOHN 17:3–5 *And this is eternal life, that they may know You, the only true God, and Jesus Christ whom You have sent. I have glorified You on the earth. I have finished the work which You have given Me to do. And now, O Father, glorify Me together with Yourself, with the glory which I had with You before the world was. (NKJV)*

key point

The concept of eternal life is hard for many people to grasp. Here Jesus makes it clear and easy to understand: Eternal life is personally knowing the one true God and Jesus Christ, his Son. Eternal life is not only what we can have after death; it's a quality of life we can enjoy now.

Jesus reported to his Father that he had brought God glory by finishing his work—dying on the cross. He spoke of it as though it had already happened, leaving no doubt he would follow through. Then he asked that God would return the glory he had before he created the world and before he came to earth. That glory is a glow or light so brilliant no human being could look at it. It would be like standing in front of the sun instead of looking at it from 93 million miles away.

At the end of his earthly life, Jesus was able to say he had completed the work God gave him to do. The apostle Paul said the same thing: "I have fought the good fight, I have finished the race, I have kept the faith" (2 Timothy 4:7 NKJV). Will you be able to say the same thing when you get to the end of your life?

God doesn't leave us in the dark when it comes to knowing the work he wants us to do. Read the following verses to find out what to do: Micah 6:8; Matthew 28:19–20; Hebrews 13:15–16; James 1:27.

Know-It-Alls

JOHN 17:6–8 *"I have manifested Your name to the men whom You have given Me out of the world. They were Yours, You gave them to Me, and they have kept Your word. Now they have known that all things which You have given Me are from You. For I have given to them the words which You have given Me; and they have received them, and have known surely that I came forth from You; and they have believed that You sent Me.* (NKJV)

After praying for himself, Jesus prayed for his disciples. He had revealed to the eleven men with him (plus Judas, who left) who God is and what he is like through the way he lived, what he taught, and the miracles he did.

The Greek word translated "manifested" in verse 6, when used with a person, means to show that person's character, to make him or her visible and clear. It also means to uncover or to lay bare. Often it was used in conjunction with the personal appearance of deity. As a result, they believed in Jesus and obeyed God's Word. They accepted what Jesus said as being the words of God, thus believing that Jesus is God.

what others say

Paul N. Tassell

Once again the towering truth of God's message comes to the forefront. Too many people are looking for a miracle when God is concerned about giving them a message.[4]

Before Jesus came to earth, God revealed himself through his names. Each name pictured an aspect of his character. Here are a few of them:

Names Reveal Aspects of God's Character

Name	Aspect
Elohim	Creator
Jehovah	Self-existent One, I Am
El Shaddai	Almighty God
Adonai	Lord, Master
Jehovah-Jireh	God provides
Jehovah-Rophe	God heals
Jehovah-Shalom	God is peace
Jehovah-Rohi	God my shepherd

something to ponder

<u>Community Property People</u>

JOHN 17:9–10 *I pray for them. I do not pray for the world but for those whom You have given Me, for they are Yours. And all Mine are Yours, and Yours are Mine, and I am glorified in them.* (NKJV)

As Jesus prayed, he focused on the disciples whom God had given him. Those men belonged to both Jesus and the Father, since they shared everything. They were the men whose lives brought glory to Jesus and would continue to do so after his resurrection from the dead.

<u>The Name That Protects</u>

JOHN 17:11–12 *Now I am no longer in the world, but these are in the world, and I come to You. Holy Father, keep through*

Your name those whom You have given Me, that they may be one as We are. While I was with them in the world, I kept them in Your name. Those whom You gave Me I have kept; and none of them is lost except the son of perdition, that the Scripture might be fulfilled. (NKJV)

predicted
Psalm 41:9

Jesus was going back to the Father, but he would leave the disciples behind in the world to tell people about him and salvation through believing in him. While Jesus was on earth, he was able to keep them safe. True, he did lose Judas Iscariot. However, it was Judas's decision to reject Jesus' protection. God had already <u>predicted</u> this action.

Jesus' leaving prompted the first of four prayer requests for his disciples: protection. When the disciples would start preaching about Jesus, they would need protection from Satan, God's enemy, who still controls this world system. Satan does everything he can to get people to turn away from God, so it was a sure thing that the disciples would be persecuted. When Jesus asked the Father to protect them in his name, he asked God to keep them with his power and authority. That's the ultimate protection; nobody is more powerful than God!

Jesus' second request for his disciples was for their oneness with him, like the Father and Son are one. The members of the Trinity live in harmony with one another and have a oneness of purpose—to do the Father's will. Jesus wants his followers to have that same relationship with him. That includes showing what Jesus is like by the way we live and what we say, even as he showed us what the Father is like by his life and teachings.

Jesus did not pray that all people who call themselves Christians would come together in one organization, regardless of what they believe. He never asked us to give up our biblical beliefs and tolerate false teachings for the sake of oneness with one another.

what others say

Leon Morris

The reference to the fulfilling of Scripture brings out the thought of divine purpose. This does not mean that Judas was an automaton. He was a responsible person and acted freely. But God used his evil act to bring about His purpose.[5]

Bring on the Joy

joy
Nehemiah 8:10

don't belong
Colossians 1:13

JOHN 17:13 *But now I come to You, and these things I speak in the world, that they may have My joy fulfilled in themselves. (NKJV)*

In light of going back to the Father, Jesus made his third request for the disciples: joy. No matter how much they would mourn his death or be persecuted after his resurrection, they could be filled with joy. Remember, joy comes from a relationship with Jesus, not from outward circumstances. He is the source of joy.

Not of This World

JOHN 17:14–16 *I have given them Your word; and the world has hated them because they are not of the world, just as I am not of the world. I do not pray that You should take them out of the world, but that You should keep them from the evil one. They are not of the world, just as I am not of the world. (NKJV)*

Because believers love God, live by different standards, teach that Jesus is the only way to God and that absolute truth exists, and expose sin, they will get plenty of hatred and persecution from the world of unbelievers and Satan. Jesus' disciples don't belong to the world, because he doesn't. Knowing this, Jesus repeated the request for protection, this time specifically from the evil one, Satan. Notice that he didn't pray that God would take his followers out of the world. He was leaving them behind to spread the good news of salvation.

what others say

D. A. Carson

The spiritual dimensions to this prayer of Jesus are consistent and overwhelming. By contrast, we spend much more time today praying about our health, our projects, our decisions, our finances, our family, and even our games than we do praying about the danger of the evil one. Materialists at heart, we often discern only very, very dimly the spiritual struggle of which Paul (for instance) was so deeply aware (Ephesians 6:10ff.).[6]

what others say

Charles U. Wagner

Clearly, our Savior was praying that His followers be kept from evil. That is, we are to be insulated from the world rather than isolated from it. When you insulate a wire, you wrap it so that when it touches other wires, the power or current of the wire won't be affected. Anything that drains our power lessens and endangers our testimony. It is possible to live in the world without taking part in its activities and values.[7]

Called into the World

JOHN 17:17–19 *Sanctify them by Your truth. Your word is truth. As You sent Me into the world, I also have sent them into the world. And for their sakes I sanctify Myself, that they also may be sanctified by the truth. (NKJV)*

Jesus' final request for his disciples was for God to sanctify them, to set them apart for him, to make them holy. There are two stages to sanctification. At the same moment we believe in Jesus, we are also set apart for God, once and for all. The disciples had already completed stage one, so there was no use praying for that. The second stage is day-by-day walking with God, separated from sin and becoming more like him. This is the process that Jesus prayed for. Daily holiness comes from knowing and obeying the truth.

key point

Three Sources of Truth

Source	Reference
God's Word	"Your word is truth"—John 17:17 (NKJV)
Jesus	"I am . . . the truth"—John 14:6 (NKJV)
The Holy Spirit	"The Spirit is truth"—1 John 5:6 (NKJV)

Just like God <u>sent his Son</u> into the world, so Jesus has sent his followers into the world. Their mission was the same as Jesus'—to tell people about God. Jesus had set himself apart for God to do his work. He, in turn, set apart his disciples for the same purpose.

Homer A. Kent Jr.

As the disciples lived for God day by day, the application of God's truth to their lives would have a purifying effect as it would call sin to their attention, and cause confession and restoration to follow. By this means they would be set apart from sin and consecrated to the ministry to which Christ had called them.[8]

For Those to Come

JOHN 17:20–21 *"I do not pray for these alone, but also for those who will believe in Me through their word; that they all may be one, as You, Father, are in Me, and I in You; that they also may be one in Us, that the world may believe that You sent Me. (NKJV)*

Jesus prayed for himself and his disciples. Then he prayed for all the people through all the ages who would become believers through his disciples' message. That includes us and others we tell about Jesus. Those eleven men spread the good news about Jesus, and some of them, like John, wrote books of the New Testament. The rest of the New Testament was written by men who became believers as a result of this original group's message.

Many people think this passage refers to Jesus' desire for Christians to have unity among themselves. Some use this passage to support their claim that Christians should not be divided into denominations or other organizations. But that is not the meaning here.

In John 10:30 when Jesus said, "I and My Father are one" (NKJV), he meant that he and the Father had a oneness. So we are to understand this as a prayer that believers might experience the same oneness with God that Jesus experienced. In the passages in John when Jesus spoke of his oneness with the Father, he talked about their unity of purpose and action. Jesus always did the Father's will and reflected his character.

Jesus did not, despite the common mischaracterization of this passage, ask that Christians experience oneness with each other—whether organizational or in a common commitment to key biblical teachings. What Jesus did pray was that Christians might experience the relationship he had with the Father. It is a oneness preserved by always seeking and doing God's will. As believers do God's will, they

something to ponder

will be united in mutual love for God. Part of doing God's will involves spreading the word about Christ to others.

go to

body
1 Corinthians
12:12–30

what others say

David Jeremiah

Jesus asked His Father that the church might be unified. . . . The Father had sent Jesus from heaven to earth to redeem a people for His very own. Jesus was now about to go to the cross to achieve that purpose. Just a few days after His resurrection, He would return to heaven, yet His mission to redeem the world would go on. The necessary sacrifice, Himself, already would have been made—but word about that sacrifice needed to be spread. How would that happen? Through the disciples. . . . Jesus' heartbeat was evangelism and missionary outreach. He had a passion that all men and women might be saved. That's what He prayed about in this remarkable prayer.[9]

When people believe in Jesus, they automatically become part of God's family, called the Body of Christ. Paul described this <u>body</u> as a unit with many parts, having unity with diversity. Although we don't all have the same gifts or abilities, we are all united in Christ.

key point

Passing on the Glory

JOHN 17:22–24 *And the glory which You gave Me I have given them, that they may be one just as We are one: I in them, and You in Me; that they may be made perfect in one, and that the world may know that You have sent Me, and have loved them as You have loved Me. Father, I desire that they also whom You gave Me may be with Me where I am, that they may behold My glory which You have given Me; for You loved Me before the foundation of the world.* (NKJV)

Even future believers will receive the glory God the Father gave his Son. Through his death, the whole world would see God's character and nature. That glory will become real to those who believe in Jesus, and they will enjoy unity with God and with one another. When believers get along, their unity makes an impact on unbelievers who see God's love in them.

The Son of God wants to be with his followers. Isn't that great? For the disciples who overheard this prayer, being with Jesus meant being in the same place—for a little while anyway. For the followers to come, being with Jesus means spending time reading the Bible and praying. That situation will change when we get to heaven and see him face-to-face; then we'll be with him in the same location. Jesus prayed that our relationship with him would include seeing his character, the glory God gave him because he loved him from eternity past.

It's Who You Know

> JOHN 17:25–26 *O righteous Father! The world has not known You, but I have known You; and these have known that You sent Me. And I have declared to them Your name, and will declare it, that the love with which You loved Me may be in them, and I in them." (NKJV)*

Jesus wrapped up his prayer time with the Father not with another request but with a final report before his death. By addressing God as "Righteous Father," he called attention to the fact that God is sinless. Jesus affirmed that the world didn't know God, but he did and so did his eleven disciples. Jesus had done his job of communicating God to them and would continue to do so in order that they would know God's love.

Since Jesus would not always be with believers in physical form, he would continue the work through the Holy Spirit. Jesus wanted his followers to know the love God had for him by experiencing that love within them. As his followers experienced his love they would become more loving people. They would be changed from inside out by the work of the Holy Spirit.

Chapter Wrap-Up

- Jesus asked God to glorify him and for his death to glorify the Father. (John 17:1–5)
- Jesus reported that he had revealed the Father to his disciples. (John 17:6–8)
- Jesus prayed that the Father would protect the disciples whom he had given to Jesus. (John 17:9–12)
- Jesus asked that God would keep his disciples safe from Satan while they were still in the world, not that he would take them out of the world. (John 17:13–19)
- Jesus also prayed for those who would believe in him in the future. (John 17:20–24)
- Jesus reported that he had made the Father known to the disciples and would continue doing so. (John 17:25–26)

Study Questions

1. What was Jesus' primary request for himself?

2. How did Jesus define eternal life?

3. What were Jesus' main requests for his disciples?

4. What did Jesus ask for future believers?

5. Why did Jesus call God "righteous Father"?

John 18: Jesus the Prisoner

Chapter Highlights:
- Leaders Arrest Jesus
- Priests Pass Judgment on Jesus
- Pilate Cuts a Passover Deal with Jesus

Let's Get Started

"It was the best of times, it was the worst of times." Although Charles Dickens didn't begin *A Tale of Two Cities* by describing Jesus' death, that sentence could apply to the night Jesus was arrested and to the next day, when he died on the cross.

That was the dark night of the soul for Jesus and his disciples. Emotions raged on all sides as Jesus was falsely arrested, then tried in a mock court before the religious leaders and Pilate, the Roman governor.

Even though it appeared on the surface that Jesus' fate was in the hands of unbelieving men, at no time did Jesus lose control. From the moment the temple priests arrived to arrest him in the garden, through a number of trials and Peter's denial, to the people's insistence that Jesus was not the prisoner they wanted released, God's plan for the salvation of the world was unfolding. Jesus could have prevented all these events or escaped at any moment. But he didn't. He voluntarily chose to go to the cross to die for our sins.

go to

Gethsemane
Matthew 26:36

Walking to the Grove

JOHN 18:1 *When Jesus had spoken these words, He went out with His disciples over the Brook Kidron, where there was a garden, which He and His disciples entered.* (NKJV)

Jesus had just spent time talking with the Father about himself, his disciples, and his future followers. The time for prayer with the disciples was over. The time for death was near, and Jesus knew it. He had prepared himself and his disciples as much as he could. So they walked across the Kidron Valley (see Illustration #11), a ravine north of Jerusalem, to a familiar olive grove. The other Gospel writers called it the Garden of <u>Gethsemane</u>.

John didn't record all the events of that evening, however. Between this verse and the next one, Jesus told Peter again that he would deny Jesus three times. Then he <u>prayed</u> privately, during which he wrestled with God over the enormity of the suffering before him and submitted to the Father's will to go through with the Crucifixion.

prayed
Matthew 26:37–46

Illustration #11
Jerusalem Area Map—This map shows the location of Gethsemane outside Jerusalem, although only the road to Bethany is shown. Before his arrest Jesus walked from Jerusalem across the Kidron Valley.

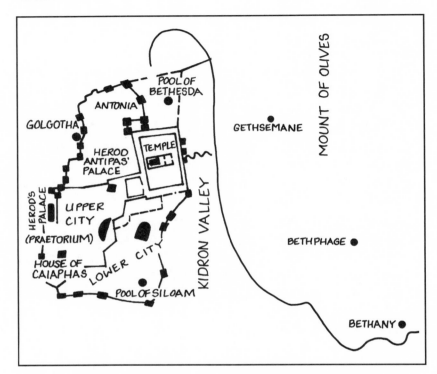

what others say

R. Kent Hughes

There is a strong poetic imagery even in the physical surroundings of moving toward the Garden of Gethsemane. . . . A drain ran from the temple altar down to the Kidron ravine to take away the blood of sacrifice. Since it was the Passover, more than 200,000 lambs would be slain in the next day. When Jesus and His band crossed the Kidron, it was red with the blood of the lambs prepared for sacrifice. Within a few hours, the blood of the Lamb of God would flow.[1]

Secret Arrest for Public Messiah

JOHN 18:2–3 *And Judas, who betrayed Him, also knew the place; for Jesus often met there with His disciples. Then Judas, having received a detachment of troops, and officers from the chief priests and Pharisees, came there with lanterns, torches, and weapons. (NKJV)*

From the beginning, Jesus' arrest and trial resembled mayhem more than justice. That was no accident. Jesus had been highly visible for three years, teaching and working miracles in public. If the temple priests and guards wanted to arrest him, they could have done it openly at any time. So where did they do it? In a private garden. And who turned him in? One of his own disciples who had been with him for those three years. Sure, it makes no sense. But it's what God had predicted hundreds of years earlier. Score one more for the reliability of God's Word.

Judas knew where Jesus likely would be. He and the disciples had spent a lot of time in that garden to escape the crowds. Judas led the soldiers and officials right to where Jesus was. It was nighttime, so the band led by the high priests and followed by a mob of excitement seekers had to search the dark garden using torches and lanterns. The knowledge that Judas had of the special places Jesus liked would have helped in finding him.

Commentators disagree on whether there were any actual Roman soldiers involved. Possibly the hysterical chief priests had asked for aid from Pilate, and he had released a detachment from the barracks in Jerusalem to tag along for the arrest. Other Bible scholars believe the translation of the word "troops" is unfortunate because the temple priests had no authority over or access to Roman soldiers. Roman soldiers would not have wanted to get involved in an internal affair. These commentators believe the "troops" were temple guards, Levites who served as civil guards in the temple under the authority of the high priests. They kept order in the temple area.

In either case, the power behind the arrest came from the Jewish leaders. But the real power came from Jesus. Even if hundreds of soldiers had turned up, Jesus could have escaped if he wanted. But he didn't. He allowed the priests to find and arrest him because it was God's will.

key point

Never Out of Control

God's name
Exodus 3:14

JOHN 18:4–6 Jesus therefore, knowing all things that would come upon Him, went forward and said to them, "Whom are you seeking?" They answered Him, "Jesus of Nazareth." Jesus said to them, "I am He." And Judas, who betrayed Him, also stood with them. Now when He said to them, "I am He," they drew back and fell to the ground. (NKJV)

In spite of the fact that he was one unarmed teacher against a batch of movers and shakers, Jesus still had power and authority as the Son of God. To let them know who was in charge, Jesus went out to meet them. He opened the conversation by asking them who they were after.

When they identified the man, Jesus answered literally, "I am." It is the same statement he had used a number of times in his teaching. It is <u>God's name</u> and a declaration that he is God. His using God's name affected the men who were there in an unusual way. We don't know for sure why they fell to the ground. Maybe it was the way Jesus took control. They were startled by Jesus' admission; they had expected him to run. Or maybe he used his power to give them a glimpse of who he is. No matter why, they knew Jesus was no ordinary man.

what others say

J. Vernon McGee

Even in this dark hour when He was yielding Himself as the Lamb of God that taketh away the sin of the world, He revealed His deity—and they fell backwards! He revealed to these men that He was absolutely in charge, and they could not arrest Him without His permission. They didn't fall forward to worship Him. They fell backward in fear and in absolute dismay.[3]

One More Time

JOHN 18:7–9 Then He asked them again, "Whom are you seeking?" And they said, "Jesus of Nazareth." Jesus answered, "I have told you that I am He. Therefore, if you seek Me, let these go their way," that the saying might be fulfilled which He spoke, "Of those whom You gave Me I have lost none." (NKJV)

Jesus repeated his question to make sure the temple guards understood they came for him, not the eleven disciples with him. He wanted to protect his men, asking that they be let go. John saw this concern as a fulfillment of Jesus' <u>prayer</u> for his disciples.

Just in case the guard didn't believe Jesus was who he said he was, Judas <u>kissed</u> him as a friend or family member would. A kiss was a sign of devotion or affection, neither of which Judas meant. This is another detail that John omitted.

go to

prayer
John 17:12

kissed
Matthew 26:48–50

healed
Luke 22:50–51

cup of judgment
Isaiah 51:17

example
Matthew 26:39–45

Wild Sword Bearer

JOHN 18:10–11 *Then Simon Peter, having a sword, drew it and struck the high priest's servant, and cut off his right ear. The servant's name was Malchus. So Jesus said to Peter, "Put your sword into the sheath. Shall I not drink the cup which My Father has given Me?"* (NKJV)

Peter had a reputation for impulsiveness and brashness. Even in this serious situation, he wasn't shy. He had guts—but not many smarts. Peter had enough courage to take on the temple police and the whole crowd with one dagger. Either Peter's aim was lousy or the guy ducked just in time! Instead of killing the servant, Peter only cut off his ear. The Greek word for "sword" and "knife" is the same. Since Peter was a fisherman, it is more likely that he had a fishing knife and not a military sword.

Luke the physician recorded that Jesus <u>healed</u> Malchus's ear, saving Peter from the consequences of his action. Then Jesus rebuked Peter for what he had done. Jesus had told his disciples plenty of times that dying was part of the plan. That's why he came to earth. He didn't need Peter to stop something he was doing willingly. The cup the Father gave him was the cross, the <u>cup of judgment</u> for the sins of humankind, which Jesus would "drink."

God rarely calls believers to be crucified today. But he does allow hard times and suffering to mold us into the kind of people he wants us to be. No matter what "cup" he gives us, we don't have to be afraid of it. Nor should we run away from it. Jesus gave us the <u>example</u> to follow by accepting God's will, even if that means being jailed and executed for our faith.

apply it

go to

cleansed the Temple
John 2:13–16

Caiaphas
John 11:49–51

D. Edmond Hiebert

The aggressive action of Peter reflected self-confidence as well as love for Jesus. It also revealed his rashness; he intended to make good on his claim that he would not fail Jesus, but he did not stop to consider the risk to himself or the futility of his single-handed action.[4]

Let the Games Begin

JOHN 18:12–14 *Then the detachment of troops and the captain and the officers of the Jews arrested Jesus and bound Him. And they led Him away to Annas first, for he was the father-in-law of Caiaphas who was high priest that year. Now it was Caiaphas who advised the Jews that it was expedient that one man should die for the people. (NKJV)*

With no doubt about whom they were arresting, the Jewish police seized and tied up Jesus. The first stop that night was Annas's house. Annas was the high priest until Pilate replaced him, but his influence continued long after his term in office. Several of his sons and a son-in-law, Caiaphas (the current high priest), succeeded him. According to Jewish law, the high priest was appointed for life. However, under Roman rule, the governors deposed and appointed high priests at will. Even though Annas didn't officially hold the office, the people still treated him as high priest.

Annas may have requested the first audience with Jesus. He was probably still mad that Jesus had <u>cleansed the Temple</u> of the merchants who sold animals for sacrifices to God at exorbitant prices. Annas had a good little racket going with the temple merchants. He got rent from the merchants, set their prices, and may have taken a percentage of the profits as well.

To be sure his readers remembered <u>Caiaphas</u>, John added a footnote that he was the one who was willing to sacrifice one man, Jesus, to keep the peace with the Romans. That was now happening.

Revell Bible Dictionary

[Annas] was deposed in AD 15 by Valerius Gratus. Yet he carried such clout that he placed five sons, one son-in-law, and a

Jewish Talmud
official body of
Jewish instruction

grandson in the high priesthood. This high priestly family was noted for vast wealth, materialism, and greed. . . . The reputation of the family was so odious that the **Jewish Talmud** contains the curse, "Woe to the family of Annas!"[5]

Follow the Leader

JOHN 18:15–16 *And Simon Peter followed Jesus, and so did another disciple. Now that disciple was known to the high priest, and went with Jesus into the courtyard of the high priest. But Peter stood at the door outside. Then the other disciple, who was known to the high priest, went out and spoke to her who kept the door, and brought Peter in. (NKJV)*

Like a good writer or movie director, John switched scenes to keep his readers in suspense. He cut away from inside the house to the courtyard surrounding the house. There Peter and another disciple tried to find out what was happening to their leader. Many Bible students believe the second man was John. Others think he was Nicodemus or Joseph of Arimathea, who helped bury Jesus, since it wasn't likely that fisherman John would know the high priest. These other two possibilities did.

Since the yard was walled and had a guarded entrance, they couldn't just walk in on the proceedings. The unnamed disciple gained entrance because he knew the high priest. Then he got permission for Peter to enter as well and went back to fetch him.

Lying by the Fire

JOHN 18:17–18 *Then the servant girl who kept the door said to Peter, "You are not also one of this Man's disciples, are you?" He said, "I am not." Now the servants and officers who had made a fire of coals stood there, for it was cold, and they warmed themselves. And Peter stood with them and warmed himself. (NKJV)*

The girl who gave permission for Peter to enter the courtyard wanted to know if he was one of Jesus' disciples. Without hesitating, Peter said no. It's hard to believe this was the same man who wasn't afraid to defend Jesus by taking out his knife and trying to kill a servant in the garden minutes before. Peter had turned into a coward who was afraid to be known as one of Jesus' disciples. He stood there with his enemies, warming himself at their fire.

No Secret Teaching

> JOHN 18:19–21 *The high priest then asked Jesus about His disciples and His doctrine. Jesus answered him, "I spoke openly to the world. I always taught in synagogues and in the temple, where the Jews always meet, and in secret I have said nothing. Why do you ask Me? Ask those who have heard Me what I said to them. Indeed they know what I said." (NKJV)*

When selecting details, John didn't mention that the religious leaders huddled behind closed doors all night, questioning Jesus and discussing how to get rid of him permanently. Alternating scenes again, he switched back to the illegal hearing in the house.

Trying to gather enough evidence for the death sentence, Annas questioned Jesus. How many disciples did he have? Who was following him? What had he taught? He was trying to figure out how big a threat Jesus really was.

Jesus had spent three years teaching publicly. Annas could have heard him in person if he'd chosen to do so. But he hadn't. Jesus had not been holding secret meetings to overthrow the leaders or the Romans. He had not formed a secret cult. If Annas wanted to know his teaching, he could ask the people who heard him; there were plenty to ask. Jesus had nothing to hide. However, he protected his disciples by leaving them out of the conversation.

Angered at His Answer

> JOHN 18:22–24 *And when He had said these things, one of the officers who stood by struck Jesus with the palm of his hand, saying, "Do You answer the high priest like that?" Jesus answered him, "If I have spoken evil, bear witness of the evil; but if well, why do you strike Me?" Then Annas sent Him bound to Caiaphas the high priest. (NKJV)*

Jesus' answer wasn't what this group wanted to hear. In fact, one of the officers was so angry that he hit Jesus across the face. It was against the law to strike a prisoner, but by this time, Annas didn't care about the law. He'd already broken it by questioning Jesus without outside witnesses and by asking incriminating questions. Jesus' answer pointed Annas back to the law, thus condemning the one who accused him of wrongdoing. Jesus didn't deserve the treatment he was getting. He only told the truth.

Annas sidestepped the issue by sending Jesus to Caiaphas, the high priest. That trial was another detail John skipped.

The Cock Crows on Time

JOHN 18:25–27 *Now Simon Peter stood and warmed himself. Therefore they said to him, "You are not also one of His disciples, are you?" He denied it and said, "I am not!" One of the servants of the high priest, a relative of him whose ear Peter cut off, said, "Did I not see you in the garden with Him?" Peter then denied again; and immediately a rooster crowed.* (NKJV)

Jumping back to the courtyard scene, John picked up the conversation around the fire. Someone else asked Peter if he was one of Jesus' disciples. For the second time, Peter forcefully denied it. One of Annas's servants recognized him from the garden, however. He may have been standing near Malchus when Peter cut off his relative's ear. For the third time, Peter denied he knew Jesus.

Immediately, the rooster crowed to announce daybreak—and fulfill Jesus' <u>prediction</u>. Luke recorded that <u>Jesus looked</u> at him on his way out of Annas's house, and Peter repented.

If you haven't discovered already, it's always easier to take a stand for Jesus when there's a crowd around to back you up. But when it's just you and no friends around to encourage and support you, it's easier to keep your mouth shut or deny the Lord, like Peter did.

Unlike Judas, who walked away from Jesus and never came back, Peter was sorry he had denied his Lord. Jesus forgave him and restored their relationship. He is willing to forgive you, too, if you've done the same thing.

go to

prediction
John 13:38

Jesus looked
Luke 22:60–62

something to ponder

Hypocrisy in Action

JOHN 18:28–29 *Then they led Jesus from Caiaphas to the Praetorium, and it was early morning. But they themselves did not go into the Praetorium, lest they should be defiled, but that they might eat the Passover. Pilate then went out to them and said, "What accusation do you bring against this Man?"* (NKJV)

The all-night trials with the religious leaders ended. They had gone as far as they could with Jesus, so they took him over to Pilate for sentencing. Pilate would have wanted to talk with Jesus and the leaders anyway to avoid a riot. He especially wanted to keep the peace during Passover, since the city was flooded with Jewish pilgrims.

Pilate didn't live in Jerusalem. He was there because of Passover. That was convenient since he was the only one around who could order a death sentence.

Those religious leaders had arrested an innocent man and had already broken a number of their own laws. But they refused to enter Pilate's palace because they didn't want to defile themselves. Entering a Gentile's house would make them religiously unclean and unable to worship in the Temple or participate in the Feast of Unleavened Bread, commonly called Passover. They obeyed the letter of God's law while plotting the death of God's Son. They wanted to stay clean for Passover while seeking to kill the Son who fulfilled the Passover rituals. What a bunch of hypocrites!

To accommodate the Jewish leaders, Pilate came out to them. The first thing he wanted to know was what Jesus was charged with.

Although the Romans allowed the Jewish people to practice their religion, they did not allow them to order anyone's execution. Rome was tolerant in many ways and permitted a great degree of self-government, including the right of **subject authorities** to have their own courts. Disputes between members of a subject people were handled in people's courts. If the dispute was between a Roman citizen and a subject person, the trial was in a Roman court. You can guess which side won such disputes!

Romans couldn't be bothered with religious disputes. To execute Jesus, the Jewish leaders fabricated new charges by accusing Jesus before Pilate not of blasphemy, but of inciting rebellion and calling himself a "king." That got the Romans' attention. They executed traitors.

Pass-the-Buck Sentencing

JOHN 18:30–32 *They answered and said to him, "If He were not an evildoer, we would not have delivered Him up to you." Then Pilate said to them, "You take Him and judge Him according to your law." Therefore the Jews said to him, "It is not lawful for us to put anyone to death," that the saying of Jesus might be fulfilled which He spoke, signifying by what death He would die.* (NKJV)

Pilate could not have cared less about the blasphemy charge against Jesus. That was not punishable by Roman law. If he was going to do anything about Jesus, there had to be a criminal reason, and he wanted to know what it was. Not only were those leaders hypocrites but also they got high marks for avoiding questions.

charge
Luke 23:1–2

Pilate was known for taking bribes, insulting the Jews, robbing the temple treasury to pay for a building project, and executing men without a trial. It was no secret that Pilate and the Jews shared a mutual hatred and contempt for one another. He clearly did not want to get involved in a religious matter, so he told the leaders to deal with Jesus under their law.

Normally the Jewish leaders would have stayed clear of Pilate, but he was their only hope of carrying out the death penalty on Jesus. Moreover, he was God's means of fulfilling Scripture as to how Jesus would die. Based on Pilate's past actions, the Jewish leaders expected him to order execution without much deliberation on the matter.

> **what others say**
>
> **Thomas Whitelaw**
>
> If Christ had only been a minor offender they could have punished Him themselves: the fact that they had delivered Him up into Pilate's hand was in their estimation proof sufficient that he was an extraordinary criminal.[6]

One Too Many Kings

JOHN 18:33–34 *Then Pilate entered the Praetorium again, called Jesus, and said to Him, "Are You the King of the Jews?" Jesus answered him, "Are you speaking for yourself about this, or did others tell you this concerning Me?"* (NKJV)

Although John didn't mention the criminal <u>charge</u> against Jesus, the Jewish leaders registered Jesus' claim to be king. That was a red flag for Pilate. Such a claim was treason against the Roman emperor and sufficient reason for the death penalty. Pilate went inside to check out the claim with Jesus.

Notice how slickly Jesus turned the conversation around. He challenged Pilate to figure out for himself what kind of king he was. The Jewish leaders used the title as referring to a religious ruler, the Messiah who would usher in God's kingdom. Pilate associated a king with a political ruler who would be a threat to his rule. Pilate thought he was trying Jesus. Little did he know Jesus put Pilate on trial.

King of Another World

JOHN 18:35–36 *Pilate answered, "Am I a Jew? Your own nation and the chief priests have delivered You to me. What have You done?" Jesus answered, "My kingdom is not of this world. If My kingdom were of this world, My servants would fight, so that I should not be delivered to the Jews; but now My kingdom is not from here."* (NKJV)

Since Pilate despised the Jews, his question to Jesus most likely dripped with sarcasm. Pilate was involved in this mess only because the Jewish leaders had pressured him into it. Since they had brought Jesus to him, there had to be some basis for the charge, and Pilate wanted to know what it was.

This time Jesus answered Pilate clearly. Yes, he was a king. But not in the way Pilate used that title. Jesus wasn't interested in taking over Pilate's rule. If he had been, his followers would have fought to keep him from being arrested. His kingship was in the spiritual realm. He would rule God's kingdom, which will one day be set up on earth.

what others say

The Life and Times Historical Reference Bible

The concept of "kingdom" in Jesus' time was rooted in the Old Testament: "kingdom" most often referred to the reign or royal authority of a king. Jewish people prayed daily for the coming of God's reign. When they prayed for His kingdom, they did not doubt that God reigned over His creation in the present. Yet they longed for the day when God would rule unchallenged and all peoples would acknowledge Him. . . .

The Romans, however, guarded the title "king." Anyone who, without the emperor's permission, claimed to be even a client king was committing the offense of high treason.[7]

The Truth, the Whole Truth, and Nothing but the Truth

JOHN 18:37 *Pilate therefore said to Him, "Are You a king then?" Jesus answered, "You say rightly that I am a king. For this cause I was born, and for this cause I have come into the* *world, that I should bear witness to the truth. Everyone who is of the truth hears My voice." (NKJV)*

truth
John 14:6

Pilate had trouble sorting out what Jesus said. He didn't understand the concept of God's kingdom. In his mind, Jesus was either a political king who threatened his rule or he wasn't. There wasn't a third option.

Jesus agreed he was a king. That much is clear. But he was King of a spiritual kingdom of truth. He was born a man, but he was also God who "came into the world." His mission was to tell people the truth about God. Those whom God had chosen to be part of his kingdom would listen to Jesus and believe in him.

When Jesus mentioned truth, Pilate might have thought he was a philosopher. It was not a crime to seek and teach about truth. Pilate must have been relieved; he could let Jesus go and get on with his life. One reason Jesus came to earth was to tell people the truth about God. Faith in him starts with reading and listening to the truth he taught.

> **what others say**
>
> ### Andreas J. Köstenberger
>
> When Jesus says, "Everyone on the side of truth listens to me," he makes Pilate palpably uncomfortable. . . . For in truth, it is not Jesus who is on trial but rather Pilate, who is confronted with the "light of the world" and must decide whether he prefers darkness or light.[8]

Free Barabbas

JOHN 18:38–40 *Pilate said to Him, "What is truth?" And when he had said this, he went out again to the Jews, and said to them, "I find no fault in Him at all. But you have a custom that I should release someone to you at the Passover. Do you therefore want me to release to you the King of the Jews?" Then they all cried again, saying, "Not this Man, but Barabbas!" Now Barabbas was a robber. (NKJV)*

Pilate's question about truth was a cynical one. The Romans, like many people today, did not believe in absolute truth. Officials like Pilate decided what was true based on the majority vote or what was practical at the time. The sad thing is, he looked at <u>truth</u> embodied in a man and didn't even see him.

Herod
Luke 23:6–12

overthrow
Mark 15:7

It didn't take Pilate long to figure out that Jesus wasn't a political threat, so he didn't want to have anything more to do with him. Under Roman law, he didn't have a charge to level against him. He could have released Jesus and been done with this matter. However, he was afraid that action would start a riot, his superiors in Rome would investigate, and he'd lose his job.

The other Gospel writers record details John left out that help to explain the events he included. While Pilate was questioning Jesus, the religious leaders outside kept up a storm of accusations. Jesus didn't defend himself, which amazed Pilate. When Pilate announced that he couldn't find a reason to convict Jesus, the religious leaders insisted Jesus was guilty of a crime, saying he had stirred up people all over the country, including Galilee.

The mention of Galilee gave Pilate a way to escape dealing with Jesus. Galilee was in Herod's jurisdiction. Between verses 38 and 39, Pilate sent Jesus to <u>Herod</u>, who was in town for the holiday. Herod, however, decided to play a game of Hot Potato and passed Jesus back to Pilate.

So Pilate devised a compromise. He offered to let a prisoner go, which was a Passover custom to make the Jews happy. The man in custody was Barabbas, a true criminal. Barabbas had acted to <u>overthrow</u> the Roman government and had committed murder. Since the religious leadership worked hard to get along with the Roman ruler, Pilate figured they would want Barabbas killed for sure.

That was a mistake. Pilate must have been shocked to hear the Jewish people clamoring for him to release Barabbas instead of Jesus. So Pilate was still stuck with a man he wanted nothing to do with and who was a political bomb.

what others say

David E. Garland

The crowd chooses the one who takes the lives of others to achieve his own selfish ends and condemns the one who gives his life for others in obedience to God. They want a king who will be comfortable with murder and mayhem, not one who refuses to resist evil with violence. It is a fatal preference.[9]

Laws Broken at Jesus' Trial

Laws About the Trial

Law	What Happened
No arrests or trials after sundown	Jesus was arrested and tried at night
No trials on holidays	Jesus tried on first day of the Feast of Unleavened Bread
Capital offense trials to be held in the Temple	Jesus was tried in high priest's house
Trials to be scheduled after morning prayers and sacrifices	Jesus' trial was right after sunrise
Governors could not try cases outside their jurisdiction	Herod, governor of Galilee, tried Jesus in Judea

Laws About Witnesses and Charges

Law	What Happened
Formal charges must be stated	Jesus was not charged during his arrest or trials
Witnesses who testify against a person must be people of integrity	Judas was a traitor and informer. False witnesses were sought
Charges were to be read at the beginning of a trial	No such charges were read
Witnesses had to agree on the answers to seven questions about the event	The questions were not asked, and the witnesses did not agree
False witnesses were to be put to death	None were
High priests could not file charges	Caiaphas acted as a witness with accusations
Written charges were to be given to the governor	None were. Plus, the Jewish leaders changed the charges from blasphemy to treason before Pilate
Governors could not sit in judgment by themselves	Pilate tried Jesus by himself

Laws About the Accused

Law	What Happened
Judges served as counsel for the accused	Annas judged Jesus by himself as an accuser
Prisoners were not to be abused	Jesus was hit and beaten

Laws About the Verdict

Law	What Happened
Voting in the Sanhedrin was to be done one person at a time, from the youngest to the oldest	Caiaphas asked for an oral vote
A unanimous vote equaled an acquittal; if the vote was unanimous, the Jews felt they had not done a good job defending the accused—the accused was released	Jesus was not let go when the Sanhedrin all voted guilty
A verdict of condemnation had made at least one day after the trial	Jesus was condemned on the same to be day he was tried
Innocent people were to be released	Pilate declared Jesus was innocent but did not release him

Chapter Wrap-Up

- Judas led a group of priests and temple guards to Jesus so they could arrest him. (John 18:1–3)
- Jesus took control of the situation and voluntarily surrendered to the mob's leaders. (John 18:4–9)
- Peter tried to defend Jesus but ended up cutting off a servant's ear, which Jesus healed. (John 18:10–11)
- While Annas was questioning Jesus in preparation for sentencing, Peter was in the courtyard denying he was one of Jesus' disciples. (John 18:12–27)
- The religious leaders took Jesus to Pilate to pronounce the death sentence, but Pilate couldn't find that Jesus was guilty of a crime that deserved crucifixion. (John 18:28–38)
- Pilate offered to release a prisoner, hoping the Jewish people would choose Jesus. Instead, they chose Barabbas. (John 18:39–40)

Study Questions

1. What happened when Jesus and his disciples went to the olive grove?

2. How did Jesus show he was in control of his arrest?

3. How did Peter respond to questions about his association with Jesus?

4. What did Jesus tell Annas about his teaching?

5. Why did the religious leaders take Jesus to Pilate?

6. What did Pilate learn about Jesus from questioning him privately?

7. When Pilate offered to release a prisoner, who did the Jewish people choose?

Part Three
Jesus' Death and Resurrection

John 19: Jesus the Sacrifice

Chapter Highlights:
- **Mock to the King**
- **Trial and Error**
- **Love on a Cross**
- **No Tomb to Call His Own**

Let's Get Started

If you lived in Jesus' day and were voting for the worst way to die, you'd pick crucifixion. You wouldn't even have to think about it for a few seconds. The cross was the most painful way to die. Nothing else came close. Amazingly, it was the way God chose for Jesus to make the final payment for our sins.

Jesus came to earth to die, to pay the penalty for our sins, so we don't have to spend an eternity separated from the God who loves us. (That's what sin does to us.) Since our sins are so monstrous in God's eyes, it took something as horrible as Jesus' crucifixion to pay the price to bring us back to God.

Mercifully, John chose not to describe all the gory details of Jesus' death on the cross. If he had, most people would quit reading at this point. It's worse than a marathon of horror movies. Instead, he gave us enough details to understand that the price for our sins was high.

In this chapter, John continued Jesus' trial before Pilate. (Remember, there were no chapter divisions in the original book.) Then he described Jesus' death and burial.

True Grit

> **JOHN 19:1–3** *So then Pilate took Jesus and scourged Him. And the soldiers twisted a crown of thorns and put it on His head, and they put on Him a purple robe. Then they said, "Hail, King of the Jews!" And they struck Him with their hands.* (NKJV)

Still not wanting to pronounce the death sentence on Jesus, Pilate had him beaten, hoping it would be enough for the Jewish people. During flogging, the victim was stripped and tied to a post. The flogger used a whip, which consisted of several pieces of leather strips fastened to a wooden handle. Each strip had butterfly-shaped metal pieces attached to the end (see Illustration #12). The whip literally shredded a person's back and was an instrument of death. Few people lived through a flogging, which saved the trouble and expense of crucifying them. Jewish law permitted a maximum of thirty-nine lashes. Roman law had no limit.

That flogging would have turned Jesus' back into one giant, open wound. The most amazing fact about it is that Jesus just stood there and took it. Anyone who could raise a dead man could zap Pilate and his soldiers in an instant. Or escape. Or at least dazzle them with an argument in his own defense. He did none of these. He took the torture.

After the flogging, the soldiers ridiculed Jesus' claim to be king by pressing a crown of thorns on his head and dressing him up in a robe. Purple dye was so expensive that only rich people owned purple garments. It was as valuable as gold. The thorns in Jesus' crown were the giant variety, an inch long and sharp as needles.

Both a crown and a purple robe were symbols of royalty. Now that he looked like a king, the soldiers repeatedly mocked him as one, using a sarcastic form of the normal greeting for the Roman emperor, "Hail, Caesar." And they beat him.

Illustration #12
Roman Whips—Jesus was beaten with whips such as these composed of leather strips with sharp pieces of metal on the ends.

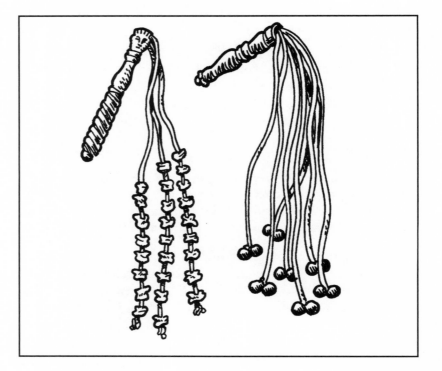

Beaten and Battered King

JOHN 19:4–5 *Pilate then went out again, and said to them, "Behold, I am bringing Him out to you, that you may know that I find no fault in Him." Then Jesus came out, wearing the crown of thorns and the purple robe. And Pilate said to them, "Behold the Man!"* (NKJV)

For the third time, Pilate went out to talk with the Jewish people. This time he brought out Jesus, who would have been unrecognizable (or close to it) from the beatings. For the second time, Pilate declared Jesus' innocence. When Pilate said, "Behold the Man!" he wasn't politely introducing Jesus to the crowd. He was mocking them. "Look at this poor man. How can you believe he is a king? Have mercy and drop the charges."

Kill the King

JOHN 19:6–7 *Therefore, when the chief priests and officers saw Him, they cried out, saying, "Crucify Him, crucify Him!" Pilate said to them, "You take Him and crucify Him, for I find no fault in Him." The Jews answered him, "We have a law, and according to our law He ought to die, because He made Himself the Son of God."* (NKJV)

The religious leaders were not about to back down. They hated Jesus with a vengeance and would not quit until they saw him dead. The courtyard scene may have been similar to a ball game today. Just like the crowds in the stadium chant for their team, the religious leaders began to shout repeatedly, "Crucify him!"

death penalty
Leviticus 24:16

message
Matthew 27:19

told him
John 18:36–37

By this time, Pilate was fed up with the Jews. He dared them to crucify Jesus even though they had no authority to do so. For the third time, Pilate pronounced him innocent.

Finally, the religious leaders clearly stated the real reason they wanted to kill Jesus: "He made Himself the Son of God." That claim carried the <u>death penalty</u>, but they couldn't execute it. Jesus didn't deserve the charge; he really was the Son of God.

Don't You Know Who I Am?

> **JOHN 19:8–10** *Therefore, when Pilate heard that saying, he was the more afraid, and went again into the Praetorium, and said to Jesus, "Where are You from?" But Jesus gave him no answer. Then Pilate said to Him, "Are You not speaking to me? Do You not know that I have power to crucify You, and power to release You?"* (NKJV)

Undoubtedly, this was the worst day of Pilate's life. Hearing that Jesus claimed to be the Son of God sent his fear temperature up another twenty degrees. Romans believed that gods came to earth, and maybe Jesus was one of them. If that were the case, it was not in Pilate's best interests to kill him. Earlier his wife had had a dream about Jesus and had sent him a <u>message</u> to have nothing to do with this innocent man. He must have been thinking about her words. Now, with the crowd chanting for crucifixion, he could sense a riot coming.

Unable to make a firm decision, Pilate went back into the house to talk to Jesus. Jesus wouldn't tell him where he was from so that Pilate would know if he was a god or not. Jesus had already <u>told him</u>. What was the point in repeating truth Pilate didn't want to know or act on?

Frustrated, Pilate changed tactics. If Jesus wasn't going to talk with him, he'd remind him of who was in charge. Pilate thought he had the power to decide Jesus' future, but the real director was God. If Pilate had all that power, why didn't he let Jesus go like he wanted to? It was a hollow boast.

Andreas J. Köstenberger

Though Roman officials may have been cynical, they also were often deeply superstitious. In pagan ears, the designation "son of god" conjured up notions of "divine men," persons believed to enjoy certain divine powers. Ancient pagans concluded commonly enough that "the gods have come down to us in human form" (Acts 14:11). If Jesus was a "son of god," Pilate may have reasoned, he might incur the wrath of the gods for having Jesus flogged (cf. Matt. 27:19).[2]

Enough Guilt to Go Around

JOHN 19:11 *Jesus answered, "You could have no power at all against Me unless it had been given you from above. Therefore the one who delivered Me to you has the greater sin." (NKJV)*

The last thing Jesus said to Pilate was a reminder that his power came from God, not from himself or the Roman government. It was useless to pull a power play with Jesus; he always wins. Pilate wasn't the only loser in this game. Caiaphas, the high priest who had handed Jesus over to Pilate for execution, committed a greater sin than Pilate was about to.

Choose Your Side

JOHN 19:12 *From then on Pilate sought to release Him, but the Jews cried out, saying, "If you let this Man go, you are not Caesar's friend. Whoever makes himself a king speaks against Caesar." (NKJV)*

Some days it doesn't pay to get out of bed. This was one of those days for Pilate. The situation just kept getting worse. The more he tried to free Jesus, the more the Jewish people argued against that action. Finally, the Jews hurled a threat that hit the target. They accused Pilate of being Caesar's enemy instead of his friend if he let Jesus go. That was a statement that would terrify any Roman governor. If word got back to Rome that Pilate had released a man whose claim to be king was a threat to Caesar's rule, he would lose his job and maybe his life. The threat was effective even though it came from hypocrites who had no allegiance to Roman rule.

idols
Exodus 20:4

Pilate ruled Israel from AD 26 to 35. As governor, he controlled the military and justice system and supervised the collection of taxes for Rome. Once a year, he visited all the provinces to hear legal cases and complaints. He was paid by Rome and forbidden to take bribes and presents. His subjects, however, could report him to the Roman emperor if he went beyond his stated duties. Since the Jewish people hated the many gods of Rome and served only God, Israel was a problem area.

Pilate made several huge errors before Jesus was brought to him for crucifixion. The first time he visited Jerusalem, Pilate brought soldiers who carried standards with busts of the Roman emperor. Since the emperor was considered a god, the Jewish people viewed those busts as <u>idols</u>, strictly forbidden in Scripture. Previous governors had had those images removed before entering the city in respect for the Jews' religious beliefs. Pilate refused to do so.

Then Pilate decided to build a new aqueduct to improve the water supply for Jerusalem. He financed it by taking money from the temple treasury. The Jewish people rioted and could have reported him to Rome.

Another time when Pilate was in Jerusalem, he had special shields made with the name of the emperor engraved on them. They were displayed in honor of the emperor, a god to the Romans. The Jewish people were enraged, but Pilate refused to remove them. That time the Jews reported him to Rome, and the emperor ordered Pilate to remove the shields.

Pilate was in danger of losing his job as governor. Consequently, he gave in to the Jewish leaders' blackmail and crucified Jesus.

Presenting His Royal Highness

JOHN 19:13–14 *When Pilate therefore heard that saying, he brought Jesus out and sat down in the judgment seat in a place that is called The Pavement, but in Hebrew, Gabbatha. Now it was the Preparation Day of the Passover, and about the sixth hour. And he said to the Jews, "Behold your King!"* (NKJV)

Pilate finally made a decision. He moved Jesus to the Fortress of Antonia, where he sat on the judgment seat in the paved courtyard and sentenced Jesus indirectly. John noted that it was about 6:00

a.m. on the day of preparation, the day the Passover lamb was killed to be eaten that night. In a mocking voice, Pilate presented Jesus to the Jewish people as their king. By then, Jesus looked like a walking dead man, not a king.

go to

washed his hands
Matthew 27:24

Choosing the Wrong King

JOHN 19:15–16 *But they cried out, "Away with Him, away with Him! Crucify Him!" Pilate said to them, "Shall I crucify your King?" The chief priests answered, "We have no king but Caesar!" Then he delivered Him to them to be crucified. Then they took Jesus and led Him away.* (NKJV)

The Jewish people, however, didn't want that king. They wanted him crucified. Instead, the leaders swore their allegiance to Caesar, rejecting God as their king. According to Matthew, Pilate washed his hands of Jesus' blood, declaring Jesus to be innocent of a political crime. But he buckled under the pressure and sold Jesus out to the religious leaders. He was more interested in keeping peace than in doing what was right. He turned Jesus over to the soldiers for crucifixion.

what others say

Manford George Gutzke

Heaven must have looked down on this scene with anguish and horror. It must have hurt the heart of God the Father to see His Son suffer. And yet salvation was being wrought out in the plan of God, as the Son was carrying out the will of the Father. Not only was the Son of God put to a shameful death by men not worthy to tie His shoelaces, but God had allowed this to come to pass.[3]

Pilate knew Jesus was innocent, but he refused to buck the crowd. Standing up for what is right isn't always easy. More often than not, it's just plain hard. But God always honors us when we take a stand for him.

something to ponder

The Darkest Day in History

JOHN 19:17–18 *And He, bearing His cross, went out to a place called the Place of a Skull, which is called in Hebrew, Golgotha,*

criminals
Isaiah 53:12

B.C.E.
before the common
era, BC

where they crucified Him, and two others with Him, one on either side, and Jesus in the center. (NKJV)

In two sentences, John summarized the worst—and best—time in history. Until he collapsed under the weight, Jesus was forced to carry his own cross from the judgment hall (Antonia) to the execution hill (Golgotha) outside the city of Jerusalem (see Illustration #11 in chapter 18). In Jesus' day, condemned criminals carried their own crosses to the site of crucifixion. Although Jesus is normally pictured with an entire cross on his back, he would have toted only the horizontal crossbeam. Several stakes already in the ground at Golgotha were reused for crucifixions. The victim was nailed to the crossbeam on the ground. Then it was lifted up and set in a groove near the top of the stake. His feet would have been only two to four feet above the ground.

There the Roman soldiers crucified him between two other criminals—an act that God had predicted hundreds of years before. Although it was a horrible time, it was also the best time. Jesus died on that cross so we can have eternal life.

what others say

J. W. Shepherd

The cross was the most disgraceful and one of the cruelest instruments of death ever invented. The Romans . . . would not allow a Roman citizen to be crucified; but reserved crucifixion for slaves and foreigners or provincials. The Jews customarily used stoning and never crucifixion. It was not only the death of greatest ignominy but of the most extreme anguish and suffering.[4]

Louis Goldberg

In Psalm 22:16 we read, ". . . they pierced my hands, and my feet." This is a Messianic psalm (it has always been regarded as such), and there is an amazing accuracy in what is proclaimed here. David wrote this Psalm about 1000 **B.C.E.**, and in that day stoning was the method of capital punishment. David spoke of Messiah's hands and feet being pierced. Under the influence of the Spirit of God, he described a manner of execution that was foreign to the people of his day. The period in which crucifixion was the common mode of execution was hundreds of years future, in the time of the Romans, who used this peculiar method. Not only was the death described, but the rest of Psalm 22 relates the suffering accompanying His death.[5]

King in Any Language

JOHN 19:19–22 *Now Pilate wrote a title and put it on the cross. And the writing was:*

JESUS OF NAZARETH,
THE KING OF THE JEWS.

Then many of the Jews read this title, for the place where Jesus was crucified was near the city; and it was written in Hebrew, Greek, and Latin. Therefore the chief priests of the Jews said to Pilate, "Do not write, 'The King of the Jews,' but, 'He said, "I am the King of the Jews."'" Pilate answered, "What I have written, I have written." (NKJV)

Jesus hung in a public place outside the city where thousands of Passover pilgrims could see him. As revenge for his political defeat, Pilate posted a notice in three languages to call attention to Jesus' humiliating crime. He made sure everyone could read it. Jewish people spoke Aramaic, Romans spoke Latin, and Greek was the common language. Labeling that beaten, crucified man as King of the Jews would embarrass and insult the Jewish people.

Of course, the chief priests took issue with the sign and asked Pilate to edit it to say Jesus claimed to be king of the Jews. They weren't going to claim him as king, so why advertise that fact? For once Pilate refused to give in to them and left it as written.

Used Clothing Division

JOHN 19:23–24 *Then the soldiers, when they had crucified Jesus, took His garments and made four parts, to each soldier a part, and also the tunic. Now the tunic was without seam, woven from the top in one piece. They said therefore among themselves, "Let us not tear it, but cast lots for it, whose it shall be," that the Scripture might be fulfilled which says:*

"They divided My garments among them,
And for My clothing they cast lots."

Therefore the soldiers did these things. (NKJV)

Unlike pictures we see of Jesus hanging on the cross while wearing a loincloth, he was naked, as was customary for crucifixions. Part of the soldiers' pay was the victims' belongings, so they divided up Jesus' clothes, which were all he had. Each of them got one piece—

go to

prophecy
Psalm 22:18

wife of Zebedee
Matthew 27:55–56

mother
Mark 15:40

honoring
Exodus 20:12

sandals, turban, robe, and sash. Since the tunic worn under the robe was seamless, they decided to throw dice for it instead of tearing it in four pieces. Little did they know that they were fulfilling <u>prophecy</u>.

Women Around the Cross

JOHN 19:25–27 *Now there stood by the cross of Jesus His mother, and His mother's sister, Mary the wife of Clopas, and Mary Magdalene. When Jesus therefore saw His mother, and the disciple whom He loved standing by, He said to His mother, "Woman, behold your son!" Then He said to the disciple, "Behold your mother!" And from that hour that disciple took her to his own home. (NKJV)*

Few of Jesus' followers stuck around for the Crucifixion. John mentioned only five: Jesus' mother, Mary; his aunt Salome, the <u>wife of Zebedee</u> and the mother of John (the writer of this book) and James; Mary, the wife of Clopas who was the <u>mother</u> of James the younger and Joses; Mary Magdalene; and John, the author.

In the midst of his pain and agony, Jesus thought about his mother. Part of <u>honoring</u> one's mother and father was providing for them when they got old. Since Jesus wouldn't be around that long, he asked John to take care of her.

While hanging on the cross, Jesus spoke seven statements, only three of which John recorded:

gospel harmony

1. "Father, forgive them, for they do not know what they do" (Luke 23:34 NKJV). Jesus forgave all those who were killing him, including the Roman soldiers who nailed him to the cross, the Jewish leaders who had him arrested, and Pilate who gave the order for crucifixion.

2. "Today you will be with Me in Paradise" (Luke 23:43 NKJV). One of the two thieves who was crucified next to Jesus believed in him as Savior from his sins while he was on the cross. As a result, Jesus told him he would go to paradise, or heaven.

3. "Woman, behold your son!… Behold your mother!" (John 19:26–27 NKJV). While he was dying, Jesus took care of his

mother by committing her to John to make sure she would be taken care of.

4. "My God, My God, why have You forsaken Me?" (Matthew 27:46 NKJV). On the cross, Jesus took on himself all of our sins. Because God is holy, he cannot look at sin. So Jesus was separated spiritually from the Father during that time. This question was a fulfillment of prophecy in Psalm 22:1.

5. "I thirst!" (John 19:28 NKJV). After three hours of hanging in the sun, Jesus' mouth would have been so parched he could barely talk. Although he didn't need the pain-deadening wine, he uttered this statement to fulfill prophecy in Psalm 69:21.

6. "It is finished!" (John 19:30 NKJV). This was a cry of victory. Jesus had completed the payment for our sins.

7. "Father, into Your hands I commit My spirit" (Luke 23:46 NKJV). As he breathed his last breath, Jesus committed himself to his Father. No one forced Jesus to die; he did it voluntarily for us.

what others say

John MacArthur Jr.

This was a beautiful gesture, and it says a lot about the personal nature of Jesus' love. Although he was dying under the most excruciating kind of anguish, Jesus, the King of love, selflessly turned aside to care for the earthly needs of those who stood by His side. Although He was occupied with the most important event in the history of redemption, He remembered to make provision for the needs of one woman, His mother.[6]

If you had lived in Jesus' day and had been one of his followers, would you have been with Judas, who betrayed him; with Peter, who denied him; with the other disciples, who scattered when he was arrested; or with the women and John, who stayed with Jesus until he died?

something to ponder

Final Payment

JOHN 19:28–30 *After this, Jesus, knowing that all things were now accomplished, that the Scripture might be fulfilled, said, "I*

go to

drink wine
Matthew 27:34

thirsty
Psalm 69:21

3:00 p.m
Matthew 27:45–50

hyssop
tall cornlike plant

*thirst!" Now a vessel full of sour wine was sitting there; and they filled a sponge with sour wine, put it on **hyssop**, and put it to His mouth. So when Jesus had received the sour wine, He said, "It is finished!" And bowing His head, He gave up His spirit. (NKJV)*

Previously, Jesus had refused to <u>drink wine</u> mixed with a painkiller that was given to victims before crucifixion. He endured all the excruciating agony of hanging on that stake. Nearing the end of his mission, and to fulfill what God had predicted earlier, he cried out, "I am <u>thirsty</u>." The soldiers soaked a sponge with sour wine, fastened it to the end of a hyssop branch (see Illustration #13), and let Jesus sip the liquid from it.

That wasn't enough wine to quench his thirst after hanging on the cross for three hours. But it was enough to permit him to shout a victory cry, "It is finished!" at <u>3:00 p.m.</u> The Greek word for this phrase means a debt is paid in full, something is accomplished, and assigned work is completed. Nothing else needed to be done for our salvation from sin. Jesus' death on the cross fulfilled all the predictions about his death and completed the payment for our sins. Then he voluntarily gave up his life. Jesus was in control of his death to his final breath.

Illustration #13
Hyssop Plant—The hyssop plant has a thick hairy stem and bunches of leaves that can trap liquid. The plant was associated with sacrifice. People used it during the first Passover in Egypt to sprinkle lamb's blood on their doorframes.

what others say

Edwin A. Blum

The wording in John 19:28 indicated that Jesus was fully conscious and was aware of fulfilling the details of prophecies (Psalms 42:1–2; 63:1). The paradox of the One who is the Water of Life (John 4:14; 7:38–39) dying in thirst is striking.[7]

Old Testament Prophecies Fulfilled in Jesus' Death

Passage	Prophecy	Fulfillment
Isaiah 50:6	Beaten and spit on	John 19:1; Matthew 27:30
Psalm 69:19	Shame	Matthew 27:28
Psalm 22:18	Clothing divided among the soldiers	John 19:24
Isaiah 53:7	Silent at the trial	Matthew 27:13–14
Isaiah 53:5–6, 10	Death by crucifixion	John 19:16
Psalm 69:3	Thirst	John 19:28
Psalm 69:21	Wine vinegar to drink	John 19:29
Psalm 22:17	Stared at	Matthew 27:36
Psalm 22:16	Hands and feet pierced	John 19:18
Zechariah 12:10	Side pierced	John 19:34
Psalm 22:14	Broken heart/blood and water	John 19:34
Psalm 22:8	Mocked	Matthew 27:43
Isaiah 53:12	Prayed for others	Luke 23:34
Psalm 22:1	Cry to God	Matthew 27:46
Psalm 22:31	Victory cry	John 19:30
Exodus 12:46	No broken bones	John 19:33, 36
Isaiah 53:12	Numbered with law-breakers	Luke 23:33
Genesis 3:15	Bruised heel	John 19:18
Isaiah 53:9	Place of burial	Matthew 27:57–60

gospel harmony

Whole Bones, Not Broken Pieces

JOHN 19:31–34 *Therefore, because it was the Preparation Day, that the bodies should not remain on the cross on the Sabbath (for that Sabbath was a high day), the Jews asked Pilate that their legs might be broken, and that they might be taken away. Then the soldiers came and broke the legs of the first and of the other who was crucified with Him. But when they came to Jesus and saw that He was already dead, they did not break His legs. But one of the soldiers pierced His side with a spear, and immediately blood and water came out. (NKJV)*

While the cross beam was on the ground, the crucifixion victim's hands or wrists were nailed in place with heavy, square nails without pulling the arms too tight. Once the cross beam was put in place on a stake, the person's left foot was pressed against the right one. With

go to

body
Deuteronomy
21:22–23

toes forced downward, a nail was driven through both arches, leaving the knees flexed.

As the victim hung there, he sagged, causing pressure on the nerves and excruciating pain shooting through his fingers and arms. It was like a fire exploding in the brain. To relieve this pain, he pushed himself up. The extra weight on the nail in his feet tore the nerves in his feet, causing more exploding pain.

His tired arms cramped, producing throbbing muscle pain and preventing him from pushing himself up. He could barely breathe and tried to raise himself again to draw air, taking some in but not being able to exhale. So carbon dioxide built up in his lungs and blood stream, temporarily relieving the arm cramps and allowing him to pull himself up to breathe. The victim could endure hours of this cycle of pain, tearing the tissue from his back each time he moved up and down on the rough wood. Slowly the sac around the heart filled with fluid, compressing his heart and causing crushing chest pain.

Finally, he reached the critical stage and died.

Part of the horror of crucifixion was a long, drawn-out death. Since it was disrespectful for the Jewish people to leave a dead <u>body</u> hanging on the Sabbath, something had to be done to make sure the three men died before sundown when the Sabbath began. The holiday made it even more urgent to clear the crosses. So the Jewish leaders asked Pilate to hasten death by having soldiers break the victims' legs. That was normal procedure to keep them from pushing up and breathing longer. With broken legs, they would suffocate in their own body fluids.

The soldiers obeyed with the two thieves. When they saw that Jesus was already dead, they didn't bother with him. Just to be sure, one of them stuck a spear in Jesus' side. The fact that blood and water had separated confirmed his death and that Jesus was a man with a human body.

what others say

Mark Bailey and Tom Constable

The flow of blood and water from His pierced side affirmed the physical reality of Jesus' death. Affirming the truth of what he wrote about Jesus' death, John then encouraged the faith of his readers by quoting Old Testament passages he saw fulfilled in the events of the Cross (Exodus 12:46; Numbers 9:12; Psalm 34:20; Zechariah 12:10).[8]

go to

broken bones
Exodus 12:46

pierced
Zechariah 12:10

Joseph of Arimathea
Mark 15:43;
Luke 23:50–51

myrrh
fragrant spice

aloes
thick leaves with a
bitter liquid inside

Scripture Clues

JOHN 19:35–37 *And he who has seen has testified, and his testimony is true; and he knows that he is telling the truth, so that you may believe. For these things were done that the Scripture should be fulfilled, "Not one of His bones shall be broken." And again another Scripture says, "They shall look on Him whom they pierced." (NKJV)*

John was an eyewitness to Jesus' death and the soldiers' actions to hasten death for the trio on the crosses. What he wrote was not secondhand knowledge or something he made up. It was true, and John included this information so readers would believe in Jesus. As with other events of the past two days, these also fulfilled Scripture. The absence of broken bones referred to the Passover lamb, which pictured Jesus as "the Lamb of God who takes away the sin of the world!" (John 1:29 NKJV). The prophet Zechariah predicted that the Messiah would be pierced.

No More Secret Believers

JOHN 19:38–40 *After this, Joseph of Arimathea, being a disciple of Jesus, but secretly, for fear of the Jews, asked Pilate that he might take away the body of Jesus; and Pilate gave him permission. So he came and took the body of Jesus. And Nicodemus, who at first came to Jesus by night, also came, bringing a mixture of* **myrrh** *and* **aloes**, *about a hundred pounds. Then they took the body of Jesus, and bound it in strips of linen with the spices, as the custom of the Jews is to bury. (NKJV)*

Crucified criminals were thrown into a common grave unless someone in the family had enough clout to request the body for proper burial. Since Jesus' arrest and sentencing happened quickly, his family didn't have time to purchase a burial tomb or make funeral arrangements. Other than John, his disciples were not around. So Joseph of Arimathea and Nicodemus quit hiding their belief in Jesus and took care of his body.

Nicodemus
John 3:1–21

Joseph asked Pilate for permission to take Jesus' body away, and Pilate granted it. He and <u>Nicodemus</u>—the same man who met Jesus at night three years earlier—picked up the body and prepared it for burial. Since shops would be closed for Passover, Nicodemus must have had the spices on hand, ready for this moment. There wasn't time to wash and anoint the body as was customary, but they wrapped it in linen strips with an enormous amount of myrrh and aloes, both expensive spices.

> **what others say**
>
> ### Ed Glasscock
>
> Joseph came and asked for the body of Christ "when it was evening," that is, some time after 3:00 P.M. on Friday but before 6:00 P.M., which would begin the high Sabbath of Passover (Luke 23:54). According to Deuteronomy 21:22–23, a criminal executed and hanged on a tree was not to be left hanging overnight. Since the coming day was a Sabbath, and a special Sabbath at that, the Jews would not allow removal of the body after sunset.[9]

Buried in a Borrowed Tomb

JOHN 19:41–42 *Now in the place where He was crucified there was a garden, and in the garden a new tomb in which no one had yet been laid. So there they laid Jesus, because of the Jews' Preparation Day, for the tomb was nearby.* (NKJV)

Jesus had not bought a tomb before he died, but Joseph had one ready for him. Since Joseph was rich, he would not have bought a tomb for himself that close to Golgotha. After all, his relatives would not have wanted to pay their respects while listening to criminals dying. And he could have afforded a better location within Jerusalem. There he and Nicodemus buried Jesus.

Jesus died and was buried. For other people, that would be the end of the story. But not for Jesus. His story is to be continued.

Chapter Wrap-Up

- Pilate had Jesus beaten, and he and the soldiers mocked him as a king. (John 19:1–5)
- The Jewish leaders continued to demand that Pilate crucify Jesus. (John 19:6–7)
- Pilate tried to pull a power play on Jesus, but Jesus reminded him that his power came from God. (John 19:8–11)
- Pilate tried to set Jesus free but bowed to the pressure of the Jewish leaders to crucify him. (John 19:12–16)
- Jesus was crucified between two thieves. (John 19:17–24)
- Before he died, Jesus arranged for John to take care of his mother. (John 19:25–27)
- Jesus voluntarily died and did not have to have his bones broken to hasten death. (John 19:28–37)
- Joseph of Arimathea and Nicodemus claimed Jesus' body and buried him. (John 19:38–42)

Study Questions

1. How did the soldiers mock Jesus?
2. What arguments did the Jewish leaders use to convince Pilate that Jesus should die?
3. Where did Pilate's power come from?
4. How did Pilate identify Jesus when he was on the cross?
5. What did Jesus do for his mother before he died?
6. Who took care of Jesus' burial, and what did they do with his body?

John 20: Jesus the Risen Lord

Chapter Highlights:
- Can't Keep a Good Man Down
- Appearing Behind Closed Doors
- Signposts to Belief

Let's Get Started

Anybody can claim to be God. There are a lot of people in mental hospitals who make that claim, but proving it is another story. That's exactly what Jesus did when he rose from the dead. His resurrection was the final proof that he is the Son of God.

Jesus' bodily resurrection is historical fact, not a myth. There is more evidence for the Resurrection than for any other event from the same time period. One of my Bible professors used to say, "If you cannot believe the Resurrection based on historical records, you cannot believe any other fact of history."

As John recorded some of Jesus' postresurrection appearances, we learn that the Resurrection gave Mary Magdalene joy, gave the disciples courage, and gave Thomas assurance of his faith. John wrapped up this chapter with his purpose statement: "that you may believe that Jesus is the Christ, the Son of God, and that believing you may have life in His name" (20:31 NKJV).

go to

seal
Matthew 27:66

guard
Matthew 27:62–65

rise
Matthew 16:21

The Case of the Missing Body

JOHN 20:1–2 *Now on the first day of the week Mary Magdalene went to the tomb early, while it was still dark, and saw that the stone had been taken away from the tomb. Then she ran and came to Simon Peter, and to the other disciple, whom Jesus loved, and said to them, "They have taken away the Lord out of the tomb, and we do not know where they have laid Him." (NKJV)*

After Joseph and Nicodemus buried Jesus, the religious leaders went back to Pilate. They asked him to <u>seal</u> and <u>guard</u> Jesus' tomb so no one could steal the body. They had acted stupidly in crucifying Jesus, but they weren't stupid. They knew Jesus had claimed he would <u>rise</u> on the third day, and they wanted to be sure no one stole the body and claimed Jesus was alive. They also wanted to be sure Jesus didn't get out of the tomb.

go to

Mary and Salome
Mark 16:1

roll away
Mark 16:3

angel
Matthew 28:2

Since Jesus had been buried hastily, Mary Magdalene showed up at the tomb early Sunday morning. She arrived shortly before <u>Mary</u>, the mother of James, <u>and Salome</u> to anoint Jesus' body for burial. They were concerned about getting someone to <u>roll away</u> the heavy stone so they could get into the tomb. But God was way ahead of them. The tomb was already open, the stone having been rolled away earlier by an <u>angel</u>.

Mary Magdalene peered into the tomb, expecting a dead body. Instead, her eyes took in a lot of emptiness. Shocked, Mary ran to Peter and John to tell them someone had taken Jesus' body. The women didn't even know where to look for it.

To explain away Jesus' missing body, people have made up several theories.

Theories of Jesus' Missing Body

Theory	Description	Evidence Against It
Fraud Theory	Someone stole it	Roman guards were posted, so no one could steal it. Disciples didn't believe Jesus was going to rise; if Jesus' enemies had taken it, they would have produced the body to show he didn't rise; disciples wouldn't have died for a fraud
Swoon Theory	Jesus didn't really die; he passed out	Jesus' wounds (hands and feet pierced with nails, side pierced with sword) were so bad he couldn't have gotten up and walked away; soldiers didn't break his legs because he was dead; after hanging on the cross, he wouldn't have had enough strength to roll away a rock that weighed two tons and fight the guards to escape
Ghost Theory	Disciples only thought they saw Jesus alive	Disciples didn't expect to see Jesus alive. Jesus had a real body after the Resurrection

what others say

Bruce Milne

The fact that the women were the first to discover the empty tomb is certainly authentic, as this alone would have discredited the story with the Jewish public (in Jesus' society, sadly, women were not even thought fit witnesses in court).[1]

Josh McDowell

After more than seven hundred hours of studying this subject and thoroughly investigating its foundation, I have come to

> the conclusion that the resurrection of Jesus Christ is one of the most wicked, vicious, heartless hoaxes ever foisted upon the minds of men, OR it is the most fantastic fact of history. . . .
>
> The resurrection of Jesus Christ and Christianity stand or fall together. A student at the University of Uruguay once said to me: "Professor McDowell, why can't you refute Christianity?" I answered: "For a very simple reason: I am not able to explain away an event in history—the resurrection of Jesus."[2]

Mary and the other women didn't have a lot to offer Jesus. Nor could they do much for him, given the restrictions of their society. But they stayed by him when he was crucified and most of his other disciples disappeared. Also, they brought ointments to anoint Jesus' body for burial after the Sabbath was over. As a result, Jesus appeared to Mary first after he rose from the dead.

You may not have much to give Jesus either. You may not have the opportunity or ability to do great things for him. But you can give him your love and devotion like these women did.

Race for the Tomb

> **JOHN 20:3–7** *Peter therefore went out, and the other disciple, and were going to the tomb. So they both ran together, and the other disciple outran Peter and came to the tomb first. And he, stooping down and looking in, saw the linen cloths lying there; yet he did not go in. Then Simon Peter came, following him, and went into the tomb; and he saw the linen cloths lying there, and the handkerchief that had been around His head, not lying with the linen cloths, but folded together in a place by itself.* (NKJV)

When Peter and John heard the news about Jesus' missing body, they took off for the tomb to see for themselves. John won the race, but he didn't enter the cave. He glanced in and saw the linen strips but no body.

When Peter arrived, he walked past John and entered the tomb. Sure enough, Mary was right. The body was missing, but evidence showed that it had been there. The grave clothes—linen strips—lay in the shape of a body as though someone had energized Jesus to another location. The napkin that had covered his head was neatly folded.

go to

Jesus had told
John 2:19

prophecies
Psalm 16:10;
Isaiah 53:10

J. Carl Laney

Whereas grave-robbers would have taken the body with the wrappings, or ripped and scattered them, John records Peter's observation that the burial cloth used on Jesus' head remained rolled or had been folded and set carefully aside.[3]

Without the Resurrection, there would be no Christianity: "If Christ is not risen, your faith is futile; you are still in your sins!" (1 Corinthians 15:17 NKJV). People in every other religion worship or look to a dead leader. Muhammad is dead. Buddha is dead. Joseph Smith (founder of Mormonism) is dead. Mary Baker Eddy (founder of Christian Science) is dead. Only Jesus is alive. Christianity is a relationship with the living God and his Son, Jesus.

Seeing Is Believing

JOHN 20:8–9 *Then the other disciple, who came to the tomb first, went in also; and he saw and believed. For as yet they did not know the Scripture, that He must rise again from the dead. (NKJV)*

When John entered the tomb, he also saw the grave clothes in the shape of a body. Like the other disciples, he wasn't expecting a missing body. But the fact that it was gone made him believe that Jesus rose from the dead. He saw and understood the evidence firsthand, making him a trustworthy witness to write this book. The empty tomb brought to mind what Jesus had told the disciples about his resurrection. However, John still didn't get the connection with the prophecies in the Old Testament Scriptures. His belief wasn't fully developed yet.

Angel Encounter

JOHN 20:10–12 *Then the disciples went away again to their own homes. But Mary stood outside by the tomb weeping, and as she wept she stooped down and looked into the tomb. And she saw two angels in white sitting, one at the head and the other at the feet, where the body of Jesus had lain. (NKJV)*

Not knowing what else to do, the disciples went home. Mary Magdalene probably returned to the tomb after they left. She stood alone, crying loudly with grief and wondering where the body was. Maybe, when she looked inside, she hoped it would be there. Instead, two angels, wearing white, sat where the body had been. We can assume from Mary's reaction that these angels looked like humans and weren't wearing wings and halos.

what others say

John Calvin

Although the apostles and the women were suffering the same disease, the apostles' stupidity was less excusable because they had profited so little by their thorough and careful teaching.[4]

Missing Body Shows Up

JOHN 20:13–14 *Then they said to her, "Woman, why are you weeping?" She said to them, "Because they have taken away my Lord, and I do not know where they have laid Him." Now when she had said this, she turned around and saw Jesus standing there, and did not know that it was Jesus.* (NKJV)

Skipping introductions and small talk, the angels asked Mary why she was crying. In one sense, it was a stupid question. What else would they expect from someone who loved the dead man and was standing at his tomb? In another sense, it was an obvious question to remind Mary that she had no reason to cry because Jesus was alive. It was a joyous occasion! She told the angels what was on her mind: Jesus' body was gone, and she didn't know where to look for it.

Then she heard something or someone behind her. She turned around to see who or what it was. Standing there was Jesus, whom she didn't recognize. Maybe she couldn't tell who he was because her eyes were blurred with tears. Or maybe Jesus temporarily blinded her. We don't know for sure.

Jesus in the Flesh

JOHN 20:15–16 *Jesus said to her, "Woman, why are you weeping? Whom are you seeking?" She, supposing Him to be the gar-*

dener, said to Him, "Sir, if You have carried Him away, tell me where You have laid Him, and I will take Him away." Jesus said to her, "Mary!" She turned and said to Him, "Rabboni!" (which is to say, Teacher). (NKJV)

"Why are you weeping?" must have been the question of the day. Jesus followed it with another one, asking Mary who she was looking for. Not knowing the man was Jesus, she figured he must be the gardener. Who else would be hanging around a tomb? So she asked him where he had taken Jesus' body. She was desperate to find him even though she could not have carried two hundred pounds (or whatever he weighed plus seventy-five pounds of spices) of dead weight back to the tomb. And what would she say if someone saw her lugging a corpse? Obviously, she was grief-stricken and wasn't thinking.

In response, Jesus spoke her name. That was enough for her to recognize him. Perhaps it was the sound of his voice. Perhaps Jesus removed her blindness toward him. Whatever it was, Mary looked at him and called him "Rabboni," the personal, informal form of "rabbi," which means teacher.

what others say

Merrill C. Tenney

One of the strange commonplaces of life is that the most penetrating utterance one can understand, no matter by whom spoken, is one's personal name. Furthermore, the way it is spoken often identifies the speaker.[5]

Jesus Is Alive!

JOHN 20:17–18 *Jesus said to her, "Do not cling to Me, for I have not yet ascended to My Father; but go to My brethren and say to them, 'I am ascending to My Father and your Father, and to My God and your God.'" Mary Magdalene came and told the disciples that she had seen the Lord, and that He had spoken these things to her. (NKJV)*

Overcome with emotion, Mary grasped Jesus. She'd lost him once; she wasn't going to lose him again. Jesus had other plans, however. He couldn't hang around the tomb. He had other people to see, and he would see her again. Besides, he had a job for her to do. Jesus told Mary to stop clinging to him and tell his disciples, whom he now called brothers, that he was alive and would ascend to his Father and God and their Father and God. He was careful to keep his relationship with God distinct from theirs.

Imagine how happy the disciples must have been when Mary delivered her news. They had spent three years with Jesus and had grown to love him. He had changed their lives. They had just been through the worst three days of their lives and thought Jesus was dead. Now they heard that he was alive. What great news!

go to

two others
Luke 24:13–32

peace
John 14:27

ghost
Luke 24:37

Peace in the Midst of Fear

JOHN 20:19–20 *Then, the same day at evening, being the first day of the week, when the doors were shut where the disciples were assembled, for fear of the Jews, Jesus came and stood in the midst, and said to them, "Peace be with you." When He had said this, He showed them His hands and His side. Then the disciples were glad when they saw the Lord. (NKJV)*

Mary had brought good news of Jesus' resurrection, but the disciples didn't fully believe it. If they had, they would not have huddled behind locked doors Sunday night, afraid of the religious leaders. Instead, they would have been out shouting the news to everyone they met. Since Jesus rose from the dead, he certainly was more powerful than the men responsible for his death and could therefore keep his followers safe.

Jesus' followers who were present—a larger group than his ten disciples with Thomas missing—had a lot to talk about together. They had Mary's report of Jesus' appearance to her, and Peter and two others had seen him that afternoon. Undoubtedly, they had also received reports from others who had seen Jesus. Now he appeared in their midst, as though he had beamed into the room. Or perhaps he walked through a wall or the locked door. However he got there, his resurrection body came in a different form than before his death and was no longer limited by the laws of nature.

key point

Standing in the midst of his frightened disciples, Jesus spoke the customary greeting: "Peace be with you." He had spoken these familiar words the night of his arrest to prepare the men for the ordeal they would face. Now Jesus showed them his hands and feet with the nail holes, since they thought they saw a ghost. That was enough evidence to convince the men that he was the same Jesus

go to

God breathed
Genesis 2:7

gospel harmony

who had died three days earlier and to fill them with joy.

For forty days after his resurrection, Jesus made a number of appearances besides the ones recorded in this chapter.

Jesus' Appearances After His Resurrection

Place	People	Scripture
Empty tomb	Mary the mother of James	Matthew 28:9–10
Jerusalem	Simon Peter	Luke 24:34
On Emmaus road	Cleopas and other disciple	Luke 24:13–32
Sea of Galilee	Seven disciples	John 21:1–24
Mountain in Galilee	Eleven disciples	Matthew 28:16–20
Galilee	More than five hundred	1 Corinthians 15:6
Unknown	Brother James	1 Corinthians 15:7
Mount of Olives	Eleven disciples and others	Acts 1:4–12

what others say

Charles U. Wagner

Christ's first words to His disciples that Sunday evening were, "Peace be unto you." He could have chosen any greeting, but he recognized their need for peace. The source of peace is the Lord, and the basis of that peace is His death and resurrection.[6]

Sent to the World

JOHN 20:21–23 *So Jesus said to them again, "Peace to you! As the Father has sent Me, I also send you." And when He had said this, He breathed on them, and said to them, "Receive the Holy Spirit. If you forgive the sins of any, they are forgiven them; if you retain the sins of any, they are retained." (NKJV)*

Once more Jesus pronounced peace on the gathered disciples. Then he commissioned his followers to go into the world and tell people about his death and resurrection like the Father had sent him. They had deserted him after his arrest, let him die almost alone, and allowed the Jewish leaders to frighten them. Nevertheless, Jesus forgave them and gave them a job to do.

In order for them to have power to do that job, he breathed the Holy Spirit on them. This action is similar to when God breathed life into Adam when he created the first man. After Jesus went back to heaven and the Spirit came on the day of Pentecost, the Spirit would automatically come to live in people at the time of their salvation. But this was still a transition time.

Jesus did not give his followers the right to forgive sins. <u>Only God</u> can do that. What he did give his followers was the right to announce forgiveness based on a person's response to the message of salvation through Jesus.

only God
Mark 2:7

Show Me the Evidence

> JOHN 20:24–25 *Now Thomas, called the Twin, one of the twelve, was not with them when Jesus came. The other disciples therefore said to him, "We have seen the Lord." So he said to them, "Unless I see in His hands the print of the nails, and put my finger into the print of the nails, and put my hand into His side, I will not believe."* (NKJV)

For whatever reason, Thomas the twin missed the meeting when Jesus appeared to a group of his disciples in an upper room. When the other disciples kept telling him they had seen Jesus, he didn't believe them. He wanted to see physical evidence that Jesus really was alive and to put his hands in the nail holes and the side wound. Thomas insisted that he had to see the proof before he would believe in Jesus' resurrection. Actually, he wasn't any different than the other people who had been in that room. They had seen Jesus in the flesh, which is what Thomas wanted to do.

Repeat Appearance

> JOHN 20:26–27 *And after eight days His disciples were again inside, and Thomas with them. Jesus came, the doors being shut, and stood in the midst, and said, "Peace to you!" Then He said to Thomas, "Reach your finger here, and look at My hands; and reach your hand here, and put it into My side. Do not be unbelieving, but believing."* (NKJV)

A week later, the disciples were locked behind closed doors again, but this time Thomas was with them. Jesus appeared like he had the week before, suddenly standing in their midst without walking through the door like a normal person. His greeting was the same too: "Peace to you!" Then he showed Thomas the evidence he wanted—the nail holes in his hand and the wound in his side. The

faith
Romans 10:17

Lord invited his disciple to touch him in those spots. Jesus wanted Thomas to believe instead of doubting his resurrection.

> **what others say**
>
> **Lawrence O. Richards**
>
> What a blessing Thomas is to Christians everywhere. He reminds us that the skeptic is not rejected by God—that doubts and uncertainty do not lose us a place in God's kingdom. He reminds us too that Jesus willingly comes to us, to show us His hands and side, that we might believe.[7]

Made a Believer out of Me

> JOHN 20:28–29 *And Thomas answered and said to Him, "My Lord and my God!" Jesus said to him, "Thomas, because you have seen Me, you have believed. Blessed are those who have not seen and yet have believed."* (NKJV)

Thomas didn't need to touch the evidence of Jesus' scars that proved he was the same man who had died. Seeing Jesus was enough for him to blurt out, "My Lord and my God!" Thomas finally believed Jesus was who he said he was—God the Messiah who rose from the dead. He first had to see for himself, though.

In another month, no one else would be able to see Jesus face-to-face before believing in him. <u>Faith</u> is not dependent on sight, however. In fact, those who believe without seeing (that's us) are "blessed," or made happy.

> **what others say**
>
> **Erwin W. Lutzer**
>
> A Buddhist in Africa who was converted to Christianity was asked why he changed religions. He replied, "It's like this. If you were walking along and came to a fork in the road and two men were there and one was dead and the other alive, which man's directions would you follow?"[8]

Jesus didn't scold Thomas for doubting that he was alive and for wanting tangible proof of his resurrection. Instead, he met Thomas where he was at spiritually and provided the evidence Thomas thought he needed. Doubts from a searching heart, not a hard heart, are not sinful. We can take those doubts to Jesus in prayer and Bible reading and get answers.

Purpose Statement

JOHN 20:30–31 *And truly Jesus did many other signs in the presence of His disciples, which are not written in this book; but these are written that you may believe that Jesus is the Christ, the Son of God, and that believing you may have life in His name.* (NKJV)

Remember writing term papers and essays in high school or college? English teachers taught us to start a paper with a thesis or theme statement—a purpose statement. John had a clear purpose statement, although he stated it near the end of the book instead of at the beginning. These verses are the key verses for the book. They explain why John wrote this Gospel: so people who read it will believe that Jesus is God's Son and gain eternal life. John didn't record every miracle Jesus did. Instead, he selected the ones that clearly point to Jesus' deity. He told us all we need to know about Jesus so we can have eternal life.

key point

what others say

F. L. Godet

He [John] aims, not at knowledge, but at faith, and through faith at life. He is not a philosopher, but a witness; his work as a historian forms a part of his apostolic ministry. In all times, those who have not seen will be able through his testimony to reach the same faith and the same life as himself.[9]

Chapter Wrap-Up

- Mary Magdalene, Peter, and John discovered that Jesus was not in his tomb. (John 20:1–9)
- Mary talked with two angels in Jesus' tomb. (John 20:10–13)
- Jesus appeared to Mary at the tomb and told her to tell his disciples that he was alive. (John 20:14–18)
- Jesus appeared to a group of disciples locked in an upper room and commissioned them to tell others about himself. (John 20:19–23)
- Thomas refused to believe Jesus was alive until he touched his wounds. Jesus appeared to him and showed him his hands and side. As a result, Thomas believed. (John 20:24–29)
- John recorded selected miracles to prove Jesus is the Son of God so people who read this book will believe in Jesus. (John 20:30–31)

Study Questions

1. What did Mary expect when she went to Jesus' tomb on Sunday morning?

2. What did Peter and John see in the tomb?

3. What message did Jesus give Mary to take to his disciples?

4. How did Jesus convince the group of disciples gathered in the locked room that he was alive?

5. What did Jesus do for his disciples to give them power to tell others about him?

6. What did it take for Thomas to believe Jesus was risen from the dead?

7. What is John's purpose statement for this book?

John 21: Jesus the Commissioner

Let's Get Started

Undoubtedly you've heard or read them: speakers who say they are concluding, then go on for another fifteen to thirty minutes; friends who wrap up with "just one more thing" and talk about another half an hour; letter writers who add postscripts that are a page or two long.

purpose statement
John 20:30–31

As a writer, John fits that category of speakers and writers who don't know when to quit. Technically, his Gospel ended with chapter 20. John recorded enough of Jesus' appearances after his resurrection to let the world know he didn't stay dead. Then he wrapped up the book with his <u>purpose statement</u>.

Sometime later, John added an epilogue, a concluding section, which we have as chapter 21. He had several reasons for doing so. John hadn't mentioned Jesus' appearance to Peter, although Luke did. Without this epilogue, readers are left hanging as to Peter's relationship with Jesus after denying him three times the night of his arrest and trials. John filled in the details of Jesus' forgiveness of Peter and assignment to feed his sheep. John also recorded Jesus' prediction of Peter's death by crucifixion, which happened about twenty years before John wrote this book. Also, there was a rumor going around that John would not die before Jesus returned, so John wanted to refute it.

Follow the Fisherman

JOHN 21:1–3 *After these things Jesus showed Himself again to the disciples at the Sea of Tiberias, and in this way He showed Himself: Simon Peter, Thomas called the Twin, Nathanael of Cana in Galilee, the sons of Zebedee, and two others of His disciples were together. Simon Peter said to them, "I am going fishing." They said to him, "We are going with you also." They went out and immediately got into the boat, and that night they caught nothing. (NKJV)*

Galilee
Matthew 28:10

Jesus had risen from the dead and was appearing to his followers before returning to heaven. One of those appearances was to seven disciples—Peter, Thomas, Nathanael, brothers James and John (whose father was Zebedee), and two others—by the Sea of Tiberias (see Appendix A).

The disciples must have felt lost as to what to do next. Jesus had told them he would meet with them in <u>Galilee</u>, although he hadn't specified a date. They returned there and waited for him while he was out talking to others. With nothing on the agenda, Peter took the lead and announced he was going fishing. The others followed right behind him. Although night fishing generally was profitable, they caught nothing.

---

what others say

Anne Graham Lotz

Peter and the other disciples obeyed the Lord's instructions and went to Galilee where they waited for Jesus to join them. And they waited. And they waited. And they waited . . . Finally, impulsive, compulsive Peter had had enough! He was not the type to sit idly around, reading magazines, completing crossword puzzles, clipping coupons, watching ESPN, and just chilling out. He hated to wait. So he announced to the others, "I'm going out to fish." . . .

I wonder if Jesus delayed joining His disciples in Galilee on purpose in order to test their patience and obedient commitment to His call in their lives. If so, Peter failed the test. Because he returned to his old lifestyle.[1]

Full of Fish

JOHN 21:4–6 *But when the morning had now come, Jesus stood on the shore; yet the disciples did not know that it was Jesus. Then Jesus said to them, "Children, have you any food?" They answered Him, "No."*

And He said to them, "Cast the net on the right side of the boat, and you will find some." So they cast, and now they were not able to draw it in because of the multitude of fish. (NKJV)

After a wasted night of fishing, the disciples headed for shore. Standing there was a man they didn't recognize. Perhaps it was their tiredness, the early morning haze, the lack of light, or the fact that their minds were on fishing and they weren't expecting Jesus. (Also remember, people didn't always recognize him after the Resurrection. <u>Mary Magdalene</u>, for example, didn't.)

When they were about a hundred yards away, Jesus asked if they had caught any fish. They hadn't. So Jesus told them to throw the net over the starboard side. When they obeyed, the net filled up with so many fish they couldn't haul it in. This was not the first time this kind of <u>miracle</u> had happened to some of the disciples. In fact, it was a close rerun from the beginning of Jesus' ministry with the twelve disciples.

Mary Magdalene
John 20:14

miracle
Luke 5:1–11

evangelists
people who tell others about Jesus

what others say

Lawrence O. Richards

The net filled with fish was a promise. It was Jesus' way of saying, "Don't worry. I can and will continue to meet every material need." The disciples would soon set out on the most insecure of all lives: they would be traveling **evangelists**, dependent on others for their food and lodging. Though these skilled fishermen had practiced their trade all night, they had caught nothing. But a single word from Jesus filled their nets.[2]

Too often we're like these disciples, trying to do things in our own strength, making decisions without praying about them. It wasn't until Jesus told the disciples where to fish that they caught any. When we reach the end of our own resources, he is standing by to share his.

Breakfast on the Beach

JOHN 21:7–9 *Therefore that disciple whom Jesus loved said to Peter, "It is the Lord!" Now when Simon Peter heard that it was the Lord, he put on his outer garment (for he had removed it), and plunged into the sea. But the other disciples came in the little boat (for they were not far from land, but about two hundred cubits), dragging the net with fish. Then, as soon as they had come to land, they saw a fire of coals there, and fish laid on it, and bread. (NKJV)*

John was the first to recognize Jesus. It may have been the repeat catch of fish that did it. Or perhaps it was Jesus' voice. Whatever the reason, he turned to Peter and identified the man on shore as their Lord, or Master. When Peter heard that, he was so excited that he

appeared
Luke 24:34;
1 Corinthians 15:5

put on his robe and dove in to swim to shore. (If he'd been thinking clearly, he would have left the robe behind.)

Peter stepped out of the water, weighed down with dripping clothes. Although Jesus had already <u>appeared</u> privately to Peter and no doubt Peter had confessed his sin of denial and received forgiveness, the two of them may not have spent much time together. Maybe this was an awkward moment for Peter. Maybe he was embarrassed by the fact that he had gone fishing instead of waiting. Maybe he was just overjoyed to see his Lord and friend. We can only speculate.

While Peter stood there, the rest of the crew rowed or sailed in, dragging a net stuffed with fish. When they hit the beach, they noticed Jesus had built a campfire and was charbroiling fish for breakfast.

what others say

Max Lucado

Peter plunges into the water, swims to the shore, and stumbles out wet and shivering and stands in front of the friend he betrayed. . . . For one of the few times in his life, Peter is silent. What words would suffice? The moment is too holy for words. . . . What do you say at a moment such as this? It's just you and God. You and God both know what you did. And neither of you is proud of it. What do you do? You might consider doing what Peter did. Stand in God's presence. Stand in his sight. Stand still and wait. Sometimes that's all a soul can do.[3]

Mark Bailey and Tom Constable

The second mention of the charcoal fire (see 18:18) is appropriate for the scene when Jesus restored Peter. Peter had denied Him three times at the first fire and then affirmed his love for the Lord three times now at the second fire.[4]

Dragging the Net Behind

JOHN 21:10–11 *Jesus said to them, "Bring some of the fish which you have just caught." Simon Peter went up and dragged the net to land, full of large fish, one hundred and fifty-three; and although there were so many, the net was not broken.* (NKJV)

When Jesus asked for some of the freshly caught fish, Peter was the first one to volunteer to bring the miraculous catch ashore. John was careful to record the exact number of fish and to mention that they were large—truly an overabundance. The catch was so big that it should have torn the net, but it didn't. Only a fisherman would have been so impressed as to note those kinds of details. If Peter hauled that catch ashore, he wasn't a wimpy lightweight. That many fish, plus a wet net, weighed about three hundred pounds.

go to

five thousand
John 6:1–13

two times
John 20:19–23,
26–29

what others say

Earl F. Palmer

These men are fishermen, and when the fish are big you count them, especially if you are poor. The fact is that John likes to note details which other narrators would ignore.[5]

Breakfast Is Served

JOHN 21:12–14 *Jesus said to them, "Come and eat breakfast." Yet none of the disciples dared ask Him, "Who are You?"— knowing that it was the Lord. Jesus then came and took the bread and gave it to them, and likewise the fish. This is now the third time Jesus showed Himself to His disciples after He was raised from the dead. (NKJV)*

Before talking with Peter, Jesus met his physical needs. He gave him breakfast, time to dry off from his swim, a chance to warm up by the fire, and time to relax with a friend. Jesus was still caring for his disciples.

By this time, the disciples had all figured out the man on the beach was Jesus. As if to confirm his identity, he offered them bread and fish. They couldn't help but recall the feeding of the <u>five thousand</u> when Jesus multiplied bread and fish and used his disciples to pass the food out to the crowd.

John noted that this was the third time Jesus appeared to the disciples. The first <u>two times</u> were in the Upper Room.

what others say

Brenda Quinn

Peter has recently failed Jesus by denying him three times. Now Jesus gives him another chance, coming to meet with him, share a meal, and express concern three times over their relationship. Jesus' care for Peter sends the message that God's grace extends to believers even when we fail God in a big way. He forgives those who are sorry and genuinely love him.[6]

go to

denied
John 18:17, 25, 27

repented
Matthew 26:75

Peter's Assignment

JOHN 21:15–17 *So when they had eaten breakfast, Jesus said to Simon Peter, "Simon, son of Jonah, do you love Me more than these?" He said to Him, "Yes, Lord; You know that I love You." He said to him, "Feed My lambs." He said to him again a second time, "Simon, son of Jonah, do you love Me?" He said to Him, "Yes, Lord; You know that I love You." He said to him, "Tend My sheep." He said to him the third time, "Simon, son of Jonah, do you love Me?" Peter was grieved because He said to him the third time, "Do you love Me?" And he said to Him, "Lord, You know all things; You know that I love You." Jesus said to him, "Feed My sheep. (NKJV)*

After breakfast, Jesus revisited the subject of Peter's love for him. Peter had denied Jesus publicly. Now Jesus restored him to service publicly.

Before Jesus was crucified, Peter had boasted of his love for the Lord: "I will lay down my life for Your sake" (John 13:37 NKJV). Although he meant those words at the time, he didn't fully understand what he was saying. Nor did he live them under the pressure of Jesus' arrest. Instead, he <u>denied</u> he ever knew Jesus but later <u>repented</u> of his sin.

When Jesus had first called Peter to follow him, he had addressed him as "Simon the son of Jonah" (John 1:42 NKJV). Coming full circle, Jesus used the same name.

Peter had denied Jesus three times. It was no coincidence that Jesus asked Peter three times if he loved him and commissioned Peter three times to take care of God's people. Peter would have quickly made the association.

Jesus asked Peter if he loved him more than the other disciples did. Before Jesus was arrested, Peter had said he did: "Even if all are made to stumble because of You, I will never be made to stumble" (Matthew 26:33 NKJV). He had not been shy then about declaring his love for Jesus; he wasn't shy now. In a straightforward manner, with no comparisons with the other disciples, he readily affirmed his love for Jesus. By the third time, he was hurt that Jesus asked him again, but he got the message. So Jesus assigned him to feed—supply with the spiritual food of God's Word—and take care of his sheep. Peter's ministry would be feeding and shepherding God's children like Jesus had. His fishing career was over.

Many Bible students have emphasized the different Greek words Jesus and Peter used for the word *love*, one meaning sacrificial love and the other, friendship love. Since John used both words as synonyms throughout the book, it's better not to make fine distinctions.

Although the word *believe* is not used in this passage, the concept is. Jesus commanded those who believe in and love him to keep on following him.

Suppose you had been in Peter's sandals that morning on the beach after Jesus' resurrection. You're sitting around the fire, talking with Jesus, when he asks you, "Do you love me?" How would you answer him?

apply it

> ### what others say
>
> #### Anne Graham Lotz
>
> Jesus reached into Peter's heart and put His finger on Peter's motivation for service. Peter's motivation to live for Jesus and to serve Jesus was not to be . . . an attempt to stave off guilt, an attempt to earn forgiveness, an attempt to avoid criticism, an attempt to measure up to the opinions of others, an attempt to prove something to someone, an attempt to gain approval or recognition, an attempt to accumulate more good works than bad works.
>
> Peter's sole motivation in service was to be his love for Jesus, pure and simple. If he did love Jesus, even a little, his mission was to do something about it. He was to get involved in the lives of others.[7]

Following Jesus to the Death

JOHN 21:18–19 *Most assuredly, I say to you, when you were younger, you girded yourself and walked where you wished; but when you are old, you will stretch out your hands, and another will gird you and carry you where you do not wish." This He spoke, signifying by what death he would glorify God. And when He had spoken this, He said to him, "Follow Me." (NKJV)*

Peter had just gotten his life straightened out when Jesus leaped to the topic of his death. He indicated how serious and important it was by beginning with the statement "Most assuredly I say to you." In a picturesque way, he contrasted the end of Peter's ministry with

follow me
Matthew 4:18–19

leaned and asked
John 13:23–25

the beginning of it and went a step further to say how he would die. "Stretch out your hands" refers to being fastened to the horizontal beam of a cross.

Peter had already died when John wrote this book. According to Jerome, one of the early church fathers, Peter was crucified upside down because he thought he was unworthy to die the same way as Jesus.

Jesus ended his commission for Peter with the same words with which he had called him three years earlier: "Follow Me." The form of the command in the Greek means to keep on following. It's not a onetime step but a lifetime walk. A lot had happened to Peter between those two commands, some of which John recorded in this book. But the command didn't change, and Peter still had the rest of his life to obey it.

Jesus still commands believers to follow him. There are no conditions attached to this command. He didn't say, "Follow me if it's convenient for you." Or "Follow me if you feel like it." Or "Follow me if you don't get a better offer." Or "Follow me if you don't have anything else to do." Following Jesus is a way of life for the rest of our lives—no matter what.

What About Him?

> JOHN 21:20–21 *Then Peter, turning around, saw the disciple whom Jesus loved following, who also had leaned on His breast at the supper, and said, "Lord, who is the one who betrays You?" Peter, seeing him, said to Jesus, "But Lord, what about this man?"* (NKJV)

Peter must have heard someone walking behind him and turned to see that it was John, the author of this book. John identified himself by where he leaned and what he asked at the Passover dinner, rather than by name. Now that his job and destiny were settled, curious Peter wanted to know what would happen to John.

None of Your Business

> JOHN 21:22–23 *Jesus said to him, "If I will that he remain till I come, what is that to you? You follow Me." Then this saying went out among the brethren that this disciple would not die.*

——————— The Smart Guide to John ———————

Yet Jesus did not say to him that he would not die, but, "If I will that he remain till I come, what is that to you?" (NKJV)

Jesus told Peter to mind his own business. He needed to stay focused on Jesus, not on other people. Jesus' question started a rumor that John wouldn't die; he would live until Jesus returned to earth. That rumor was one reason John added this chapter to the book. Jesus didn't say John wouldn't die. It was none of Peter's business if John lived or died. He was responsible for following Jesus regardless of what happened to the other disciples.

go to

selected miracles
John 20:30–31

Yeshua
Jesus

what others say

David H. Stern

Yeshua rules out curiosity about matters that do not concern us or help us live a holy life, although he does not rule out scientific inquiry into how the world works. Likewise he excludes unhealthy, jealous competition concerned with comparing our lives, tasks, gifts, accomplishments, interests and calling with those of others. In both matters Yeshua's central point is: You, follow me![8]

The End

JOHN 21:24–25 *This is the disciple who testifies of these things, and wrote these things; and we know that his testimony is true. And there are also many other things that Jesus did, which if they were written one by one, I suppose that even the world itself could not contain the books that would be written. Amen. (NKJV)*

Greek, Roman, and Jewish legal documents ended with a testimony by witnesses. As John concluded this Gospel, he added his endorsement that what he wrote was true since he had been an eyewitness to the events. "We know that his testimony is true" may have been added by someone who was a contemporary of John. It was similar to a seal of approval. Since John was writing for the second generation of believers who didn't know Jesus personally and hadn't seen any of his miracles, this statement would have been important in judging the accuracy of his words.

But what John recorded in this one book was only a fraction of what Jesus did and said in three years. He had already written that he selected miracles that supported his purpose for writing. By the time John penned this book, there were three other **Gospels** in existence, each containing events the other writers omitted. We can read all the words Jesus spoke that are recorded in the four Gospels in about three hours. There is no question that Jesus said and did much more—so much that many more books could have been written.

John's book has ended, but Jesus' work continues today. If you want to find out what happened in the early years after his resurrection, read the Book of Acts.

what others say

John Calvin

Christ's majesty, because it is infinite, swallowed up (so to speak) both human understanding and heaven and earth as it demonstrated a miraculous display of its own splendor in those deeds. If the evangelist, looking at Christ's brightness, exclaims in astonishment that even the whole world does not have room for a complete narrative, who can be surprised?[9]

Chapter Wrap-Up

- Seven disciples met together. When Peter decided to go fishing, they went with him but didn't catch anything. (John 21:1–3)

- When the disciples followed Jesus' instructions, they caught a net full of fish. (John 21:4–11)

- Jesus invited his disciples to join him for breakfast on the beach. (John 21:12–14)

- Jesus restored Peter to service and assigned him the ministry of caring for believers. (John 21:15–19)

- When Peter wanted to know what would happen to John, Jesus told him it was none of his business. Then Jesus predicted Peter's death. (John 21:20–23)

- John concluded this book with a statement about its truthfulness since he was an eyewitness of the events. (John 21:24–25)

Study Questions

1. What did Peter lead the disciples to do while they were waiting for Jesus?

2. How did John recognize the man on shore as Jesus?

3. How did Jesus meet Peter's needs before talking with him about a serious subject?

4. Why did Jesus ask Peter the same question about loving him three times?

5. What ministry did Jesus assign Peter to do?

6. When Peter wanted to know what would happen to John, what did Jesus answer?

Appendix A—Map of Israel

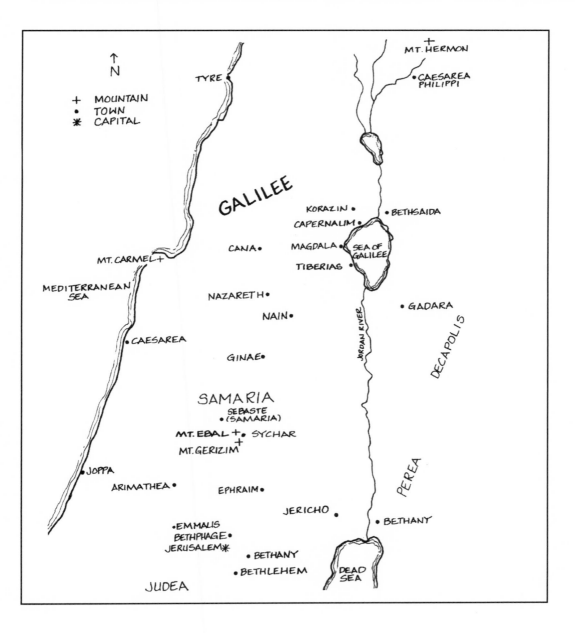

Appendix B—The Answers

JOHN 1: JESUS THE WORD

1. John described Jesus as the Word, as God, as the one who made all things. John also called Jesus life, the light of men, and the true light. (John 1:1–9)

2. John the Baptist was a witness to the light, but he wasn't the light. The passage also demonstrates John's willingness to let his own disciples follow Jesus, the one whom they were announcing. His whole point was to bring others to belief in the true light. (John 1:6–9, 35–39)

3. All who trust Jesus as a sacrifice for their sin become children of God—receiving him, believing on his name, reaching out and accepting the supernatural gift from God. (John 1:10–13)

4. Everything John the Baptist said pointed to Jesus. John testified of him, spoke of how Jesus surpassed him. He said, "I am not the Christ," and prepared the way for Jesus. (John 1:15–23, 29–31)

5. John and Andrew followed Jesus immediately. Then Andrew looked for Simon to tell him about Jesus. Philip answered Jesus by finding Nathanael and bringing him to Jesus. Their immediate response and contagious attitude demonstrated their belief in Jesus. (John 1:35–46)

JOHN 2: JESUS THE AUTHORITY

1. By telling Jesus that they had run out of wine, Mary demonstrated her understanding of his authority. She knew he wasn't only her son but was also the Son of God. By telling the servants, "Whatever He says to you, do it," she further pointed out her faith in Jesus. (John 2:3–5 NKJV)

2. Jesus responded first by distancing himself as her son and helping her transition from seeing him as her child to seeing him as the Messiah. (John 2:4–5)

3. Jesus changed the water into wine so his disciples as well as Mary would believe. The servants, too, also knew what he had done. (John 2:11)

4. Jesus drove all the animals and vendors out of the Temple with a whip, scattering money and overturning tables. He knew how much God longed to be with his people, and he was furious that the money changers kept the people from worshiping the God who loved them so much. (John 2:13–17)

5. Jesus answered them with the statement "Destroy this temple, and in three days I will raise it up" The Jews didn't understand and thought he was talking about the literal temple building. They missed the point entirely. (John 2:18–22 NKJV)

6. The people loved the miracles and professed to believe in Jesus as a result. However, Jesus didn't put much stock in their commitment. (John 2:23–25)

JOHN 3: JESUS THE CHOICE GIVER

1. Nicodemus had lived all his life knowing and teaching God's Word and keeping the rules. But now miracles were happening (though not in his life), and he needed to get some straight answers. Unfortunately, he got sidetracked with his literalism. (John 3:1–8)

2. We are born physically alive but spiritually dead. "Born again" means facing that death—the sin in our hearts—and repenting and letting God through Jesus Christ make us alive again. (John 3:3–8)

3. The new birth is supernatural and unseen, like the wind, but you see the impact of both. Birth helps us visualize the "new life" of the Spirit, and the snake pole shows the choice we have—to look to Jesus and live. (John 3:3–15)

4. He loved us so much that he didn't want us to die. We are his beloved creation! So he sent Jesus, his only Son, on a rescue mission. There was no other way. (John 3:16–18)

5. John joyfully cleared the path for Jesus. He happily saw his ministry and mission as decreasing. He fully acknowledged that Jesus was above all. (John 3:27–33)

JOHN 4: JESUS THE GIVER OF SPIRITUAL LIFE

1. Jewish people avoided Samaria, even though it meant a detour of many miles, because they loathed the Samaritans. For Jesus not only to go through Samaria but also to stop there was unheard of. Jews and Samaritans had been enemies for seven hundred years. (John 4:4–6)

2. "Living water" symbolizes eternal life, the soul-satisfying experience of life through Jesus. (John 4:10–15)

3. The woman didn't get it at first, but she wanted not to be thirsty: "Sir, give me this water, that I may not thirst, nor come here to draw." She was miserable enough with her life to want something to change. (John 4:13–15 NKJV)

4. Jesus was saying, in essence, "Open your eyes! There are people all around who need my love!" He used food as a way to broaden their understanding of ministry and God's love. (John 4:31–38)

5. The Samaritan woman went out and told the townspeople (people who despised her, rejected her, avoided her): "Come, see a Man who told me all things that I ever did." Many of them believed. (John 4:27–42 NKJV)

6. The official's faith was evidenced in his long walk. Jesus warned him about only believing because of miracles, then he healed the son long-distance. (John 4:48–53)

7. Jesus has power over distance. We don't have to see the miracle—or even the Son of God—to receive his healing love. (John 4:50–53)

JOHN 5: JESUS THE HEALER

1. They hoped a miracle might occur at those waters, and so they gathered there day after day. They were desperate for anything that might work. (John 5:1–3)

2. Dependency is a difficult lifestyle to break, especially after thirty-eight years. Jesus rightly challenged the man: How badly do you want to be healed? (John 5:6–8)

3. The Scriptures don't indicate how Jesus healed him, but it's clear from the man's obedience to Jesus' command that the healing was instantaneous. (John 5:6–8)

4. The Jewish leaders were upset about any healing they didn't perform. They were bent on punishing rule breakers, and this man had been healed on the Sabbath, when work was prohibited. (John 5:10–13)

5. He wanted the man to not only be healed physically but to be healed spiritually as well. Perhaps, too, he wanted to be sure that God received the glory for the healing. Jesus also knew that, when he sought out the man in the Temple, the man would both identify him and report him to the Jews and persecution would begin. (John 5:14–18)

6. He called God "My Father," implying a close and familiar connection, and he identified himself as the Son of God. He also said, essentially, that because God was always working, Jesus was always working, making himself the same as God. (John 5:14–18)

7. God, Moses, and John all testify about Jesus. (John 5:31–40, 45–47)

8. His final statement about Moses, whom the Jews revered, closed the case. The Jews knew very well that Moses testified about Jesus. (John 5:45–47)

JOHN 6: JESUS THE MIRACLE WORKER

1. The people were hungry for the miraculous. They followed him because they'd seen him do such dramatic miracles. (John 6:1–4)

2. Even though he was tired from the crowds and constant ministry, Jesus was gracious. He asked his disciples, "How can we buy food for these people?" (John 6:5–9)

3. This miracle made it clear that Jesus was more than your average lay preacher. The people believed after this that he was the Prophet they'd been waiting for. (John 6:14–15)

4. The people loved this miracle. They were so captivated by it that they wanted to make him king by force. (John 6:14–15)

5. When the disciples got halfway across the sea, a storm blew up quickly and violently. The frightened disciples rowed for several miles in the wind and waves. Then they saw Jesus walking across the water to them. He got in the boat, and immediately the boat reached shore. (John 6:16–21)

6. Jesus' walking on the water and bringing the boat ashore instantly proved he was the Lord—indeed, the Creator—of the wind and waves. He was not held back by material or natural things. (John 6:19–21)

7. Jesus let them know he saw through their flattery. They wanted the food he could provide. They wanted the miracles, not the life he was offering. (John 6:26–27) Furthermore, he clarified exactly what he offered: a deep soul satisfaction of their hunger and thirst. (John 6:35–40)

8. The people kept obsessing about the physical food, taking everything literally. As soon as Jesus said, "I am the bread that came down from heaven," they got caught up in the logistics. "Isn't this Joseph's son? "He can't be from heaven" (John 6:41–42). Even the disciples griped about it (John 6:60–65). Many of those professing to be his followers left after this teaching (John 6:67–71). To follow Jesus would require more faith than these people wanted to

invest. It's much easier to just have miracle food appear on your plate daily (John 6:67–71).

JOHN 7: JESUS THE DIVIDER

1. Jesus' brothers wanted him to make a grand entrance at the feast to prove that he was indeed the Messiah. "If you're real, then show yourself," they seemed to be saying. They, too, believed in the miracles but not in the man, the Son of God. (John 7:1–5)

2. Some people said Jesus was a good man; others said he was a deceiver (John 7:10–13). Some said he was demon-possessed (John 7:20–24). Many figured Jesus couldn't be the Messiah because they knew his parents, and they had decided the Messiah would just show up without a background (John 7:25–27).

3. The religious leaders saw Jesus as a lawbreaker (John 7:16–19). The people liked all the miracles but were not certain he was the Messiah, and the Jewish leaders were such tyrants that the people were afraid to take sides in public (John 7:10–13).

4. Jesus challenged people to check him out. He said that if you want to do God's will, you'll find out if his teaching comes from God or not. The true test is this: Whom do you honor with your teaching? Jesus didn't gain honor for himself through his teaching but gave honor to God. (John 7:16–19)

5. The Feast opened with the proclamation from Zechariah that living water would flow out from Jerusalem. When Jesus announced that he could quench their thirst and that living waters could flow out of them if they believed in him, he basically was saying, "I'm the one you've been waiting for! I'm the Messiah, the Christ, the fulfillment of the prophecy." (John 7:37–39)

6. The fact that Nicodemus stood up for Jesus indicates that his earlier conversation with Christ had taken root. As one of the Pharisees, Nicodemus knew the law and probably wanted to give Jesus a fair hearing. (John 7:50–53)

JOHN 8: JESUS THE FREEDOM GIVER

1. The religious leaders wanted to trap Jesus. The law demanded stoning for the sin of adultery. If Jesus condemned her to stoning, his teachings of mercy would be thrown in his face. If he let her go, the Jews would accuse him of disobeying God's Word. (John 8:3–8)

2. The leaders' attitude toward the woman was one of condemnation, but Jesus said, "Neither do I condemn you." He saw her as a child of God with sins as serious as everyone else's. He showed his love for her by forgiving her. (John 8:6–11 NKJV)

3. Jesus meant that he was God. The use of "I AM" made it clear, and the Jewish people understood both that statement and the use of the word "light." Light stood for God's holiness. (John 8:12)

4. Jesus knew that something was proved by two witnesses, so he used himself and his Father. (John 8:13–18)

5. Knowing the truth sets us free. (John 8:31–32)

6. Because children follow their fathers. If the Jews were in fact Abraham's children, then they would be doing the things Abraham did, not trying to kill Jesus (John 8:39–41). Besides that, Abraham rejoiced at the thought of the coming Messiah (John 8:54–56).

7. Jesus said their father was the devil, a murderer and a liar. They proved that relationship because they wanted to kill Jesus. (John 8:42–44)

8. At Jesus' last words, "I am," when he again equated himself with God, the Jews picked up rocks to stone him. Making oneself equal to God was blasphemy, deserving of death. (John 8:57–59)

JOHN 9: JESUS THE SIGHT GIVER

1. The disciples wanted to figure out who was to blame for the man's blindness. Was it because he sinned or because his parents sinned? (John 9:1–2)

2. The man's blindness was more about displaying God's glory than about the man's problem or even his sin. His life could become a place where God's work was displayed. (John 9:3–5)

3. He made mud out of dirt and saliva, packed it on the man's eyes, and told him to go and wash in the Pool of Siloam. (John 9:6–7)

4. The people were upset, disturbed, and critical of the healer. Their questioning of the man showed no joy or thankfulness, only prodding about Jesus. The fact that Jesus had healed on the Sabbath again became an issue. (John 9:8–12)

5. The man just told the facts: He put mud on my eyes; I washed; now I see. (John 9:13–15)

6. Jesus had freed the man from a lifetime of blindness. He credited the healing to God and told the Pharisees, "He is a prophet." (John 9:16–17). Later, the man argued that someone with sin couldn't have done such a miracle, so Jesus had to be from God. (John 9:30–34).

7. Jesus knew the man had stood up for him and was being persecuted by the Pharisees. He

wanted to solidify the man's experience with fact. So he introduced himself as the Son of Man, giving the former blind man a chance to believe and worship him. (John 9:35–38)

8. When Jesus said he was the Son of Man, the former blind man instantly responded, "Lord, I believe!" and worshiped Jesus. (John 9:35–38)

9. Because the Pharisees claimed they could see, Jesus told them they were guilty. The truly blind, who acknowledge they have no sight, are given spiritual sight by believing in Jesus. The Pharisees, with their self-righteousness, couldn't acknowledge any spiritual lack and thus condemned themselves to blindness. (John 9:39–41)

JOHN 10: JESUS THE GOOD SHEPHERD

1. The sheep Jesus is talking about are all who belong to him, who listen to his voice. (John 10:4–6)

2. The shepherd is Jesus. (John 10:11)

3. The thieves and robbers are all the religious leaders who came before Jesus, pretending to lead the people. (John 10:7–8)

4. A good shepherd would literally die to keep his sheep safe. Jesus, good from the inside out, would ultimately lay down his life for his sheep. (John 10:11)

5. Jesus is a gate, in that anyone who enters into relationship with God through him will be saved. (John 10:9–10)

6. People follow Jesus, the Good Shepherd, because they know his voice, recognize the love in his voice, and know he wants only good for them. (John 10:14–16)

7. The Jewish leaders wanted to know if Jesus were truly the Christ. "Tell us plainly." (John 10:22–24)

8. Jesus answered by saying he'd already told them, and they wouldn't believe. They didn't recognize his voice because they weren't his sheep. (John 10:25–26)

9. Jesus' response did not go over well with the leaders. They picked up stones to stone him with, not because of the miracles, but because he claimed to be God. (John 10:31–39)

JOHN 11: JESUS THE RESURRECTION AND THE LIFE

1. Jesus wanted, again, to be sure that God got the glory in the Lazarus situation. (John 11:3–4)

2. Martha told Jesus that Lazarus wouldn't have died if he'd gotten there sooner. But her faith seemed intact because she added, "I know that God will give you whatever you ask." (John 11:21–22)

3. Jesus is the one who has power over both life and death. His statement, "I am," again made him equal with God, the Life-giver. He gives eternal life and raises us from spiritual death. (John 11:25–27)

4. Jesus was deeply moved at Mary's grief. Troubled, he wept over Lazarus's death. Jesus mourned with Mary. (John 11:33–35)

5. He prayed, gave God glory and thanks, and called Lazarus to come out of the tomb. (John 11:41–44)

6. Once again, Jesus' miracles produced a divided camp. Some of the people believed in him and put their faith in him. Others, however, went tattling to the Pharisees. Those religious leaders felt terribly threatened and called a meeting of the Sanhedrin, which would sentence Jesus to die. (John 11:45–53)

JOHN 12: JESUS THE KING WHO WILL DIE

1. Mary took a container of expensive perfume and poured it on Jesus' feet, then wiped them with her hair because her heart overflowed with love for him (John 12:3). This was an act of worship and also a means of preparing Jesus' body for burial (John 12:7–8).

2. Judas had a different response than Jesus, who accepted her love gift. Judas, who kept the money bag, jealously asked, "Shouldn't we have sold this and [wink, wink] given the money to the poor?" John makes it clear that Judas dipped into the reserves when he wanted money. (John 12:4–6)

3. The crowd rushed out to greet Jesus with palm branches and loud praises, shouting "Hosanna! Blessed is He who comes in the name of the LORD! The King of Israel!" They wanted to make him their literal, political, reigning king. (John 12:12–13)

4. Jesus rode into the city on a donkey to fulfill the prophecy that the king would come on a donkey as a servant. The people expected him to ride in on a huge horse or in a chariot, as befitted an earthly king. (John 12:14–15)

5. If we want to gain our lives, we must give them over to God's care, trusting him with all that we are and have. When we let go of our own lives and focus on God's priorities, God takes over and grants us eternal life. (John 12:23–26)

6. The Jews didn't expect a king who would die; they knew that the Messiah would live forever. So when Jesus said he would be lifted up (die), they didn't get it. (John 12:34)

JOHN 13: JESUS THE SERVANT

1. During the Passover dinner, Jesus took the role

of a servant by washing the disciples' feet to demonstrate humility. (John 13:1–5)

2. When Peter protested about getting his feet washed, Jesus confronted him with the truth that he must be cleansed to be united with him. (John 13:6–10)

3. By washing the disciples' feet, Jesus taught that his followers need to receive cleansing from sin and that they must reflect his lifestyle of humble servanthood. (John 13:12–17)

4. Upon hearing that one of them would betray Jesus, the disciples were stunned and began to question which one of them would be the traitor. (John 13:22–25)

5. Jesus said that the mark of his followers would be the quality of their love for one another, which reflected his unconditional, humble, and sacrificial love. (John 13:34–35)

6. Jesus predicted that Peter would betray him by disowning him three times before the rooster crowed. (John 13:37–38)

JOHN 14: JESUS THE COMFORTER

1. After Jesus leaves the earth, he will prepare a place in heaven for his followers and then return to bring them to their eternal dwelling place with him. (John 14:1–4)

2. As he spoke with Thomas, Jesus described himself as "the way, the truth, and the life." Jesus explained that anyone who has seen him has seen the Father. (John 14:5–7)

3. Jesus' followers will do greater works than he did by reflecting his power and greatness while being weak, sinful humans. Through the Holy Spirit, the number and extent of his workings in his followers will be greater than what he did alone on earth. (John 14:12–14)

4. We prove we love Jesus by obeying his commands and receiving his Holy Spirit to continually teach us his truths. (John 14:15–17)

5. Jesus said he would send his Holy Spirit when he went back to heaven. The Holy Spirit is our Helper, Comforter, and the Spirit of truth. (John 14:16–17)

6. The kind of peace that Jesus gives his followers is directly and uniquely from him, confident of God's care and not dependent on situations. His peace includes wholeness and fulfillment because it is a fruit of a relationship with God through Jesus. (John 14:27)

JOHN 15: JESUS THE VINE

1. Jesus used an object familiar to the disciples—the vine—to describe his relationship with them. He called himself the "true vine." God the Father is the vinedresser, and believers are the branches. (John 15:1–2)

2. When we abide in Jesus, we produce the fruit of his character. As we become more and more like him, we realize our utter dependency on him. (John 15:4–6)

3. To be sure we are productive, God "prunes" us like a gardener who cuts back the vine. God's "pruning" removes anything that hinders his life from bearing fruit in our lives. (John 15:1–2)

4. Jesus calls his disciples friends because he entrusted his followers with everything he learned from his Father and also because he desires a loving, intimate bond with his followers. (John 15:14–15)

5. Jesus told his followers to expect the world's hatred, persecution, and rejection toward them after he was gone. (John 15:18–19)

JOHN 16: JESUS THE TEACHER

1. People who believe in Jesus can expect to be persecuted because those who reject Jesus may think that they are righteous in rejecting, harming, or even killing his followers. Jesus was not spared from persecution, so his followers will not be spared either. (John 16:1–3)

2. The Helper will aid believers and convict unbelievers in relation to sin, righteousness, and judgment. (John 16:8–11)

3. After Jesus returns to heaven, the Spirit of truth will help believers understand God's Word and know Jesus with an increasing passion. (John 16:12–15)

4. When Jesus taught that he was going away, his disciples questioned each other about what he meant because they did not understand. (John 16:16–18)

5. Asking in Jesus' name means requesting what Jesus desires in order to serve and honor God. This involves bringing God a yielded and moldable heart. (John 16:23–24)

6. Jesus' followers can be sure of having peace because Jesus promised them his peace and because he is victorious over everything that may attempt to cause a troubled heart. (John 16:33)

JOHN 17: JESUS THE PRAY-ER

1. As Jesus prayed, his main request for himself was that he would glorify the Father. (John 17:1–2)

2. Jesus defined eternal life as intimately knowing God and himself. He explained that through this relationship eternal life can be experienced on earth as well as in heaven after death. (John 17:3–5)

3. Jesus prayed for his disciples to be protected by the power of God's name and to be closely united with God. He also prayed that the disciples would be filled with his joy and be set apart for daily walking with God and fulfilling his purposes. (John 17:11–19)

4. Jesus asked the Father that future believers would be unified in love with a close bond similar to the oneness he and the Father shared. (John 17:20–23)

5. Jesus called God "righteous Father" to express that God is sinless and that his children must approach him with reverence through knowing Jesus. (John 17:25–26)

JOHN 18: JESUS THE PRISONER

1. Judas showed up with a group of priests and temple police to arrest Jesus. (John 18:2–3)

2. Jesus showed he was in control of his arrest when he identified himself with God's name, "I am." Jesus also revealed his divine authority when he healed Malchus's ear after Peter had cut it off. (John 18:4–6, 10–11)

3. When Peter was questioned about his association with Jesus, he denied being one of his disciples. (John 18:17–18)

4. Jesus told Annas to question the people he had taught in public. By doing so, Annas would then know more about Jesus' teachings, which were not secret. (John 18:19–21)

5. The religious leaders took Jesus to Pilate because, as the Roman governor, Pilate was the only one who could order the death sentence. (John 18:28–29)

6. When Pilate questioned Jesus privately, he learned that Jesus was a king. However, Pilate didn't understand that Jesus' kingdom was a spiritual one rather than a political one. (John 18:33–37)

7. When Pilate offered to release a prisoner, the Jewish people chose Barabbas, a criminal who had been arrested for murder and rebellion against the government. (John 18:38–40)

JOHN 19: JESUS THE SACRIFICE

1. The soldiers mocked Jesus by jamming a crown of thorns on his head, clothing him in a purple robe, and calling him "King of the Jews." (John 19:1–3)

2. They said Jesus claimed to be the Son of God and a king who opposed Caesar. (John 19:7, 12)

3. Pilate's power came from God, who chose to give that power to him. (John 19:11)

4. Pilate identified him in three languages as "JESUS OF NAZARETH, THE KING OF THE JEWS." (John 19:19)

5. Jesus entrusted his mother to John's care as though John were her real son. (John 19:26–27)

6. Joseph of Arimathea and Nicodemus, two secret disciples, handled Jesus' burial. They got permission from Pilate to take the body off the cross, then they wrapped it in spices and linen strips and buried it in Joseph's tomb. (John 19:38–42)

JOHN 20: JESUS THE RISEN LORD

1. Mary expected to see Jesus' dead body in the tomb. (John 20:1–2)

2. Peter and John saw strips of linen in the shape of a body as though Jesus was beamed out of them. (John 20:5–8)

3. Jesus told Mary to tell his disciples that he was alive and would return to his Father. (John 20:17)

4. Jesus appeared to his disciples without walking through the door, and he showed them his wounded hands and feet. (John 20:19–20)

5. Jesus breathed the Holy Spirit on them. (John 20:22)

6. Thomas had to see Jesus for himself. He also wanted to put his finger in the nail holes in Jesus' hands and put his hand in the wound in Jesus' side. (John 20:25, 27–28)

7. John wrote this book to encourage people to believe in Jesus. (John 20:31)

JOHN 21: JESUS THE COMMISSIONER

1. Peter led the other disciples to go fishing. (John 21:3)

2. John probably recognized the man as Jesus because the miracle of the fish was similar to one Jesus had performed before. (John 21:5–7)

3. Jesus fed Peter breakfast and gave him time to dry off and warm up by the fire. (John 21:9, 12–13)

4. Jesus asked Peter if he loved him three times because Peter had denied him three times. (John 18:17, 25, 27)

5. Jesus assigned Peter to feed and take care of his "sheep," the people who believed in him. (John 21:15–17)

6. Jesus told him to mind his own business and follow him. (John 21:22)

The Experts

Bailey, Mark—Associate professor of Bible exposition, vice president of academia, and dean of faculty at Dallas Theological Seminary.

Barclay, William—Minister of Trinity Church, Renfrew, Scotland, professor of divinity and biblical criticism at the University of Glasgow, and author of numerous commentaries.

Barton, Bruce B.—Editor of the *Life Application Bible Commentary* series.

Beasley-Murray, George R.—Principal of Spurgeon's College of London, professor of New Testament interpretation at Southern Baptist Theological Seminary, Louisville, Kentucky.

Blackaby, Henry—Best-selling author and speaker, and special consultant to the presidents of the North American Mission Board and LifeWay Christian Resources of the Southern Baptist Convention.

Blum, Edwin A.—Associate professor of historical theology at Dallas Theological Seminary.

Boice, James Montgomery—Former pastor of the Tenth Presbyterian Church in Philadelphia and speaker on the "Bible Study Hour," and author of numerous commentaries.

Borchert, Gerald L.—Professor of New Testament interpretation at Southern Baptist Theological Seminary, Louisville, Kentucky, and author of several books.

Bruce, F. F.—Former Rylands professor of biblical criticism and exegesis at Manchester University, England, and author of numerous books and commentaries.

Buksbazen, Victor—Former missionary, commentator, and author.

Burge, Gary M.—Professor of New Testament at Wheaton College.

Calvin, John—One of the Reformation's most influential Bible teachers and author of commentaries on most of the Bible books.

Carson, D. A.—Professor of New Testament at Trinity Evangelical Divinity School, Deerfield, Illinois, and author of numerous books.

Constable, Tom—Department chairman and senior professor of Bible exposition at Dallas Theological Seminary.

Fredrikson, Roger L.—Retired pastor of First Baptist Church, Wichita, Kansas.

Garland, David E.—Professor of New Testament at Southern Baptist Theological Seminary.

Geldenhuys, Norval—Former minister in South Africa and director of publications of the Reformed Church of South Africa in Cape Town.

Glaser, Mitch and Zhava—Mitch is minister-at-large for Jews for Jesus, San Francisco, California, and Zhava has served as a Jews for Jesus missionary.

Glasscock, Ed—Vice president of academics and director of biblical studies at Southeastern Bible College, Birmingham, Alabama.

Godet, F. L.—Swiss theologian in the 1800s, professor of New Testament in the University of Neuchâtel. Louis Goldberg—Former pastor and professor of Jewish studies and Bible/theology at Moody Bible Institute, currently serving with Jews for Jesus.

Gutzke, Manford George—Author of two dozen books in the *Plain Talk Bible* commentary series.

Harrison, Everett F.—Professor emeritus of New Testament at Fuller Theological Seminary and collaborator on various theological works.

Hendriksen, William—Pastor emeritus of the Creston Christian Reformed Church in Grand Rapids, Michigan, and former professor of New Testament literature at Calvin Seminary.

Henry, Matthew—Seventeenth century biblical expositor, expelled from the Church of England in 1662; Puritan, Presbyterian pastor, author of multivolume Bible commentary still used today.

Hiebert, D. Edmond—Former professor of Greek and New Testament at Mennonite Brethren Biblical Seminary, Fresno, California.

Hobbs, Herschel H.—Past president of the Southern Baptist Convention, speaker on the "Baptist Hour" radio program, and former pastor.

Hughes, R. Kent—Senior pastor of College Church, Wheaton, Illinois, and author of several books.

Jeremiah, David—Pastor of Shadow Mountain Community Church in San Diego, California, and speaker on the "Turning Point" radio program.

Keener, Craig S.—Professor of New Testament at Hood Theological Seminary, Salisbury, North Carolina, and author of several books.

Keller, Phillip—Best-selling author who spent many years as a shepherd and agricultural researcher.

Kent, Homer A., Jr.—Former president and professor of New Testament and Greek at Grace Theological

Seminary, Winona Lake, Indiana, and author of several books and commentaries.

Köstenberger, Andreas J.—Professor of New Testament and Director of Ph.D./Th.M. studies at Southeastern Baptist Theological Seminary.

Laney, J. Carl—Professor of biblical literature at Western Conservative Baptist Seminary, Portland, Oregon, and the author of numerous commentaries and other books.

Lewis, C. S.—Former writer, scholar, and lecturer at Oxford and Cambridge universities.

Little, Paul—Served with InterVarsity Christian Fellowship for twenty-five years and former associate professor of evangelism at Trinity Evangelical Divinity School, Deerfield, Illinois.

Lotz, Anne Graham—Evangelist, author of several books, and founder of AnGel Ministries.

Lucado, Max—Pastor of Oak Hills Church of Christ in Texas and best-selling author and speaker on the radio program "UpWords."

Luther, Martin—Father of the German Reformation. Erwin W. Lutzer—Senior pastor of Moody Church in Chicago, speaker, and author of numerous books.

MacArthur, John, Jr.—Pastor of Grace Community Church, Sun Valley, California, speaker on "Grace to You" radio program, and popular author and conference speaker.

MacLaren, Alexander—One of Britain's most famous preachers in the late 1800s, known as the "prince of expository preachers."

McDowell, Josh—Internationally known speaker, author, and traveling representative for Campus Crusade for Christ.

McGee, J. Vernon—Former radio broadcaster for "Thru the Bible," as well as teacher, speaker, author of numerous books, and pastor.

Milne, Bruce—Minister of First Baptist Church, Vancouver, British Columbia.

Morris, Leon—Former president of Ridley College in Melbourne, Australia, and author of numerous books and commentaries.

Myers, Bill—Award-winning writer/director for TV and film, youth worker, author of numerous books.

Myers, Ruth—Staff member with the Navigators.

Pentecost, J. Dwight—Professor of Bible exposition at Dallas Theological Seminary and author of several books, primarily dealing with prophecy.

Pink, Arthur W.—Former conference speaker, pastor, and author of various books on Bible exposition.

Quinn, Brenda—Staff editor for Serendipity House and editorial coordinator for MOPS International, Inc.

Richards, Lawrence O. (Larry)—General editor for *The Bible Smart Guides*™ series and author of more than 175 books, including Christian education, Bible, theology, and devotional works.

Richards, Sue—Wife of Larry; retired English teacher and women's Bible study teacher in her church.

Ridenour, Fritz—Youth editor for Gospel Light curriculum.

Scroggie, W. Graham—Pastor of several churches in England and Scotland.

Spurgeon, Charles H.—London's most popular preacher in the 1800s.

Stalker, James M.—Scottish scholar, pastor, and professor of church history in the United Free Church College, Aberdeen.

Stern, David H.—Messianic Jew living in Jerusalem, author of several books, former professor at Fuller Theological Seminary, and former officer of the Messianic Jewish Alliance of America.

Tasker, R. V. G.—Former dean of faculty of theology, King's College, University of London, professor of New Testament exegesis, and author of several books.

Tassell, Paul N.—Former national representative of the General Association of Regular Baptist Churches and author of several books.

Taylor, Hudson—Pioneer missionary to China and founder of the China Inland Mission.

Tenney, Merrill C.—Professor emeritus of Bible and theology and former dean of the graduate school at Wheaton College.

Wagner, Charles U.—A prolific author with more than thirty years of pastoral experience and past president of Grand Rapids Baptist College and Seminary, Grand Rapids, Michigan.

Whitelaw, Thomas—Former Scottish minister and biblical scholar.

Wiersbe, Warren W.—Writer-in-residence at Cornerstone College in Grand Rapids, Michigan, distinguished professor of preaching at Grand Rapids Baptist Seminary, and author of numerous books.

Yancey, Philip—Editor-at-large for *Christianity Today* and award-winning author of numerous books.

Witherington III, Ben—Professor of New Testament Interpretation at Asbury Theological Seminary.

To the best of our knowledge, all of the above information is correct. We were unable to obtain information for those experts that are missing.

—The Editors

Endnotes

Introduction

1. Merrill C. Tenney, *New Testament Survey* (Grand Rapids, MI: Wm. B. Eerdmans Publishing Co., 1961), 185.

2. Warren W. Wiersbe, *Be Alive* (Colorado Springs: ChariotVictor Books, 1986), 10.

John 1: Jesus the Word

1. Lawrence O. Richards, *Victor Bible Background Commentary* (Wheaton, IL: Victor Books, 1994), 212.

2. Manford George Gutzke, *Plain Talk on John*(Grand Rapids, MI: Zondervan Publishing House, 1968), 12–13.

3. J. Dwight Pentecost, *The Words and Works of Jesus Christ* (Grand Rapids, MI: Zondervan Publishing House, 1981), 30.

4. Leon Morris, *The Gospel According to John* (Grand Rapids, MI: Wm. B. Eerdmans Publishing Co., 1971), 90.

5. Ibid., 96.

6. Merrill C. Tenney, *John: The Gospel of Belief* (Grand Rapids, MI: Wm. B. Eerdmans Publishing Co., 1976), 70.

7. Edwin A. Blum, "John" in *The Bible Knowledge Commentary*, vol. 2: New Testament, eds. John F. Walvoord and Roy B. Zuck (Wheaton, IL: Victor Books, 1983), 273.

8. Warren W. Wiersbe, *Be Alive* (Colorado Springs: ChariotVictor Books, 1986), 15.

9. James Montgomery Boice, *The Gospel of John*, vol. 1 (Grand Rapids, MI: Zondervan Publishing House, 1975), 127–28.

10. William Barclay, *The Gospel of John*, vol. 1, rev. ed. (Philadelphia: Westminster Press, 1975), 87–88.

John 2: Jesus the Authority

1. Warren W. Wiersbe, *Be Alive* (Colorado Springs: ChariotVictor Books, 1986), 24–25.

2. Craig S. Keener, *The IVP Bible Background Commentary: New Testament* (Downers Grove, IL: InterVarsity Press, 1993), 268.

3. D. Edmond Hiebert, *An Introduction to the New Testament*, vol. 1: *The Gospels and Acts* (Chicago: Moody Press, 1975), 227–28.

4. William Hendriksen, *The Gospel of John* (Grand Rapids, MI: Baker Book House, 1953), 122.

5. D. A. Carson, *The Gospel According to John* (Grand Rapids, MI: Wm. B. Eerdmans Publishing Co., 1991), 180–81.

6. Wiersbe, *Be Alive*, 32.

John 3: Jesus the Choice Giver

1. Manford George Gutzke, *Plain Talk on John* (Grand Rapids, MI: Zondervan Publishing House, 1968), 32.

2. Philip Yancey and Brenda Quinn, *Meet the Bible* (Grand Rapids, MI: Zondervan Publishing House, 2000), 420.

3. Craig S. Keener, *The IVP Bible Background Commentary: New Testament* (Downers Grove, IL: InterVarsity Press, 1993), 270.

4. Bill Myers, *Jesus: An Eyewitness Account* (Wheaton, IL: Victor Books, 1988), 26.

5. Leon Morris, *The Gospel According to John* (Grand Rapids, MI: Wm. B. Eerdmans Publishing Co., 1971), 231.

6. William Barclay, The Gospel of John, vol. 1, rev. ed. (Philadelphia: Westminster Press, 1975), 141.

7. R. V. G. Tasker, *The Gospel According to St. John* (Grand Rapids, MI: Wm. B. Eerdmans Publishing Co., 1960), 73.

John 4: Jesus the Giver of Spiritual Life

1. Bruce Milne, *The Message of John* (Downers Grove, IL: InterVarsity Press, 1993), 83.

2. Philip Yancey and Brenda Quinn, *Meet the Bible* (Grand Rapids, MI: Zondervan Publishing House, 2000), 424.

3. Paul N. Tassell, *That Ye Might Believe* (Schaumburg, IL: Regular Baptist Press, 1987), 40–41.

4. Anne Graham Lotz, *Just Give Me Jesus* (Nashville: Word Publishing, 2000), 110.

5. Max Lucado, ed., *The Inspirational Study Bible: The Gospel of John* (Nashville: Word Publishing, 1994), 7.

6. Craig S. Keener, *The IVP Bible Background Commentary: New Testament* (Downers Grove, IL: InterVarsity Press, 1993), 274.

7. Henry Blackaby, *Experiencing the Word Through the Gospels* (Nashville: Holman Bible Publishers, 1999), 222.

8. Matthew Henry, *Matthew Henry's Commentary on the Whole Bible*, vol. 4: *Matthew to John* (McLean, VA: MacDonald Publishing Co., 1721), 915–16.

9. Erwin W. Lutzer, *Seven Convincing Miracles* (Chicago: Moody Press, 1999), 72.

John 5: Jesus the Healer

1. Anne Graham Lotz, *Just Give Me Jesus* (Nashville: Word Publishing, 2000), 117.

2. R. Kent Hughes, *Behold the Lamb* (Wheaton, IL: Victor Books, 1984), 94–95.

3. Dana Gould, ed., *Shepherd's Notes: John* (Nashville: Broadman & Holman, 1998), 31.

4. Leon Morris, *The Gospel According to John* (Grand Rapids, MI: Wm. B. Eerdmans Publishing Co., 1971), 309.

5. Roger L. Fredrikson, *The Communicator's Commentary: John* (Dallas: Word Publishing, 1985), 117.

6. Paul Little, *How to Give Away Your Faith* (Downers Grove, IL: InterVarsity Press, 1988), 131.

John 6: Jesus the Miracle Worker

1. Erwin W. Lutzer, *Seven Convincing Miracles* (Chicago: Moody Press, 1999), 109.

2. Ibid., 126.

3. Herschel H. Hobbs, *An Exposition of the Four Gospels* (Grand Rapids, MI: Baker Book House, 1968), 129.

4. Warren W. Wiersbe, *Be Alive* (Colorado Springs: ChariotVictor Books, 1986), 73–74.

5. Lawrence O. Richards, *The 365-Day Devotional Commentary* (Wheaton, IL: Victor Books, 1990), 773.

6. W. Graham Scroggie, *The Gospel of John* (London: Pickering and Inglis Ltd., 1976), 45.

7. Bruce B. Barton, ed., *Life Application Bible Commentary: John* (Wheaton, IL: Tyndale House Publishers, 1993), 131.

8. Philip Yancey and Brenda Quinn, *Meet the Bible* (Grand Rapids, MI: Zondervan Publishing House, 2000), 474–75.

9. D. A. Carson, *The Gospel According to John* (Grand Rapids, MI: Wm. B. Eerdmans Publishing Co., 1991), 295.

10. James Montgomery Boice, *The Gospel of John*, vol. 2 (Grand Rapids, MI: Zondervan Publishing House, 1976), 219.

John 7: Jesus the Divider

1. J. Vernon McGee, *John Chapters 1–10* (Nashville: Thomas Nelson Publishers, 1991), 119.

2. John Calvin, *John* (Wheaton, IL: Crossway Books, 1994), 183–84.

3. J. Carl Laney, *Moody Gospel Commentary: John* (Chicago: Moody Press, 1991), 141.

4. F. F. Bruce, *The Gospel of John* (Grand Rapids, MI: Wm. B. Eerdmans Publishing Co., 1983), 177.

5. Mitch and Zhava Glaser, *The Fall Feasts of Israel* (Chicago: Moody Press, 1987), 179.

John 8: Jesus the Freedom Giver

1. Bill Myers, *Jesus: An Eyewitness Account* (Wheaton, IL: Victor Books, 1988), 63–64.

2. Everett F. Harrison, *John: The Gospel of Faith* (Chicago: Moody Press, 1962), 52.

3. David H. Stern, *Jewish New Testament Commentary* (Clarksville, MD: Jewish New Testament Publications, 1992), 181.

4. Dana Gould, ed., *Shepherd's Notes: John* (Nashville: Broadman & Holman, 1998), 44.

5. Ibid., 46.

6. Charles U. Wagner, *This Is Life* (Schaumburg, IL: Regular Baptist Press, 1981), 46.

7. James Montgomery Boice, *The Gospel of John*, vol. 2 (Grand Rapids, MI: Zondervan Publishing House, 1976), 365.

8. George R. Beasley-Murray, *Word Biblical Commentary: John* (Nashville: Thomas Nelson Publishers, 1999), 139.

John 9: Jesus the Sight Giver

1. Roger L. Fredrikson, *The Communicator's Commentary: John* (Dallas: Word Publishing, 1985), 168.

2. Anne Graham Lotz, *Just Give Me Jesus* (Nashville: Word Publishing, 2000), 188.

3. Everett F. Harrison, *John: The Gospel of Faith* (Chicago: Moody Press, 1962), 58–59.

4. Gerald L. Borchert, *The New American Commentary* (Nashville: Broadman & Holman, 1996), 321.

5. R. V. G. Tasker, *The Gospel According to St. John* (Grand Rapids, MI: Wm. B. Eerdmans Publishing Co., 1960), 125.

6. Andreas J. Köstenberger, *John* (Grand Rapids, MI: Baker Academic, 2004), 295.

7. Erwin W. Lutzer, *Seven Convincing Miracles* (Chicago: Moody Press, 1999), 152, 154.

John 10: Jesus the Good Shepherd

1. Phillip Keller, *A Shepherd Looks at the Good Shepherd and His Sheep* (Grand Rapids, MI: Zondervan Publishing House, 1978), 169.

2. Manford George Gutzke, *Plain Talk on John* (Grand Rapids, MI: Zondervan Publishing House, 1968), 109.

3. Philip Yancey and Brenda Quinn, *Meet the Bible* (Grand Rapids, MI: Zondervan Publishing House, 2000), 483.

4. Matthew Henry, *Matthew Henry's Commentary on the Whole Bible*, vol. 4: Matthew to John (McLean, VA: MacDonald Publishing Co., 1721), 1032.

5. William Barclay, *The Gospel of John*, vol. 2, rev. ed. (Philadelphia: Westminster Press, 1975), 63.

6. Louis Goldberg, *Our Jewish Friends* (Chicago: Moody Press, 1977), 59.

7. Victor Buksbazen, *The Gospel in the Feasts of Israel* (Fort Washington, PA: Christian Literature Crusade, 1954), 63.

8. J. Carl Laney, *Moody Gospel Commentary: John* (Chicago: Moody Press, 1991), 194.

9. Herschel H. Hobbs, *An Exposition of the Four Gospels* (Grand Rapids, MI: Baker Book House, 1968), 170.

10. Paul Little, *How to Give Away Your Faith* (Downers Grove, IL: InterVarsity Press, 1988), 114.

John 11: Jesus the Resurrection and the Life

1. James Montgomery Boice, *The Gospel of John*, vol. 3 (Grand Rapids, MI: Zondervan Publishing House, 1977), 186.

2. Bruce Milne, *The Message of John* (Downers Grove, IL: InterVarsity Press, 1993), 160.

3. Erwin W. Lutzer, *Seven Convincing Miracles* (Chicago: Moody Press, 1999), 169.

4. Charles H. Spurgeon, *The Treasury of the Bible*, vol. 2 (Grand Rapids, MI: Zondervan Publishing House, 1962), 456.

5. Hudson Taylor, quoted in Bruce Milne, *The Message of John* (Downers Grove, IL: InterVarsity Press, 1993), 158.

6. D. A. Carson, *The Gospel According to John* (Grand Rapids, MI: Wm. B. Eerdmans Publishing Co., 1991), 411.

7. F. F. Bruce, *The Gospel of John* (Grand Rapids, MI: Wm. B. Eerdmans Publishing Co., 1983), 243.

8. Max Lucado, *Life Lessons with Max Lucado Book of John* (Nashville: Word Publishing, 1996), 71.

9. Bruce B. Barton, ed., *Life Application Bible Commentary: John* (Wheaton, IL: Tyndale House Publishers, 1993), 233.

10. Anne Graham Lotz, *Just Give Me Jesus* (Nashville: Word Publishing, 2000), 213.

11. Max Lucado, *Life Lessons with Max Lucado Book of John* (Nashville: Word Publishing, 1996), 72.

12. John Calvin, *John* (Wheaton, IL: Crossway Books, 1994), 281.

13. F. L. Godet, *Commentary on the Gospel of John* (Grand Rapids, MI: Zondervan Publishing House, 1893), 189.

14. Erwin W. Lutzer, *Seven Convincing Miracles* (Chicago: Moody Press, 1999), 168.

15. Charles U. Wagner, *This Is Life*, Senior Instructor (Schaumburg, IL: Regular Baptist Press, 1981), 61.

16. Alexander MacLaren, *Expositions of Holy Scripture: St. John*, vol. 10 (Grand Rapids, MI: Wm. B. Eerdmans Publishing Co., 1944), 108.

John 12: Jesus the King Who Will Die

1. Gary M. Burge, *The NIV Application Commentary: John* (Grand Rapids, MI: Zondervan Publishing House, 2000), 351.

2. James Montgomery Boice, *The Gospel of John*, vol. 3 (Grand Rapids, MI: Zondervan Publishing House, 1975), 304.

3. Arthur W. Pink, *Exposition of the Gospel of John* (Grand Rapids, MI: Zondervan Publishing House, 1945), 244.

4. David E. Garland, *The NIV Application Commentary: Mark* (Grand Rapids, MI: Zondervan Publishing House, 1996), 428.

5. Norval Geldenhuys, *The New International Commentary on the New Testament: The Gospel of Luke* (Grand Rapids, MI: Wm. B. Eerdmans Publishing Co., 1983), 480.

6. William Barclay, *The Gospel of John*, vol. 2, rev. ed. (Philadelphia: Westminster Press, 1975), 118.

7. Bill Myers, *Jesus: An Eyewitness Account* (Wheaton, IL: Victor Books, 1988), 94.

8. Bruce B. Barton, ed., *Life Application Bible Commentary: John* (Wheaton, IL: Tyndale House Publishers, 1993), 258.

9. J. Vernon McGee, *John Chapters 11–21* (Nashville: ThomasNelson Publishers, 1991), 52.

10. Everett F. Harrison, John: *The Gospel of Faith* (Chicago: Moody Press, 1962), 78.

11. F. F. Bruce, *The Gospel of John* (Grand Rapids, MI: Wm. B. Eerdmans Publishing Co., 1983), 275.

John 13: Jesus the Servant

1. Philip Yancey and Brenda Quinn, *Meet the Bible* (Grand Rapids, MI: Zondervan Publishing House, 2000), 512.

2. Fritz Ridenour, *Tell It Like It Is* (Glendale, CA: Regal Books, 1968), 138.

3. J. Carl Laney, *Moody Gospel Commentary: John* (Chicago: Moody Press, 1991), 240–41.

4. Philip Yancey and Brenda Quinn, *Meet the Bible* (Grand Rapids, MI: Zondervan Publishing House, 2000), 510.

5. Herschel H. Hobbs, *An Exposition of the Four Gospels* (Grand Rapids, MI: Baker Book House, 1968), 214.

6. David E. Garland, *The NIV Application Commentary: Mark* (Grand Rapids, MI: Zondervan Publishing House, 1996), 526.

7. Leon Morris, *The Gospel According to John* (Grand Rapids, MI: Wm. B. Eerdmans Publishing Co., 1971), 628.

8. Bill Myers, *Jesus: An Eyewitness Account* (Wheaton, IL: Victor Books, 1988), 99.

9. Larry and Sue Richards, *The Teen Study Bible* (Grand Rapids, MI: Zondervan Publishing House, 1993), 1452.

10. W. E. Vine, *Vine's Expository Commentary on John* (Nashville, TN: Nelson Reference, 1997), 164.

John 14: Jesus the Comforter

1. James Montgomery Boice, *The Gospel of John*, vol. 4 (Grand Rapids, MI: Zondervan Publishing House, 1978), 95.

2. Homer A. Kent Jr., *Light in the Darkness* (Grand Rapids, MI: Baker Book House, 1974), 173.

3. C. S. Lewis, *Mere Christianity* (New York: Macmillan Publishing Co., Inc., 1960), 56.

4. Gary M. Burge, *The NIV Application Commentary: John* (Grand Rapids, MI: Zondervan Publishing House, 2000), 351.

5. Henry Blackaby, *Experiencing the Word Through the Gospels* (Nashville: Holman Bible Publishers, 1999), 252.

6. John Calvin, *John* (Wheaton, IL: Crossway Books, 1994), 344.

7. Lawrence O. Richards, *The 365-Day Devotional Commentary* (Wheaton, IL: Victor Books, 1990), 797.

8. R. Wade Paschal Jr., quoted in *The Bible for Everyday Life*, ed. George Carey (Grand Rapids, MI: Wm. B. Eerdmans Publishing Co., 1996), 211.

9. John MacArthur Jr., T*he Legacy of Jesus* (Chicago: Moody Press, 1986), 88–91.

10. Ben Witherington III, *John's Wisdom: A Commentary on the Fourth Gospel* (Louisville, KY: Westminster John Knox Press, 1995), 253.

John 15: Jesus the Vine

1. Lawrence O. Richards, *The 365-Day Devotional Commentary* (Wheaton, IL: Victor Books, 1990), 798.

2. R. Kent Hughes, *Behold the Man* (Wheaton, IL: Victor Books, 1984), 69–70.

3. Wayne Jacobson, *In My Father's Vineyard*, adapted by Anne Christian Buchanan (Dallas: Word Publishing, 1997), 16.

4. Henry Blackaby, *Experiencing the Word Through the Gospels* (Nashville: Holman Bible Publishers, 1999), 255.

5. John Calvin, *John* (Wheaton, IL: Crossway Books, 1994), 356.

6. William Barclay, *The Gospel of John*, vol. 2, rev. ed. (Philadelphia: Westminster Press, 1975), 178.

7. Jacobson, *In My Father's Vineyard*, 20.

8. John MacArthur Jr., *The Legacy of Jesus* (Chicago: Moody Press, 1986), 135.

9. Herschel H. Hobbs, *An Exposition of the Four Gospels* (Grand Rapids, MI: Baker Book House, 1968), 231–32.

John 16: Jesus the Teacher

1. William Hendriksen, *The Gospel of John* (Grand Rapids, MI: Baker Book House, 1953), 321.

2. Matthew Henry, *Matthew Henry's Commentary on the Whole Bible*, vol. 4: *Matthew to John* (McLean, VA: MacDonald Publishing Co., 1721), 1134.

3. Everett F. Harrison, *John: The Gospel of Faith* (Chicago: Moody Press, 1962), 96.

4. D. A. Carson, *The Farewell Discourse and Final Prayer of Jesus* (Grand Rapids, MI: Baker Book House, 1980), 157–58.

5. Ibid., 160.

6. Philip Yancey and Brenda Quinn, *Meet the Bible*

(Grand Rapids, MI: Zondervan Publishing House, 2000), 516.

7. Leon Morris, *The Gospel According to John* (Grand Rapids, MI: Wm. B. Eerdmans Publishing Co., 1971), 708.

8. Ruth Myers, *The Satisfied Heart* (Colorado Springs: WaterBrook Press, 1999), 48.

9. J. Vernon McGee, *John Chapters 11–21* (Nashville: Thomas Nelson Publishers, 1991), 117.

10. Dana Gould, ed., *Shepherd's Notes: John* (Nashville: Broadman & Holman, 1998), 76.

John 17: Jesus the Pray-er

1. Martin Luther, quoted in J. Vernon McGee, *John Chapters 11–21* (Nashville: Thomas Nelson Publishers, 1991), 119.

2. Arthur W. Pink, *Exposition of the Gospel of John* (Grand Rapids, MI: Zondervan Publishing House, 1945), 95.

3. R. Kent Hughes, *John* (Wheaton, IL: Crossway Books, 1999), 395.

4. Paul N. Tassell, *That Ye Might Believe* (Schaumburg, IL: Regular Baptist Press, 1987), 112.

5. Leon Morris, *The Gospel According to John* (Grand Rapids, MI: Wm. B. Eerdmans Publishing Co., 1971), 728.

6. D. A. Carson, *The Farewell Discourse and Final Prayer of Jesus* (Grand Rapids, MI: Baker Book House, 1980), 191.

7. Charles U. Wagner, *This Is Life*, Senior Instructor (Schaumburg, IL: Regular Baptist Press, 1981), 104.

8. Homer A. Kent Jr., *Light in the Darkness* (Grand Rapids, MI: Baker Book House, 1974), 192.

9. David Jeremiah, *Prayer: The Great Adventure* (Sisters, OR: Multnomah Publishers, Inc., 1997), 201.

John 18: Jesus the Prisoner

1. R. Kent Hughes, *Behold the Man* (Wheaton, IL: Victor Books, 1984), 126–27.

2. Edwin A. Blum, "John" in *The Bible Knowledge Commentary*, vol. 2: *New Testament*, ed. John F. Walvoord and Roy B. Zuck (Wheaton, IL: Victor Books, 1983), 334.

3. J. Vernon McGee, *John Chapters 11–21* (Nashville: Thomas Nelson Publishers, 1991), 136.

4. D. Edmond Hiebert, *Mark: The Portrait of a Servant* (Chicago: Moody Press, 1979), 365.

5. Lawrence O. Richards, ed., *The Revell Bible Dictionary* (Grand Rapids, MI: Fleming H. Revell, 1990), 69.

6. Thomas Whitelaw, *Commentary on John* (Grand Rapids, MI: Kregel Publications, 1993), 384.

7. *The Life and Times Historical Reference Bible* (Nashville: Thomas Nelson Publishers, 1997), 1440.

8. Andreas J. Köstenberger, *John* (Grand Rapids, MI: Baker Academic, 2004), 529.

9. David E. Garland, *The NIV Application Commentary: Mark* (Grand Rapids, MI: Zondervan Publishing House, 1996), 579.

John 19: Jesus the Sacrifice

1. James M. Stalker, *The Trial and Death of Jesus Christ* (Grand Rapids, MI: Zondervan Publishing House, 1961), 59.

2. Andreas J. Köstenberger, *John* (Grand Rapids, MI: Baker Academic, 2004), 534.

3. Manford George Gutzke, *Plain Talk on John* (Grand Rapids, MI: Zondervan Publishing House, 1968), 188.

4. J. W. Shepherd, *The Christ of the Gospels* (Grand Rapids, MI: Wm. B. Eerdmans Publishing Co., 1946), 480.

5. Louis Goldberg, *Our Jewish Friends* (Chicago: Moody Press, 1977), 127.

6. John MacArthur Jr., *The Murder of Jesus* (Nashville: Word Publishing, 2000), 216.

7. Edwin A. Blum, "John" in *The Bible Knowledge Commentary*, vol. 2: New Testament, eds. John F. Walvoord and Roy B. Zuck (Wheaton, IL: Victor Books, 1983), 340.

8. Mark Bailey and Tom Constable, *The New Testament Explorer* (Nashville: Word Publishing, 1999), 191.

9. Ed Glasscock, *Moody Gospel Commentary: Matthew* (Chicago: Moody Press, 1997), 543.

John 20: Jesus the Risen Lord

1. Bruce Milne, *The Message of John* (Downers Grove, IL: InterVarsity Press, 1993), 294.

2. Josh McDowell, *The New Evidence That Demands a Verdict* (Nashville: Thomas Nelson Publishers, 1999), 203–4.

3. J. Carl Laney, *Moody Gospel Commentary: John* (Chicago: Moody Press, 1991), 360.

4. John Calvin, *John* (Wheaton, IL: Crossway Books, 1994), 444.

5. Merrill C. Tenney, "John" in *Zondervan NIV Bible Commentary*, vol. 2: *New Testament*, ed. Kenneth L. Barker and John Kohlenberger III (Grand Rapids, MI: Zondervan Publishing House, 1994), 369.

6. Charles U. Wagner, *This Is Life*, Senior Instructor (Schaumburg, IL: Regular Baptist Press, 1981), 124.

7. Lawrence O. Richards, *The 365-Day Devotional Commentary* (Wheaton, IL: Victor Books, 1990), 811.

8. Erwin W. Lutzer, *Seven Convincing Miracles* (Chicago: Moody Press, 1999), 188–189.

9. F. L. Godet, *Commentary on the Gospel of John* (Grand Rapids, MI: Zondervan Publishing House, 1893), 436.

John 21: Jesus the Commissioner

1. Anne Graham Lotz, *Just Give Me Jesus* (Nashville: Word Publishing, 2000), 317, 319.

2. Lawrence O. Richards, *The 365-Day Devotional Commentary* (Wheaton, IL: Victor Books, 1990), 812.

3. Max Lucado, ed., *The Inspirational Study Bible: The Gospel of John* (Nashville: Word Publishing, 1994), 35.

4. Mark Bailey and Tom Constable, *The New Testament Explorer* (Nashville: Word Publishing, 1999), 193.

5. Earl F. Palmer, *The Intimate Gospel: Studies in John* (Dallas, TX: Word Books, 1978), 176.

6. Philip Yancey and Brenda Quinn, *Meet the Bible* (Grand Rapids, MI: Zondervan Publishing House, 2000), 532–33.

7. Anne Graham Lotz, *Just Give Me Jesus* (Nashville: Word Publishing, 2000), 330–31.

8. David H. Stern, *Jewish New Testament Commentary* (Clarksville, MD: Jewish New Testament Publications, 1992), 214.

9. John Calvin, *John* (Wheaton, IL: Crossway Books, 1994), 472.

Index

bread, physical vs. spiritual, 70
   See also Jesus: as bread of life
Bruce, F. F.
   on judgment, 156
   on Martha, 132
   on Sabbath law, 84
Buksbazen, Victor
   on Hanukkah, 122
Burge, Gary M.
   on Jesus' disciples' greater works,
     177–78
   on Mary of Bethany, 144
burial customs
   anointing body, 258, 259
   how bodies prepared, 131
   how caves prepared, 135
   wrapping with spices, 253–54
burial, of Jesus, 253–54

C

Caesar, and Jesus, 243
   See also Pilate
Caiaphas
   greater sin than Pilate, 243
   on Jesus dying for the people,
     139–40
   relation to Annas, 224
   trying Jesus, 224, 225–27
   See also Pharisees and Jesus;
     Temple
Calvin, John
   on apostles doubting the
     Resurrection, 261
   on Christ's love, 189
   on Christ's majesty, 278
   on hatred of Jesus, 82
   on Jesus and death, 136
   on rule by Spirit, 180
Cana of Galilee, 21, 49, 50
Capernaum, 26, 49, 50, 68, 74
Carson, D. A.
   on cross, 199
   on disciples' grief, 200
   on Jesus cleansing the Temple,
     28–29
   on Lamb of god, 74
   on Lazarus' death, 132
   on spiritual struggle, 212
casting the first stone, 92–93
Cephas, 16
ceremonial cleansing, 140
Chahin, Jesus, 53
charoset, 167
children of God, 8
   See also belief; believers
Christ, the, 47, 49, 87, 121
   See also Jesus; Messiah
Christianity, 177
circumcision, 83
communion, 74–76
condemnation for sin, 94

   See also forgiveness of sins
Constable, Tom
   on Jesus' pierced side, 252–53
   on Peter, 272
Court of Women, 96
courtyard, in Jesus' day, 174
Creator, as Jesus, 3–4
   See also Father; God; Jesus
cross, carrying cross to execution, 246
crown of thorns, 239–40
crucifixion, 239, 251–52
   prophesied by David, 246
   See also Jesus; Jesus fulfilling Old
     Testament prophecies

D

darkness
   as evil, sin, 5
   as sin, 95
David, 165, 246
death, 143
   Enoch and Elijah as not dying, 127
   followed by resurrection, 59–60
   life after death, 6
   See also Jesus' prophecies; Lazarus
death penalty
   as Roman prerogative, 228
   for treason, 229
demon possession, 121
   accusation against Jesus, 83, 101–2
devil, 99
devil, his children, 100–101
   See also Pharisees and Jesus; Satan
Dickens, Charles, 219
disability
   and sin, 105–6
   See also Jesus' miracles in John
disciples mentioned in John.
   See Andrew; James; John; Judas;
     Judas [not Iscariot]; Nathanael;
     Peter; Thomas
donkey, as king's mount, 148
dove descending on Jesus, 14

E

Elijah
   as announcing the Messiah, 12
   as not dying,127
   See also John the Baptist
empty tomb, 257–59
Enoch
   as not dying, 127
Ephraim (town), 140
eternal life, 39, 59, 150, 208–9
   and belief in Jesus, 74
   communion with Jesus, 74–75
   as Jesus' promise, 173–77, 179
   resurrection to eternal life, 59
   resurrection to judgment, 59
everlasting life

manna vs. bread of life, 73–74
   See also eternal life
execution.
   See crucifixion; death penalty

F

faith, 266
false teachers, 84
Father
   "Father is in me," 125
   as glorifying Son, 207–8
   as greater than Jesus, 182
   Jesus comes in Father's name, 61
   knowing Jesus means knowing
     Father, 96
   loves those who love Jesus, 180
   as vinedresser, 185
   wills salvation for all, 72, 155
   as witness to Jesus, 60–61, 95–96
   See also: Jesus' teachings: on the
     Father; Son of God; Son of Man
Feast of Dedication, 121–22
Feast of Lights, 122
Feast of Tabernacles, 79, 80, 86
   as week-long celebration, 80
Feast of Unleavened Bread (Passover),
   228
   donations to poor, 168
feeding five thousand
   crowd wants Jesus for king, 67–68
   disciples unsure, 75–75
   Jesus calls self bread of life, 69–72
   Jesus predicts Judas' betrayal
   loaves and fishes multiplied, 66–67
   walks on water, 69
   See also Jesus' miracles in John
feet, washing feet, 164
flogging, 239–40
forgiveness of sins
   offered by Jesus, 94, 95, 264
   sin after salvation, 163
Fredrikson, Roger L.
   on assigning blame, 106
   Father revealed in Jesus, 58
freedom, 91, 99
friends of God, 190
fruit of the Spirit, 185, 189

G

Gabbatha, 244
Galilean, as term of abuse, 88
Galileans, as doubters, 50
Galilee
   as haven from Pharisees, 41, 79–80
   as not source of prophets, 88
Garden of Gethsemane, 185
Garland, David E.
   on crowd's preferring Barabbas, 232
   on importance of table fellowship,
     167

arresting party falls to ground, 222
heals Malchus' ear, 223
trial before high priests, 224–25
trial before Pilate, 227–33
laws broken at his trial, 226, 228, 233–34
mocked and scourged, 239, 240–41
crown of thorns, 239–240
presented as "king," 244–45, 247
his crucifixion, 245–53
carrying cross, 246
crucifixion procedure, 251–52
lots cast for his clothing, 247–48
gives his mother to John, 248–49
seven last statements, 248–49, 250
legs not broken, 251, 253
his burial, 253–54
post-Resurrection appearances, 257–78
empty tomb, 257–60
appears to Magdalene at tomb, 260–63
shows disciples his wounds, 263–64
Resurrection appearances listed, 264
Jesus, breathing the Holy Spirit, 264–65
appearing at Sea of Galilee, 269–77
abundance of fishes, 270–71
in heaven, 175
return in glory, 180–81
See also Jesus, describing himself
Jesus, describing himself
as bread of life, 67–72
as choosing his friends, 190–91
as come to give more abundant life, 117
as Creator, 3–5
as drinking cup of judgment, 223
as door, 117–18
as from above, 97
as Gate, 117
as God, 10–11, 58–62
as God's agent, 4
as Good Shepherd, 118–23
as hated without cause, 192
as I AM, 72, 93, 94–95, 102–3, 133, 175, 222
as image of Father, 176
as judge, 155–56
as king, 122, 229–31, 247
as Lamb of God, 13–14, 253
as laying down life willingly, 120
as life, 5, 175
as lifted up, 152
as light, 153
as light of men, 5
as light of the world, 94–95
as Lord, 163
as man and God, 8–10
as Messiah, 7, 8, 28, 46, 84, 148, 152–54
as observant Jew, 54

as offering forgiveness, 93
as one with the Father, 214
as only way to God, 117
as overcoming world, 204
as prophet, 45
as rabbi, 81–84
as resurrection and life, 133
as sacrifice for sin, 8
as savior, 155–56
as seeking God's glory, 82
as sending Holy Spirit, 173–83
as servant, 159, 161–71
as Son of God, 14, 111–13, 124, 242, 243
as Son of Man, 17–18, 34, 59, 150, 153, 168
as Teacher, 163
as true light, 7
as true vine, 185
as truth, 175, 231
as vine, 185–94
as way, 175–76
as witness to truth, 60–61, 95–96, 230–31
as Word, 4, 9, 11
See also Jesus fulfilling Old Testament prophecies
Jesus fulfilling Old Testament prophecies
betrayal, 165
casting lots for his clothing, 247–48
cleansing Temple, 26
disbelief of the people, 153–54
hated without cause, 192
legs not broken, 251, 253
opening eyes of blind, 113
pierced side, 252–53
prophecies fulfilled listed, 251
restoring sight, 115
Resurrection, 260–61
riding a donkey, 148
thirst on cross, 250
See also Jesus' miracles in John
Jesus' miracles in John, 29
feeding of the five thousand, 65–71
finding fishes, 270–71
healing lame man, 53–57
healing official's son, 49–51
man born blind, 105–13
miracles not recorded in John, 267
raising Lazarus, 127–41
walking on water, 68
Jesus' prophecies
crucifixion as method of death, 152
death and resurrection, 28, 57, 75–76, 97–98, 120–21, 150–52, 182–83, 199, 200–201, 202
disciples scattered, 203
disciples' grief will become joy, 200–201
greater works for disciples, 177

Judas will betray him, 76, 97–98, 162, 165, 167–68
persecution of Christians, 191–92, 195, 204
Peter's betrayal, 170, 219–20, 227
Peter's death, 269, 275–76
See also Jesus fulfilling Old Testament prophecies; Jesus' teachings
Jesus' teachings
on consequence of disbelief, 97
on dying for sins, 163
on eternal choice, 39
on evangelism, 215
on Father 4, 57–62, 96–97, 176–77
on figurative language, 202
on friends vs. servants, 189–90
on God's glory, 208–9
on God as vinedresser, 185–86
on his body and blood, 74–76
on his body as temple, 28
on his death, 150
on his flesh, 74–75
on his kingdom, 230–31
on his life and mission, 202
on his promises, listed, 124
on Holy Spirit, 178, 181, 193
on laying down life for friends, 189
on love, 188–89, 190–91
on loving one another, 169
on obedience, 183, 189–90
on peace, 181–82
on the poor, 146
on his promises, listed, 124
on servanthood, 163–64
on who is greatest, 161
See also Son of God
Jewish courts, 228
See also laws broken at Jesus' trial
Jewish people
as Abraham's descendants, 98–103
mixed responses to Jesus, 8, 79, 81–82
John 3:16, 35–36
John (author of book of John)
as author, vi, 149, 273
as disciple of John the Baptist, 15
at final Passover, 166
as friend of Jesus, v-iv, 166
at Jesus' arrest, 225
as Mary's new "son," 248–49
as member of inner circle, v
on own death, 276–77
his purpose in writing, 26, 267
with risen Jesus, 269, 270, 271, 272–73
at tomb of Jesus, 257–58, 259
John the Baptist
baptizing Jesus, 13–14
baptizing Jews as scandal, 12

seeing Lazarus raised, 137, 139
at Simon the Leper's home, 143
Mary (of Bethany)
anointing Jesus' feet, 144–46
asking Jesus to help Lazarus,
127–28
grief for Lazarus, 131–37
meeting Jesus on way to tomb, 134
at Simon the Leper's house, 143
Mary (mother of James), 257
Mary (mother of Jesus)
at Cana wedding, 21–25
at Capernaum, 26
as coming from Nazareth, 84
Jesus gives her to John, 248–49
Mary (wife of Clopas), 248
Mary Magdalene
at foot of cross, 248
her loyalty, 259
Jesus' body is gone, 257–59
Jesus calls her by name, 262
meeting the risen Jesus, 261–63
telling disciples of Resurrection,
262–63
matzah, 167
McDowell, Josh
on Resurrection, 258–59
McGee, J. Vernon
on Feast of Tabernacles, 81
on Jesus' deity, 222
on peace of Christ, 204
on willful blindness, 154
menorah
at Feast of Tabernacles, 94
at Festival of Lights, 122
Jesus' "light of the world"
statement, 94–96
menorah illustrated, 95
See also Jesus, describing himself
Messiah
born in Bethlehem, 87
crowd's wrong expectations,
147–48, 152–53
Jesus declares self Messiah, 46
Jewish vs. Roman views, 229–30
John says Jesus is Messiah, 12
many believe in Jesus as Messiah,
29
Philip says Jesus is Messiah, 16–17
See also Jesus; Jesus fulfilling Old
Testament prophecies
Milne, Bruce
on God's delays, 128–29
on prejudice against women, 42
on women discovering empty tomb,
258
miracles, v
in book of John, listed, 25
and laws of nature, 107
reason for John's choice, 25
results of miracles, 25

See also Jesus' miracles in John
moneychangers at Temple, 26–27
Morris, Leon
on God as Father, 57
on Jesus coming home to Israel,
8–9
on Judas, 168, 211
on judgment, 37
on prayer, 201
on testimony, 7
Moses
as friend of God, 190
Jesus as greater than Moses, 75
as judge, 62
as lawgiver, 82–83
lifting up the serpent, 34–35
and manna, 71–72
Pharisees as Moses' disciples,
110–11
prophesying Jesus, 62, 67
seeing God's glory, 9
Mount Gerizim, 45
Mount of Olives, 91, 185
mourning customs, 131
Myers, Bill
on Jesus writing in the dirt, 93
on loving one another, 169
on Nicodemus, 34–35
on sacrificial death, 150
on triune God, 203
Myers, Ruth, 203
on triune God, 203
myrrh, 253, 254

N

Nathanael
doubts Jesus is Messiah, 17–18
and Jacob's bridge to God, 18
meets risen Jesus, 269–70
nature, iv
Nazareth, 87
as Jesus' hometown, 17
new birth, 33
New Testament, iii, 214
See also Gospels
Nicodemus
came to Jesus by night, 31–35
counseled to be born again, 31,
31–35
defended Jesus, 88
provided spices for Jesus' burial,
253
put body in tomb, 257
nobleman, Jesus healing his son, 50
See also Jesus' miracles in John

O

obedience, 179–80
Old Testament, iii

See also Jesus fulfilling Old
Testament prophecies;
Jesus' prophecies

P

palm branches, 147
Palm Sunday origin, 143, 147–49
Palmer, Earl F.
on John's eye for detail, 273
parables, 100
Paschal, R. Wade, Jr., 182
on peace Jesus offers, 182
Passover
commemorating escape from
slavery, 26, 72
as Feast of Unleavened Bread, 228
Jesus driving out moneychangers,
26–29
Jesus' third and final Passover, 140
as pilgrimage holiday, 26
unleavened bread, 72
See also bread of life
Passover customs
avoiding defilement, 227–28
ceremonial cleansing, 140
criminals' bodies not left hanging,
251, 253
dinner rituals, 147
donations to poor, 168
food served, 167
reclining at Passover, 166
seder supper, 160
Passover lambs, 220, 245
Jesus as lamb, 253
Pavement, the, 244
Pentecost, 264–65
Pentecost, J. Dwight
light as knowledge of God, 5–6
persecution of Christians
Jesus overcoming the world, 204
persecutors hope to please God,
195–96
predicted by Jesus, 191–93
Satan engineering persecutions, 211
world's values vs. Jesus' values, 212
See also Satan
Peter
asking who would betray Jesus, 166
commission from Jesus, 274–75
confessing Jesus as giving eternal
life, 76
cutting off Malchus's ear, 223
denying Jesus once, 225
denying Jesus three times, 227
his own crucifixion prophesied,
275–76
Jesus prophesies his betrayal, 170,
173, 219–20
Jesus' three questions, 274–75
at Jesus' tomb, 257–58, 259
meeting Jesus, 16

protesting his loyalty, 170
protesting Jesus' washing his feet,
162–63
restored after betrayal, 271–77
return to fishing, 269, 270–72
wondering about John's fate,
276–77
Pharisees and Jesus, 85–86
arresting Jesus, 220–24
believing Pharisees, 154–55
called blind by choice, 112
called Devil's children, 100–101
cleansing the Temple, 26–28
Feast of Tabernacles, 87–88,
95–103
as fundamentalists, 32
healing on the Sabbath, 55–57, 83
as hirelings, 119
as keepers of the faith, 108
and man born blind, 80, 108–11
as Moses' disciples, 110–11
Pharisees as bad shepherds, 119–20
raising of Lazarus, 138–40, 149
as thieves and robbers, 117
threat to stone Jesus, 129
who they were, 32
woman caught in adultery, 91–94
See also Jesus: trial before high
priests
Philip
describing Jesus, 16–17
and feeding of five thousand, 66
Gentiles ask to see Jesus, 149
wishes to see Father, 176–77
Pilate, and Jesus
displays scourged Jesus to crowd,
241–42
fears charge of disloyalty, 243
gives permission to break legs, 251
has Jesus scourged, 239–41
hears request for tomb guard,
257–58
Jesus brought for death sentence,
227–29
on Jesus as "god," 242–43
lets Joseph have body, 253–54
maneuvers to save Jesus, 241–45
must avoid Passover riot, 227–28
offers crowd Barabbas, 231–32
sentences Jesus to crucifixion,
244–45
talks to crowd first time, 227–29
talks to crowd second time, 231–32
talks to crowd third time, 241
talks to Jesus first time, 229–31
talks to Jesus second time, 242–43
washes his hands, 245
writes inscription for cross, 247
See also laws broken at Jesus' trial;
Pilate, as governor
deposes Annas, 224

misdeeds as governor, 229
Pilate's view of truth, 231
why unpopular, 244
pillar of fire, 94
Pink, Arthur W.
on Jesus' last day, 208
on Sadducees, 146
Place of a Skull, 245
Pool of Bethesda
as curing waters, 54–55, 80
illustrated, 55
Jesus heals lame man, 53–57
Pool of Siloam, 106–8
poor people, Jesus' view, 145–46
power, in Jesus' view, 121
prayer, as revealing oneself, 208
prayer, in Jesus' name
meaning of term, 201–2
in Upper Room discourse, 195
Preparation Day (for Passover)
and bodies of criminals, 251
and burials, 254
as day of Jesus's death, 244–45
hastening executions, 251–52
prophecy. *See* Jesus fulfilling Old
Testament prophecies
Prophet, the
Jesus hailed as such, 67, 87
John the Baptist denies title, 12
as not from Galilee, 87
See also Jesus: as Messiah; Messiah
purification, 23
purple dye, 240

Q

Quinn, Brenda
on Jesus distrusting sensation-
seekers, 73
on Jesus forgiving Peter, 273
on Jesus' servanthood, 164
on love of God, 43

R

raising of Lazarus. *See* resurrection of
Lazarus
religion, earning God's favor, 70
repentance, 7
and being born again, 33
resurrection of believers, 133
resurrection to eternal life, 59
Resurrection of Jesus
and access to God, 202
importance to Christianity, 260
missing body issue, 257
as proof of Jesus' claims, 257
and resurrection of believers, 133
skeptical theories, 258
resurrection to judgment, 59
resurrection of Lazarus, 136–38

as demonstrating Jesus' power, 59
as galvanizing Jesus' enemies,
138–39
See also Lazarus
Revell Bible Dictionary
on Annas, 224–25
Richards, Larry and Sue
on loving one another, 169
Richards, Lawrence O.
on God as pruning us, 186
on Holy Spirit, reminding us of
Jesus' teaching, 181
on Jesus meeting needs, 271
on logos, 4
on materialism, 70
on skepticism, 266
Ridenour, Fritz, 161
Roman citizen, 228
Roman courts, 228
See also laws broken at Jesus' trial
Roman sandal, 13
Roman soldiers, 221

S

Sabbath, 108
and executed criminals, 252, 254
Jesus healing lame man, 55–57
Sabbath observance, 55–57, 83
See also Pharisees and Jesus
sacrifice, at Temple, 26
See also lambs
Sadducees, 146
saliva, 106–7
Salome
at foot of cross, 248
at Jesus' tomb, 258
as John's mother, v
salvation
as Father's will, 72
as God's plan, 219
as limited time opportunity, 37
loss of salvation, 187–88
Samaria, 50
Samaritan, as insult, 101
Samaritan woman
argues with Jesus, 42–47
declares Jesus to be prophet, 45
Jesus declares self Messiah, 46
Jesus offers living water, 43
as outcast, 42, 44, 47
testifies to Jesus, 48–49
Samaritans
avoided by Jews, 41–42
declare Jesus savior of the world, 49
their beliefs, 45–46
sanctification, 213
sandal, 13, 161
Sanhedrin, 32
Satan
entering Judas, 167

his choke hold on world, 204
his names listed, 152
as murderer and liar, 100–101
as persecutor, 211
as ruler of this world, 151–52, 183, 197
as turning people from God, 211
See also demon possession; devil
scourging, 239, 240–41
Scripture (see Bible)
Scroggie, W. Graham
on heavenly bread, 71
Sea of Galilee
feeding five thousand, 65
Jesus walking on water, 69
Resurrection appearances, 269–77
Sea of Tiberias (Galilee), 65
second birth, 33
seder, 160
separation from God, 95
servanthood
Jesus demonstrating servanthood, 161
Jesus' discourse on servanthood, 161–71
sheep, 115
image for God's people, 115–23
Old Testament references, 119
sheepfold, 116
Sheep Gate, 53
sheep pen, 116
Shepherd, J. W.
on crucifixion as punishment, 246
shepherds
in country, 117
images in Old Testament, 119
in town, 116
See also Jesus, describing himself: as Good Shepherd; Pharisees and Jesus: Pharisees as bad shepherds
Simon Peter. *See* Peter
Simon the Leper, 143
sin, 105–6
redeemed by Jesus, 250
seen as darkness, 95
sin after salvation, 163
slavery to sin, 98–99
See also forgiveness of sins
Son of God
can do nothing by himself, 58
does Father's will, 98
glorifying Father, 207–8
knows the Father, 119
only Son has seen Father, 73–74
power to execute judgment, 58–59
raises believers to eternal life, 72
seeks Father's will, 59
unbelievers condemned, 35–36, 97
will die for life of world, 74
See also Father; Jesus; Jesus:

describing himself; Son of Man
Son of Man
and angels, 17–18, 153
as glorified in death, 150, 168
in Heaven, 34
his right to judge, 59
as Messiah, 152–53
returning to Heaven, 75–76
whoever believes has eternal life, 34
See also Jesus; Jesus: describing himself; Son of God
Sons of Thunder (James and John), v
spikenard, 144
Spirit, 14, 33
See also Holy Spirit
spiritual death, 97
spiritual fruit, 87
spiritual life, 97
spit, 107
Spurgeon, Charles H., 130
on strengthening of faith, 130
Stalker, James M.
on mockery of Jesus, 241
Stern, David H.
on curiosity, 277
on Jesus and woman caught in adultery, 94
stone water jar, 24
stoning
after I AM statement, 102
as Jewish form of execution, 152
threats to stone Jesus, 102, 124, 129
woman caught in adultery, 92
suffering, 105–6
cause vs. purpose, 106
man born blind, 106
pruning as symbol, 186
Sychar, 41, 42, 47
synagogue, 26
expulsion from synagogue, 109, 154–55
synoptic Gospels, iv, 166

T

Tasker, R. V. G.
belief, as matter of life or death, 39
on rejecting grace, 111
Tassell, Paul N., 45, 210
on alienation from God, 45
on truth of God's message, 210
Taylor, Hudson
on trials, 131
Temple in Jerusalem
abuses, 26–28
as architectural wonder, 149
Jesus expels merchants, 26–29
in Jesus' day, 27
Pilate and the Temple, 244
Temple guards, 221

Temple tax, 26–28
Tenney, Merrill C.
on importance of one's name, 262
on Jesus as human, 9
on uniqueness of John, v
Thomas
asks way to God's house, 175
demands proof, 265–67
famous as doubter, 130
given assurance by Resurrection, 257
meets Jesus at Sea of Galilee, 269, 270
not at first Upper Room meeting, 263
offers to die with Jesus, 130
sees risen Jesus, 265–67
Tiberias (city), 69, 70
Tlacote, Mexico, 53
tomb, of Jesus, 254
as guarded, 257
tribulation, 204
Trinity, 178, 203, 211
See also God; Holy Spirit; Jesus; Jesus' teachings: on the Father
troops, as arresting Jesus, 224
truth
sources for Christians, 213
truth shall make you free, 98
See also Jesus: as truth

U

unbelief
hardening in unbelief, 154
as self-condemned, 35–36
See also belief
unbelievers
as dead branches, 187
as dying in their sins, 97
See also believers
unity among Christians, 214
unleavened bread, 72
Upper Room
Passover, 159–217
Resurrection appearances, 273
Upper Room discourse, 159–217

V

Vine, W. E.
on Peter, 170
vines, pruning, 185–86

W

Wagner, Charles U.
on Abraham's descendants, 99
on insulated vs. isolated, 213
on Jesus' peace greeting, 264

on raising of Lazarus, 138
walking on water, 69
washing feet, 161–63
Water Gate, 86
water
  as God's word, 33
  healing water, 53
  as John's baptism, 33
  living water, 86–87
  water and the spirit, 33
  water as symbol, 42–47
  water into wine. *See* wedding at
    Cana
water jar, 24
wedding at Cana
  as first sign miracle, 25
  Jesus turns water to wine, 23–25
  Mary asks Jesus' help, 21–23
  See also Jesus: miracles in John
wedding customs, 22–24
whipping, 239–40
whips, Roman whips, 240
  See also scourging
Whitelaw, Thomas, 229
Wiersbe, Warren W.
  on grace before Jesus, 11
  on Jesus' distrust of the crowds,
    29
  on Mary at Cana, 22
  on meaning of Gospel events, v
  on trusting the Lord, 69
wine
  at Cana in Galilee, 22–24
  at Jewish festivals, 23–24
Witherington, Ben, III, 183
witnesses
  two witnesses for valid testimony,
    95–96
woman caught in adultery, 91–94
women, restrictions, 47
Word
  Jesus as Word, 4, 11
  Word, becoming flesh, 9
  See also Jesus; Jesus, describing
    himself
Word of God. *See* Bible
world
  and Christians, 212
  its enmity to Jesus, 191
  See also persecution of Christians;
    Satan

Y

Yahweh, vi
  See also God
Yancey, Philip, 32, 73, 118–19, 160,
    164, 201
  on grief turning to joy, 201
  on Jesus distrusting sensation-
    seekers, 73

on Jesus fulfilling Old Testament,
    118–19
on Jesus' love and servanthood,
    73
on Leonardo's *Last Supper*
    painting, 160
on Nicodemus, 32

Z

Zebedee, as John's father, v
Zechariah, 253
Zechariah 14:8, 86